A COUNTRY WITHIN

A JOURNEY OF
LOVE AND HOPE
DURING THE REFUGEE
CRISIS IN GREECE

KIM MALCOLM

A Country Within: A Journey of Love and Hope During the Refugee Crisis in Greece

Copyright © 2018 by Thunderhooves Press. All Rights Reserved.

For information about this title or to order other books and/or electronic media, contact the publisher:
Thunderhooves Press
ThunderhoovesPress@gmail.com

ISBN: 978-9995896-0-1 (print)
         978-0-9995896-1-8 (eBook)

Printed in the United States of America

As once the winged energy of delight
carried you over childhood's dark abysses,
now beyond your own life build the great
arch of unimagined bridges.

Wonders happen if we can succeed
in passing through the harshest danger;
but only in a bright and purely granted
achievement can we realize the wonder.

To work with Things in the indescribable
relationship is not too hard for us;
the pattern grows more intricate and subtle,
and being swept along is not enough.

Take your practiced powers and stretch them out
until they span the chasm between two
contradictions ... For the god
wants to know himself in you.

— RAINIER MARIA RILKE

Table of Contents

For My Gabe

Prologue

THE WORLD IS IN A permanent state of war, heedless of the effects — increasingly global in nature — on innocent people. Sometimes, in unexpected ways, war unites the noncombatants, the nonpoliticians, and the victims, and brings out the best in them. I experienced this unintended consequence of war in a small corner of the world when I traveled to Greece in late 2015 to help with what has been called "the refugee crisis" there.

My story is personal, but its setting is global. The geopolitical context for my story goes back thousands of years, but a good starting point is early 2015, when hundreds of refugees began arriving every day on the beaches of the Greek Island of Lesvos from war-torn Syria, Iraq, and Afghanistan. Traveling across a treacherous stretch of the Aegean Sea from the Turkish coast, the refugees arrived on rubber rafts and rotting fishing vessels — wet, cold, hungry, and traumatized — on a path to Germany, Scandinavia, or any place that would take them. By the end of 2015, more than 500,000 people had arrived on Lesvos — a rural community of fewer than 90,000 residents.

For most of the year and with almost no support from the European Union, the United Nations, or the world's large charitable organizations (NGOs), the residents of Lesvos offered food, clothing, transportation, and shelter to their transient guests. They also provided expressions of respect, encouragement, and compassion. They acted according to the Greek value called *philotimo,* literally, "friend of honor," but evoking a higher purpose and inner sense of duty to community and humanity. In September of that same year, the image of the drowned body of three-year-old refugee Aylan Kurdi made headlines. After that, the people of Lesvos got some relief. Volunteers and NGOs showed up with funds, energy, and a sense of mission. As the relief efforts on the island became more organized — and international attention grew into international controversy — the residents of Lesvos appeared able to resume their normal lives.

Greece was never a final destination for the refugees who began arriving in 2015. They knew the Greek economy could not support them. At that time, a number of European states, in particular Germany and the countries of Scandinavia, welcomed more than a million refugees in less than a year. That changed in early 2016, when the EU embarked on a campaign to stop the refugees from entering Europe. The EU cut a deal with Turkey that would leave millions of refugees stuck in Turkey, a country that provided few opportunities for non-citizens and had become increasingly hostile to democratic values. Those who had been able to escape the violence of their respective homelands now were subjected to harassment and dire conditions in Europe. Thousands of children who had arrived without parents or guardians (called "unaccompanied minors") were left to their own devices. Many refugees died from abuse, exposure, or, in hopelessness, acts of suicide.

The refugee crisis — more aptly referred to as a "humanitarian crisis" — is changing the face of many European nations, highlighting cultural and political differences of its member nations in how they have reacted to the crisis and how they would resolve it. The refugee crisis is not going away, and the way the world responds to it will be a test of our common humanity and ability to adapt to global demographic change.

This is the story of the time I spent in Greece between late 2015 and late 2017. I originally set out to write about the quiet heroism of the residents of Lesvos at a time when I naively believed Lesvos represented Europe's response to the ongoing humanitarian crisis. As sentiments of EU member citizens and states changed in ways that affected the circumstances on Lesvos, the nature of my own journey changed, and I knew there was much more to write about. The real story, as always, is partly optimistic and partly tragic. For me, personally, it was one of enrichment. Through a series of small gestures and events, I felt connected with something that felt large and important, and later became a part of an ad hoc family of young people from four countries. I couldn't change the world, but I could make a small difference in the lives of a few. There were many who certainly made a difference in mine.

A note on the book's structure and my use of certain terms:

This book is a memoir, which means it presents my subjective view of things. Out of necessity, I have had to add detail or make some assumptions about motives or feelings, especially in retelling the events that occurred before 2016. The geopolitical context I provide tells only a very small part of the story, mainly those parts that were relevant to what was going on around me. I refer to the island of "Lesvos" rather than "Lesbos" because the former is what the Greeks call it.

Some of the people I write about were not the most obvious subjects. For example, the people of Lesvos whose stories I share do not include the heroic fishermen of Skala Sykamania or the dedicated volunteers who committed their times and resources to helping refugees. I wanted to write about people who did not get attention for their effort but whose lives were changed by it. Most of the names I use are fictional, in order to avoid compromising safety or privacy.

When I refer to "refugees," I do so partly for reasons of convenience. It is too difficult to say "immigrants and refugees" at every turn. And I believe that virtually all the people coming to Lesvos from Turkey were refugees in the strictest sense and according to international law, escaping bombs, persecution, torture, conscription by extremists, or explicit threats. Some have argued that many of the people entering Europe from the Middle East and Africa are "economic migrants" and "only" seek a better life. To me, you are a refugee if you are part of any group that is unable to provide the most basic human needs to your children. You are a refugee if you are willing to risk your life to escape your homeland.

Although I believe the term "refugee" is more accurate than "immigrant" for my purposes here, it is important to remember that "refugees" are people with diverse backgrounds, personalities, and dreams. Refugee is a circumstance, not a person.

The Friends on Lesvos

Michalis — *Greek member of Hellenic Coast Guard in Molyvos; son of Papa Stratis*

Papa Stratis — *Greek Orthodox priest who dedicated himself to helping refugees arriving on the island*

Panagiotis Vati-Mariola — *Greek hotel owner in Molyvos; married to Aphrodite*

Aphrodite Vati-Mariola — *Greek hotel owner in Molyvos; married to Panagiotis*

Natasha — *Greek resident of Molyvos; employee of Starfish NGO*

Sofie — *Norwegian volunteer*

Taxia — *Greek restaurant owner in Molyvos*

Ilektra — *Greek owner of gift store in Molyvos*

Melinda McRosti — *British owner of Captain's Table in Molyvos; founder of Starfish*

Eric and Philippa Kempson — *British couple living on Lesvos who dedicated themselves to helping refugees arriving on the island*

The Extended Family in Greece

Arian (Arian) Akbar Hashimi — *Afghan refugee, married to Rana and father of three children; previously in banking and a television actor in Kabul*

Rana — *Afghan refugee, married to Arian and mother of three children*

Shayan — *oldest son of Arian and Rana*

Jamal — *middle son of Arian and Rana; disabled by severe cerebral palsy*

Amir — *youngest son of Arian and Rana; "Little Monkey"*

Hashem — *Syrian refugee living at Skaramangas Camp; previously a math teacher and sports coach*

Farshad — *Afghan refugee living at Skaramangas Camp waiting to reunite with his mother in Germany; previously a soccer professional*

Marzia — *Kurdish refugee from Syria living at Skaramangas Camp, waiting for reunification with her husband in Germany; mother of three children — Jahan, Sarah, and Hamza; traveling with and guardian of her nephew, Ramesh*

Lorin — *Kurdish refugee from Syria living at Skaramangas Camp with Hashem, Marzia, and Marzia's children*

Rafiq — *Algerian national living with a resident visa in Greece; volunteered at Piraeus and worked for an Apple contractor and, later, a large NGO providing refugee services*

Nanci — *American volunteer from Oakland, California; one of the "moms"*

Anne-Lene — *Norwegian volunteer from Oslo; one of the "moms"*

Timeline

October 7, 2001: United States invades Afghanistan.

March 20, 2003: United States invades Iraq.

December 2010: Arab Spring, the protesting and/or over-throwing of authoritarian regimes in the Middle East, begins in Tunisia and spreads to five other countries.

Mid-2011: Assad regime in Syria begins to heavily use military in key Syrian cities to fight anti-regime forces.

Early 2015: Large numbers of refugees begin arriving on the island of Lesvos, escaping war-torn Syria, Iraq, and Afghanistan.

September 2, 2015: The body of 3-year-old Alan Kurdi washes ashore in Lesvos and makes international news. Volunteers and NGOs begin arriving on Lesvos to help to alleviate the growing humanitarian crisis.

October 28, 2015: A boat carrying approximately 300 refugees sinks off the coast of Lesvos, killing an estimated 200 passengers. This further motivates and mobilizes NGOs and volunteers to help ease the refugee crisis.

Late December 2015: More than half a million refugees had migrated to and through Lesvos.

January 14, 2016: Greek coast guard arrests five Spanish lifeguards who rescued refugees from waters off the coast of Lesvos on suspicion of "migrant trafficking"

February 21, 2016: Macedonia closes its borders to Afghans; other Eastern European countries begin limiting refugee crossings, leaving thousands stranded in Greece.

March 8, 2016: The European Union announces a "deal" with Turkey that would end the "flow of human beings into Europe."

March 9, 2016: Macedonia closes its border with Greece.

April 16, 2016: Pope Francis visits Moria, on the island of Lesvos.

Spring 2016–Summer 2017: Refugees, living mostly in isolated camps, wait for the results of their asylum claims; on Lesvos and Chios, refugees continue to live in squalor and like prisoners as boats begin arriving in increasing numbers.

Summer 2017: The Greek government begins issuing final decisions on asylum claims and makes a commitment to closing the squats and camps, and integrating refugees into local communities.

The Region of the Aegean Sea

I

DYOS VARKAS

Two Boats

Chapter 1

December 2015

Dust of My Feet

I WENT TO GREECE IN THE winter of my 62nd year, and what happened there changed me. Maybe not enough for anyone to notice — and maybe, at some point, even I will not notice — but the gifts from my time in Greece will always be with me. And if the endings were not what I might have hoped for, I learned that there are no endings — just changes and complications.

I went to Greece without any special expectations, except to explore the world beyond the one that had rewarded my powers of analysis and muted the power of my heart. At the time, I had been traveling for most of two years. I traveled to learn about the ways other people live and their relationships to the land, the air, and the water. I searched for differences and connections. I traveled to be surprised. My journey in Greece provided all of this, as all my travels had, but what happened in Greece allowed me to explore more than just the land and the people. It allowed me to explore something inside me, almost as if it were another country. It began when boats of refugees were arriving on the Greek Island of Lesvos and continued in Athens, where I became a part of an unlikely family of refugees.

My path to Greece did not place me in the ranks of the explorers and risk-takers of the world, although in my life I had occasionally taken advantage of my good fortune to make a few unconventional decisions. As a young adult, I spent a year on an island without electricity, running water, or cars, where I helped build a log house and lived among a group of dreamers and salmon fishers. A few years later, I chose a career in a corner of government dominated by men. Just before I turned 40, I adopted a black baby boy as a single mother.

Reaching these slightly unusual decisions didn't require much more from me than the confidence of a person leading a privileged life, which I had. I was a white American, born to my good fortune. While not rich, my parents were among the beneficiaries of the booming economy of post-World War II America. Because of that, I had grown up with opportunities most of the world can only imagine. I always had a loving family, good friends, and good health. My career in government and nonprofit organizations provided titles of privilege — judge, executive director, chief of staff. I wasn't rich by American standards, but I was certainly rich by the standards of the rest of the world. I had raised my son, Gabe, in a small but elegant house in an affluent neighborhood, drove nice cars, and vacationed in places like France and Italy. Gabe went to summer camp, had exceptional healthcare for his knee problems, took piano lessons, and eventually graduated from a private college.

As Gabe grew into a young adult and began to steer his own path, I could have retired and led a comfortable life. I was grateful for all of it, but there was something missing in my life that made me restless. I wanted to feel connected to something bigger. I wanted some perspective on my good fortune. And I had a case of wanderlust.

The last job of my career — as a director for a program of the City of San Francisco — opened a door. Although I loved my work, I was increasingly aware that I would have to choose between being effective and staying true to my ethics. Choosing one would have unacceptably compromised the other. I wasn't going to choose. One sun-drenched San Francisco morning on my way to work, I got off the bus in front of my office building and called Gabe. Over the noise of traffic and the whistle of the city's famous wind, I asked him how he would feel if I quit my job to travel around the world. He said, "Yes, Mom — I will support whatever you do. I think this is what you need to do." That was August, 2014.

A few days later, I bought a ticket to Madrid and a ticket home from Hong Kong, with no plans for the places in between. I put everything in storage that didn't fit into a 22-inch bag and traveled for four months. Shortly after I returned home, I left again. And over the next year, again and again. In 16 months, I visited 14 countries. Because most of my friends did not have the freedom (or urge) to travel as I did, I was mostly alone, and, at times, I felt very lonely. But traveling solo made me more curious and more observant. Because I couldn't rely on people like me for conversation and companionship, I connected with local people — not well, I should say. I am friendly and social but not very adept with strangers. Still, I ultimately began to think of the people I met everywhere as part of a very large extended family, and that simple revelation was, for me, a profound discovery.

In early 2015, I returned home to the San Francisco Bay Area and reluctantly began working as an independent consultant, a prosaic change of pace from my latest six months of travel. I consoled myself that I loved my work and would still be able to travel, if not as a nomad then as a tourist. That fall, Gabe told me he planned to be in Hawaii with his girlfriend for the Christmas holidays. With little to keep me at home, I decided to spend the holidays on another continent. At the time, I had a long list of places I wanted to visit, but I chose Greece because it satisfied a few simple criteria — it was a place I had never visited, its December weather would not be too harsh, and I could get there using frequent-flyer miles. I booked a flight to Athens with a plan to wander the Greek countryside and learn Greek mythology.

In preparing for my trip, I read a lot about Greece, including articles from all over the world that were delivered to me electronically. Many of the articles referred to "the refugee crisis" in Europe. What I learned reading European news articles shocked me. By November 2015, almost a million refugees from Syria, Iraq, and Afghanistan had migrated to Europe under the most difficult conditions, mostly from Turkey through Greece. About half of those arrived through the Greek island of Lesvos, a place I knew almost nothing about. The stories I read described people so desperate to escape war that they left their homes, communities, and families to travel as much as 3,000 miles on a path of uncertainty and danger, sometimes on foot and ultimately on overcrowded rafts across a rough stretch of the Aegean Sea.

People were in desperate circumstances all over the world. What made this tragedy different for me was the response of the people of Lesvos, who were trying to serve the needs of as many as 6,000 refugees arriving in a single day, with little help from the outside world. After reading these stories, mythology didn't seem so important. I canceled my plans to travel on the Greek mainland so that I could spend time on the island of Lesvos as a volunteer.

But you would not understand what is important about my story if I began there. It really begins with the story of my Armenian grandfather, who was himself a refugee from the 20th century's first genocide. As I grew up, he was a special person in my life and a man of great mystery. He was reflective and kind, and I knew at an early age he had secrets he could not share, secrets that had made him large in spirit and humble in presentation. As a 19-year-old and years after my grandfather died, I asked my father to write about my grandfather's life during the time before he arrived in America. It was a story that had never been discussed between the competitive rounds of backgammon and the delivery of grease-spitting shish kebabs from the barbecue to the table at my grandparents' modest Pasadena home. My father, intellectual and romantic, was delighted by my request. Over the subsequent 30 years, he wrote more than a thousand pages, portions of which he periodically presented to his family in manageable, numbered volumes, each titled *Dust of My Feet*. Only a few of those pages shared the story of my grandfather. The rest were about everyone else in my father's life.

My father didn't need to apologize for allowing the story of my grandfather to be overtaken by his own. He just didn't know much about my grandfather, and no one else in the family did, either. I had asked him for a biography too late for meaningful research.

What we do know about my grandfather is that he was born Melcon Najarian. In 1913, he left his family and his home in Chunkush, a town of Armenians in a part of Turkey called Anatolia. He was 17. He left with a few dollars and a little knowledge of English. He never saw his family again. Along with hundreds of thousands of other Armenians in Anatolia, his family perished at the hands of the Turks. My grandfather made his way to America and changed his name to Thomas Malcolm. He married, owned a small dry-cleaning business, and raised four children who became successful professionals. He died in 1965 and, according to my sisters, subsequently returned to the world as a dolphin.

We don't know much about my grandfather's journey to America except that he arrived on Ellis Island on a ship he'd boarded in Marseille, France. My grandfather never told his family about how he got from Chunkush to Marseille. But it is reasonable and important for me to believe that, before he arrived in France, he left Turkey in a small boat that landed on the island of Lesvos, where, 100 years later, I saw the dolphins in the fierce Aegean Sea as I waited for boats of refugees.

In the same year I first arrived on Lesvos, a young man named Arian crossed that same sea of dolphins with his wife and three young sons. Arian would later become like a son to me and, by implication, the great-grandchild of my Armenian grandfather.

The story of how my grandfather arrived in Europe is imagined, as it must be. I could have imagined it only after learning about the story of Arian, which is Arian's own and true. The story of how the events in Greece connected these two people and how they transformed me is my own.

Chapter 2
February 1913
Melcon, My Grandfather

STANDING IN THE ARCHED doorway of the church, Melcon could barely hear Father Gregor over the sound of the church bells announcing the end of Sunday mass. Father Gregor rested a hand on Melcon's left shoulder. "Safe journey, my son. You may at times feel that you are traveling alone, but you are not alone." Melcon lowered his head and thanked him. He pulled his woolen cap over his ears and jogged toward his family and the trail of neighbors making their way down the rutted road that connected the church and the village. Whitewashed houses draped over the lower part of the hillside. The valley below spread out under a ceiling of dense clouds. The rocky soil of the valley's small farms was unplanted at this time of year except for the vineyards and the olive trees lining pastures dotted with brown- and white-fleeced sheep.

As he approached his brothers on the road, Melcon could hear the muffled voices of his parents walking ahead of him. He guessed they were speaking of preparations for Sunday dinner or plans for his older brother's wedding. He wasn't listening. He was thinking about how he would miss these Sundays, the liturgical chanting, the feeling of belonging, and the smell of incense his mother would take home in the curls of her black hair. He had not been able to think about how he would miss his family, especially his father.

Melcon heard the song of a skylark and looked up in time to see it swoop across the contour of the hillside and then dive out of sight. Comforted by this distraction, he remembered the Wordsworth poem he had learned in his English class:

> Whence thou dost pour upon the world a flood
> Of harmony, with instinct more divine;
> Type of the wise who soar, but never roam;
> True to the kindred points of Heaven and Home!

The week before, Melcon's father had returned home from America. He had been gone for almost three months. It had been a dangerous and lonely journey through Cairo to America's eastern coast. For more than a month, he had stayed in a small community of Armenians outside of Boston, Massachusetts. The family had been grateful for his safe return and, on his first night home, had eagerly listened to stories of his travels. The same night, he proposed a new life for his family in America, safe and full of opportunities. As an engraver, he said, he would be able to find work with a publisher or newspaper, and there would be Armenian neighbors and good schools and shops with Armenian foods. For the previous three months, Melcon's mother had considered how she would respond to her husband's plan, knowing he would propose it when he arrived home. She told him she would not leave her church and her family. She could not live in another country with strange customs and leave her parents to take care of themselves as they aged. She told Melcon's father that his worries about the family's safety were unfounded: the massacres of the Armenians by the Turks were a thing of the past.

Melcon understood his mother's hesitation to leave Chunkush. The journey would be long and dangerous, and the future uncertain. Melcon's mother had no ambitions to live a better life as his father did. She loved the traditions of her community and the emotional security her family provided. But Melcon also understood his father's instinct to leave Armenia. Life in Anatolia had always been unpredictable for Armenians. In the years just before Melcon was born, the Turkish sultan had systematically murdered thousands in the villages around Chunkush. More recently, the Turkish government had overseen the massacre of 30,000 Armenians in the city of Andana, 100 miles south. Everyone in the village had heard rumors that the new government of "Young Turks" had begun persecuting Armenians again and had plans to rid Anatolia of them. Turkey had lost a large amount of territory during the Balkan Wars, which had forced thousands of Muslim refugees to resettle in Anatolia, many of them in and around Chunkush. Throughout Anatolia, there was a growing feeling of unease between the Muslim refugees, most of whom struggled to feed their children, and their Christian Armenian neighbors, who owned vast tracts of land and most of the small businesses in the eastern provinces. Melcon had heard Turks refer to Armenians as *gavur,* which he knew meant "infidel."

For the previous two years, Melcon had attended Euphrates College in Harput, 50 miles north, where he studied literature. He had planned to study for two more years and then apply for a position as a teacher in the local middle school. His plans had changed. Although the family would not be traveling to America together, his father had begged Melcon to leave Chunkush in the days after he returned from his travels. "You must go. Haig is too young, and Azad insists on staying with your mother. You will have many opportunities in America. We are not safe here for long."

Melcon knew his father was right, but he struggled with the thought of leaving his family and his community for the uncertainty of life in a new country. Yet Melcon and his father did not speak of loss or fears. Their conversations turned instead to the practicalities of the journey. After returning home from church that Sunday, Melcon's father had spread a large map of Europe on the walnut dining table and traced a route for Melcon's journey with the stub of a pencil. Although there were no official restrictions on Armenians traveling out of the country, the path through Cairo was no longer safe. Turkish border officials had recently begun antagonizing Armenian travelers, and some were being detained at the borders. Melcon would need to find passage from the Turkish coast, where Ottoman Greeks were sending boats of Greek and Armenian Christians to Greece. From there, he could get passage on a ship to Marseille, and from Marseille on another ship to New York harbor.

At dinner that night, Melcon's mother was silent. His 14-year-old brother, Haig, handed Melcon a copy of Victor Hugo's *Les Miserables*, Melcon's favorite book. It was a rare volume printed in Armenian, leather bound and unread. Haig stared at Melcon as he held the book to his chest. "Thank you, Haig. I will see you in America someday. I love you, my brother." Haig raised his arm to hide his face and left the room. Melcon heard his heart pounding in his head. His cheeks burned. Melcon's father placed his hand on Melcon's forearm and pushed a small leather pouch into Melcon's hand. It held the money he needed for his train ticket and passage through Europe to New York.

The next morning, Melcon woke before sunrise to travel to Harput, where he would board a train for the 1,000-mile journey across Anatolia to Turkey's western coast. Melcon met his mother in the kitchen, where the air had been warmed by the fire that heated the oven. She busied herself at the stove and invited him to sit at the table, where she had placed a mug of dark tea and a plate of hot bread and salted cheeses. Melcon was grateful that his brothers were still sleeping. He couldn't eat and apologized. His mother gave him a weak smile and wrapped his breakfast in a small linen bag. She had already packed enough oranges, loaves of bread, and roasted chicken to last him several days. He pushed the linen bag into his knapsack on top of laundered shirts and a pair of gabardine pants, extra mittens, and a black woolen cap.

His father had arranged for Melcon to ride to Harput with Aram, a neighbor who owned a silk mill. Aram had planned to travel to Harput that day to deliver undyed fabrics to the market there. When Melcon heard the truck pull up in front of the house, he felt his stomach flip. He rose from the table and hugged his mother. She seemed to be shaking, and he knew it would not be wise to prolong his farewell. In the yard, his father greeted Aram with a strained smile and handed him several coins. Melcon pulled himself up into the passenger seat and pulled a heavy woolen blanket over his lap. He had never seen his father with tears in his eyes.

The ride through the hills was slow and bitterly cold, but they arrived in Harput before sundown and in time for the day's last train to Smyrna. When Aram dropped Melcon off at the station, the train was boarding. Melcon got on a second-class car and settled into a seat next to an older man in a black suit and a silk tie. The man had nodded off. He smelled like garlic and cigar smoke. The steam whistle blew. Melcon felt the top of his knapsack for the lump that was the breakfast his mother had packed and imagined his family around the dinner table. Maybe someday he would return to Armenia an educated and successful man.

Melcon kept to himself and read for most of the journey. On the third day, he woke when the man in the silk tie nudged him gently. The sun was coming up over the horizon, and the porter yelled "Smyrna, next stop!" A few minutes later, he pulled his knapsack over his shoulder and climbed out of the rail car into a blast of cold air. The station was full of people coming and going, some with trunks or children or both. He had never seen such a crowd, so much rushing. The stationmaster stood at the end of the platform in a blue suit and square cap. Melcon approached him. "Excuse me, sir. How do I get to the harbor?" The stationmaster looked at the knapsack and then startled Melcon by responding in Armenian. "Son, if you are trying to get to Greece, the best way is through Cesme to the west, but you won't get to Greece from Cesme. Not anymore. The next train to Dikili leaves in an hour. At the far end of the port in Dikili, you will find Greek fishing boats that will take you to one of the islands. Be careful, and good luck to you."

Melcon was disappointed by the change in plans, but he didn't doubt the station-master, who spoke in a way that reminded Melcon of his father. Melcon boarded the train to Dikili when it arrived and stepped off of it in Dikili as the sun sat low in a clear winter sky. Dikili was a modest fishing village that appeared to have once been prosperous. Large trees lined paved roads, and many of the houses had automobiles. Some stood empty, and some of the shops were closed.

As Melcon walked toward the harbor, he saw hundreds of people with suitcases and knapsacks in groups along the waterfront. He saw the fishing boats the station-master had described. None was rigged for its original purpose. Fishing nets and winches had been left in piles along the harbor road. Three small boats were bobbing toward the horizon, full of people in heavy coats. Two boats were entering the harbor empty. The whine of several boat engines created a wall of sound as backdrop for voices of men yelling and the occasional wailing of a baby.

Melcon approached an older man at the furthest dock. The man was moving through a small crowd toward one of the fishing boats. He was unshaven, with weathered skin and a fisherman's cap. Melcon caught his eye. The man didn't wait for him to speak. "Are you trying to get to Greece, son?" Melcon nodded and put his hand to the brim of his cap. "I can pay."

"The sardine launch at the north end of the harbor is leaving in about an hour. The cost is 3,000 drachmas. The smaller boats are leaving every 20 minutes or so. The fare is 1,000 drachmas, and you'll probably get wet." Melcon asked why so many people were at the docks. "We have heard that the Turkish frontier guards are on their way to Dikili. The boats that leave today could be the last to leave safely." The boats were going to an island called Lesvos about 20 kilometers west. The trip would take about three hours, depending on the winds and the tide.

Melcon thanked the man and walked toward the village to find something to eat — bread, maybe some cheese or fruit. He paused to watch a young man in an unfenced field on the opposite side of the road. The man was with a large chestnut horse. Slowly, the man removed the horse's bridle and saddle and placed them under an alder tree. The horse stood quietly while the man emptied a bag of grain on the ground in front of her. He stroked her neck, and the horse bumped his shoulder with her nose. She lowered her head to take a mouthful of grain and then chewed slowly while she watched the man walk back toward the docks. Melcon saw that the man was crying.

Melcon forgot about finding food and headed back toward the docks. He walked toward the larger boat, a turquoise-and-black 60-foot sardine launch. It was nothing elegant and still smelled of its catch, but it would be very seaworthy, with its large draft and inboard engine. It was getting ready to sail. The people boarding it were wearing clean, tailored clothes and carrying small pieces of leather luggage. In contrast to those waiting at the other end of the harbor, they seemed composed. Melcon had money to board this boat but decided against it. He needed to save what he had for the uncertain weeks and months ahead.

Melcon walked to the docks, where small groups of Greeks and Armenians were waiting to board one of the dozen white-and-blue wooden fishing boats. He felt the anxiety there, a sense of urgency. The air was full of fumes from the tiny engines. Melcon noticed that, except for the sardine launch, the largest of the boats at the dock could not have been more than 30 feet. Men on the docks were taking cash from other men and helping women and children board. A couple of men were arguing with one of the boat owners about payment. Women in layers of woolen shawls and heavy skirts were holding young children close.

Every minute or so, one of the men on the docks yelled, "No suitcases, no animals!" A suitcase could mean a person left behind. Occasionally, one of the men helping people into the boats grabbed a suitcase from a passenger and threw it into the water. A young woman behind Melcon opened a cage sitting beside her on the dock. She pulled a large gray cat out and held him like a baby. She rubbed her cheek across the top of the cat's head. Then she walked away from the crowd and let him go.

Melcon watched as the anxious people on the docks boarded the boats, some moving awkwardly as the boats bobbed in the water. When they were seated, they were pushed together shoulder-to-shoulder from bow to stern. Children and knapsacks were perched on laps, half-hidden by flaps of heavy coats and crisscrossed arms. By the time the boats were pushed away from the docks, there was nothing of the boat to see except a few inches of freeboard. The boats were solid masses of passengers. Some were holding each other. Some were holding their heads in their laps. Melcon watched a man pull a whiskey flask from his hip pocket and pour a few drops of its contents into a baby's mouth and then offer it to the woman holding the baby. A small Greek flag flapped on the stern of each boat.

Two boats set out as Melcon waited in line, shivering. He recognized two young men from the train ride to Dikili from Smyrna as they got into one of the boats. Although there was still time to get across the water before sunset, Melcon was relieved when it was his turn to board. He was directed to one of the smaller boats. It was probably less than 20 feet. He took a place on an outside seat and smiled meekly at the family who were sitting across from him on a makeshift bench. One of the men untied the boat after 25 adults boarded with five children. The boat smelled of rotting fish and fear. Melcon felt nauseous as the boat pulled away from the dock.

The wind in the harbor had died down, and the tide was with them, so the boat moved easily toward the open sea. As they pulled out of the harbor and away from the shelter of the hills to the south, a gust of wind caused the boat to lunge. Water splashed over the gunwales. Melcon heard screams and slowly adjusted his weight. He and several of the other men had been given large cans, and each began carefully scooping up water in the bottom of the boat and throwing it into the growling sea. The process was slow because getting the cans between the passengers' legs without tipping the boat was difficult.

The engine pulsed and sputtered as the boat made its way across the tiny stretch of the Aegean Sea that connected the Turkish coast with Europe. The tiny stretch might as well have been an endless expanse. Over the engine noise, Melcon could hear whimpers and occasional crying and screams. For unpredictable periods, the boat held steady. Then it would hit a swell, and its wood planks and beams groaned under the strain. Melcon wondered how many on the boat knew how to swim. No one had a life jacket. The boat had four lifesaving rings hanging on the outside of the boat along the gunwales. These might help five or six passengers, although not for very long. He consoled himself that he might be able to swim to shore, depending on where the boat capsized. He watched the horizon and, minute by minute, tried to calculate the distance to shore.

The sun was starting to set in front of them, making it difficult to recognize the contours of the island. The departure from the Turkish coast seemed a lifetime ago, but, seeing land, Melcon felt a surge of hope that he would survive this journey. The wind off the water was pushing the boat faster toward shore. The boat was heading toward a small village at the base of a hill. Melcon could make out a small beach and a handful of fishing boats at a dock.

As the boat neared shore, its captain yelled to his passengers, "Good people, welcome to Greece! Lesvos Island is just ahead. Do not move or stand up! Do not try to jump into the water! We do not want the boat to capsize. We will try to land on the beach."

As he spoke, another gust of wind lurched the boat slightly north. About 300 meters from shore, the boat headed straight for a rock the size of a tiny island. Two of the men thrashed the water with the paddles to turn the bow toward shore. The boat spun slightly with the tide and hit the rock hard. The jolt threw all of the boat's passengers forward. Melcon could hear the planks cracking and splintering among screams and cries. The bow collapsed and began taking in water. The men in the bow grabbed women and children and tossed them on to the rocks above the water line. Two of the men in the stern jumped into the freezing water as the bow tipped forward. Melcon and a man across from him ripped the lifesaving rings off the gunwales and threw them toward the men trying to swim to the tiny island from the stern.

Everyone was able to reach the rock, some with bleeding gashes. Some might have broken limbs, concussions, or hypothermia. Their injuries could wait, but they could not spend the night here in the sea wind. Those who were wet would not survive.

The captain faced the shipwrecked passengers as they huddled in a dark mass, shivering. "We need two of you to swim to shore to get help. It's about 200 yards, and the tide will be with you. Who is able to swim that distance?" Melcon stood up and nodded. Melcon had swum longer distances many times in the Euphrates River, east of the village. But he knew this was different. Even in the sheltered bay, the sea was icy cold, and the journey across the Aegean had caused an unfamiliar kind of exhaustion.

As the men began removing their shoes, someone in the group offered them small handfuls of wild berries from a small leather bag. Someone else had a flask of fresh water to share. The men spent a few minutes eating the berries. Together, they climbed over the black, shiny rocks along the water line and entered the cold, turbulent water together. The sun was setting.

Melcon could barely feel his hands or feet in the icy water, but his body propelled him toward the shore almost effortlessly. He told himself the swim was short, that he was strong, that others were counting on him. Ten minutes later, Melcon felt the pebbles of the beach under his feet. As he collapsed on the shore, he saw that the other young man was pulling himself out of the water. The beach was empty except for two fishermen running toward them with heavy blankets. A third had already pushed off in a large trawler to pick up the passengers waiting on the tiny island. As Melcon looked out toward the island, an older woman approached him with a large cup of hot tea. She stretched out her arm toward him. It was draped with clean pants and a heavy sweater. One of the fisherman put his arm on Melcon's shoulder and held out his hand, saying, "*Kalosorises, filo mou.*"

Chapter 3
Winter 2015–16
Arian

"YOU MAY DIE ONE SECOND at a time or die in a second, but you may also find freedom. You must decide for yourself." When Arian asked his father about whether he should leave Afghanistan for Europe, he knew his father could not provide an answer, only perspective. Anwar Hashimi himself had left his family in Kabul because of threats on his life, retreating once to Pakistan and another time to Iran. At different times over the previous 35 years, Afghanistan was a place of either little security or great danger for members of the Shi'a minority. Arian's father worried about the safety of the other members of the household. In addition to threatening Arian, the Taliban had threatened to burn down the family house with everyone in it.

As his father spoke, Arian sat silently. He thought about how a life in exile might be the price he would pay for who he was — too outspoken, too independent, not religious enough. Arian longed to be free to choose the rules of his life, free from the Taliban's false and confining interpretations of the Koran.

He had always known the world his teachers presented at the *madrassah* was not science, not history, not literature. It was not truth — just a way to control his thinking. He wanted to know more and had pursued his education of the world outside of school. When he was 14, he had met a shopkeeper who let him borrow books for 100 Afghanis a month. He rode his bike three miles to the shop every week through the alleyways and roads that seemed safest from explosions, snipers, and petty thieves. He read books about WWII and the Nazis and the holocaust, about France and England and America. When he could not pay, the shopkeeper let him borrow books for free.

When Arian was 15, the Americans arrived in Kabul with tanks and guns, unleashing all kinds of violence along the roads and alleyways to the bookstore. Arian stopped riding his bike across town for the books. But something else happened when the Americans came. Slowly, the programs he watched on the tiny television in his family home changed. They were no longer just the government's partial truths or the sermons of *imams*. They showed people laughing together, women in short dresses without headscarves, people fighting corruption and the drug trade, people who had contrary opinions. And wealth. Nice cars, nice houses, beautiful clothes. Arian knew that, if he learned English, he might be able to learn more, have more, do more. At the *madrassah*, he had learned only a few phrases, some grammar, some vocabulary. It was not enough, so he read whatever English-language books and papers he could find and watched English-language television. After watching 81 episodes of *Prison Break*, he called his sister "sleepyhead" when she yawned.

Arian's work on his English-language skills was rewarded shortly after he graduated from high school. The British military had hired him to help with the war effort in Helmand Province, where he had translated electronic messages intercepted in the field. When the Taliban discovered Arian's betrayal, they had threatened his family in Kabul. Fearing for his family's safety, Arian had returned home to Kabul, where he found work as a cashier and sales associate for two Afghan banks.

A few years later, Arian was hired to play the part of "Bashir" in a television series that highlighted women's rights and education, and disparaged corruption and human trafficking. The program aired on a station supported by a Western government and was produced by a NATO contractor. Arian's new work acknowledged his charisma, intelligence, and good looks. His role affirmed his views of the world and some of the ideas he had learned in the books he had read. Previously, those views had made him an outsider in his community. Now they were helping him support his family. But this would not last. One night on his way home from work, he was jumped by five men wearing masks and brass knuckles. The beating left him with deep gashes on his face, the beautiful face of "Bashir." A week later, he received a note from local Taliban thugs threatening to burn down his family home if he did not join them or quit his work.

Other Tolo TV employees were receiving similar threats, and the company advised them that it might not be able to protect them. Arian sadly quit the acting job he loved and found contract work with a property developer in Dubai. For a short time, Dubai provided a life of wealth and enjoyment as a reward for his work. It didn't last. A month after he arrived, he returned home to Afghanistan because the government of the United Arab Emirates would not grant work permits to Afghan nationals.

Because his face was known all over Afghanistan, Arian knew he could not live there. The Taliban would always present a risk to him and his family, which by now included his young wife, Rana, and their three young sons. Arian knew many Afghan men who had left Afghanistan with smugglers, among them two cousins and several friends. His uncle was in Sweden, and Rana's brother was in Germany. Arian had considered leaving Afghanistan at other times but did not want to leave his family. His brothers were in college and did not have jobs to help support the family. His father's job with the Afghan government did not pay much, and his mother was not well, which would probably require her to retire from her nursing career soon.

Arian returned to his family's part of the house and found Rana holding two-year-old Jamal, disabled by cerebral palsy. They were sitting at the end of the small couch across from the bed where his other young sons, Shayan and Amir, were sleeping. Arian told Rana about what his father had said. He told her he could not continue to live in Afghanistan. The family would not be safe there for as long as the Taliban remained in control. As he spoke, he opened the window over the bed and then closed it. Should they go together, or should Arian go alone? Rana knew the journey would be dangerous, especially with three young children, and yet she did not hesitate. "We live together, and we die together." Arian sat down and then stood up. He opened the window again.

He reminded Rana that the winter weather would make the journey more dangerous. Should they wait until the weather improved? "No," she said. "The borders are open. That could change by spring. We must go now."

Arian did not respond. He kissed Rana gently and walked out the door into the fog and drizzle of the December night. He paused on the cement porch, feeling his heart pounding in his ears. He pulled the hood of his jacket over his head and raised his right hand to massage the gash on the top of his right cheek and then the one trailing off under his lip. They were finally healing. He looked up and down the road in front of the house, as he always did to avoid an encounter with Taliban members. But now the road was empty. Patches of yellow and blue light were falling on the pavement from small windows of modest houses. He could not decide what would be more dangerous — the journey to Europe or remaining at home. He shivered uncontrollably and took a gulp of air to fight back the tears. He could not cry. He tried to focus on the hope that Europe would provide a safe, prosperous life for his children.

He put on his headphones and turned on the Afghan music he had downloaded onto his phone. He walked, quickly and without thought, without regard for his destination. An hour later, he found himself in Qambar Square. The stress of his decision was overtaken by the stress of the moment. The neighborhood was full of drug users and desperate people. He pulled the headphones out of his ears and increased his stride. He found himself talking out loud. "You're brave. You'll be OK. *Inshallah.*"

A few days later, Arian contacted smugglers to get his family to Europe. He met with them in the back room of a run-down café. One of the men spread out a frayed map on a rickety metal table and traced his finger along the route from Kabul to the Greek Islands. The journey was 3,000 miles through dangerous territory — armed soldiers, armed Taliban, armed police, thieves, deserts, and mountains. The journey would be by jeep, by foot, by bus, and, finally, by boat to the Greek Islands. They told him he did not have to pay until his family arrived in Greece. If he did not pay when he arrived in Greece, his family in Kabul would be in danger.

A week later, he and Rana left the house with full backpacks. Arian's friend Hamid picked them up in his cab to take them to the location where they would board a bus for the first leg of their journey. When Hamid realized where he was taking the family, he protested. "Arian, no. The smugglers — they're all bad, and the way out is dangerous. It's cold, man. How are you going to do it with the children?" Arian replied, "Thank you, Hamid, but we do not have a choice now."

At the edge of the city, Arian pointed out an abandoned lot, where dozens of people stood anxiously next to an old-looking bus. As the family crawled out of the car, Arian could see Hamid fighting back tears. "Let me know when you get there, Arian. Allah be with you."

The bus left Kabul spewing fumes and bouncing on its aging suspension. Arian could not talk to Rana over the noise of the engine. Their six-year-old son, Shayan, played a video game on Arian's phone while the two younger boys nodded off. The bus stopped abruptly at the edge of the city. Arian knew by the flags waving from a tiny tin kiosk that they had stopped at a Taliban checkpoint. Arian could hear several of the passengers whisper and tried to ignore the tightening in his chest. Three men in fatigues and black masks boarded the bus. The sound of their heavy boots seemed to shake the bus. They moved down the middle aisle of the bus slowly, waving AK-47 rifles over the passengers' heads. Arian heard Rana gasp for air. He wanted to reach for her hand but knew he should not move. He held Amir tighter. One of the men surveyed the faces of the terrified passengers, using the butt of his rifle to poke the bags and backpacks perched in overhead racks. He gestured to the two others. They said something to the driver and got off the bus.

An hour later, the sound of an explosion tore through the bus. Passengers were screaming, crying. The bus lurched and came to a stop. The bus driver turned around, "It is the tire. We will fix it. Do not worry." But Arian did worry. Even while they could still see the hills of Kabul, they had already faced two types of danger. He whispered to Rana, "Perhaps this is a sign that we should turn back." Rana paused and ran her hand over Jamal's hair. She looked up at Arian. "We began this journey. We will finish it."

Later that day, the bus arrived on the edge of the desert, where four jeeps were lined up along the roadside. Four smugglers boarded the bus and checked each of the 60 passengers' documents. Then the passengers were directed to board one of the jeeps. The convoy would cross Afghanistan's desert to the Pakistan border, 26 hours off-road without water or food except what the passengers were able to bring with them.

The women and children rode inside. Arian sat outside on the tailgate with four other men. He covered his head and mouth with a red-striped *keffiyeh* to keep out the dust and muffle the engine noise. The jeep was traveling at full speed on the crumbling asphalt road. At first, Arian felt a sense of exhilaration and freedom. He loved adventure, the idea of a new life. The loud, bumpy ride in the sweltering heat seemed like a small price to pay. But fear overcame his initial exhilaration when, only an hour's drive from the border, the jeep broke down. Arian knew this was treacherous territory, far from even small villages and full of thieves and Taliban militia. He wondered how his family would survive in the desert that night and then get to the smugglers' hotel on the other side of the border. They were out of food and water.

Rana and the boys stayed in the jeep that night with nine other passengers, but there was no room for the five men who had ridden on the back of the jeep. Arian was frozen with fear, knowing he could not survive the desert cold that night in his blue jeans and jacket. As the sun set, Arian noticed that the nearby sand dunes protected the jeep from the fierce desert winds. He nodded to the other men shivering in the shelter of the jeep. For an hour, the five men dug into the side of the dunes with their hands and then slipped into five narrow pockets of sand, still warm from the heat of the day's sun. Arian wrapped his *keffiyeh* around his head and slept fitfully until the sun rose.

The next morning, while the driver prodded at engine parts under the jeep's hood, a local Taliban group pulled up in a truck. Two of them jumped out of the back and approached the jeep, waving semi-automatic weapons. They were wearing black scarves and jackets. Arian could see Rana pulling the boys closer and turning their heads away from the window. Arian worried that one of the men would recognize him from his appearances on Afghan television. He pulled his sunglasses over his eyes and the *keffiyeh* over his forehead. The men spoke with the driver. Arian could hear that they offered, for a substantial sum, to provide tents and food, and to take the family to the border the next morning. Arian knew the gesture was not one of kindness but of business practicalities. The Taliban made substantial sums from the smuggling operation. Its members were there to make sure it survived.

The jeeps arrived at the Pakistan border the next day, where the convoy was confronted by the Pakistani military. A dozen men approached the jeeps and directed the passengers to get out. Crawling out of the jeep, Rana began sobbing uncontrollably, clinging to the sleeve of Arian's jacket while she held Jamal. She and Arian had heard stories of how the Pakistani military treated refugees trying to cross the border. They would rape the women, kidnap the children to sell to sex traffickers, and then shoot the men. Arian could smell the terror of his fellow travelers. Most had run for cover in a thicket behind the jeeps. He took Jamal from Rana's arms and stepped forward with his free hand in the air. He spoke to the soldiers in Urdu. "Please, I have a sick baby. You see him here. He must get to Europe to survive." Jamal did indeed look sick. His complexion was gray from lack of sleep, and the cerebral palsy had left him abnormally thin and unable to hold his head up. Arian heard Shayan giggle and say in Farsi, "Baba, I think their guns look like plastic." Shayan was shaking uncontrollably. Arian noticed that the men with the guns did not acknowledge Shayan's statement. He realized in that moment that they didn't understand Farsi.

One of the soldiers told Arian to tell the group hiding in the thicket to come forward. Arian knew this directive was a death sentence for anyone who obeyed. He nodded and slowly turned toward the people hiding in the thicket. In Farsi, he yelled, "Do not come forward. They will kill you!" He said it again, with authority, hoping to convince the soldiers he was following their instructions. Several moments passed in silence. No one moved. Arian looked at the soldiers and, believing they had given up, slowly pulled a wad of bills out of his pocket. He showed the soldiers 200 euros. One of them took the money. The soldiers returned to their military jeeps and drove off.

After crossing the border that night, a group of smugglers met them and directed the family to a small hotel room, which they shared that night with a small herd of sheep. The smell was overpowering, but the family's exhaustion was more powerful. They slept. In the morning, the smugglers arrived with motorcycles, and the family rode for four hours through the mountains to Iran's border. There, the family boarded a public bus with 60 other Afghans to get to Tehran. Several hours later, they arrived at the bus station in Tehran, where the Iranian police were searching the buses for Afghan refugees. Carrying the three children, Arian and Rana slipped out the back door of the bus and through an opening in the metal siding of the bus terminal.

The family stayed in Tehran for several weeks, which provided a break from the fear and hardship of their travels. They found a room in a run-down hotel in a crumbling neighborhood. The hotel was safe but filthy and overpriced. The aging heating system barely kept the room above freezing temperatures, but the family wore layers and blankets. Arian was grateful for the tiny hot plate in the room that Rana used to make simple Afghan meals — rice pilaf with a little lamb, chicken stewed in yogurt. Sometimes they found spinach to cook with potatoes. Arian cleared out garbage and made small repairs. Rana scrubbed the floors and bathroom. Arian found a doctor for Jamal in case he developed seizures. Although he knew Rana and the children needed more rest, Arian worried about the news reports of border closures, beatings by border patrols, and claims of right-wing politicians that refugees were terrorists. He was relieved when he got a call from one of the smugglers telling him a car would pick them up in the morning for the journey to Maku on the Turkish border.

The car was small, and the family shared it with two young men. The drive to Maku was more than 500 miles. The pace was slow, interrupted by stops that lasted for hours while the smugglers checked the roads ahead for police. Just outside of Maku, the family walked three hours around a hill to avoid a police checkpoint. After they arrived in Maku, Arian's family joined 50 other refugees on a bus, which took them to a mountain road. Just before sunset, the bus stopped. One of the smugglers directed the passengers to get out of the bus with their belongings. He pointed to a narrow dirt road and told them to follow it for "20 minutes" to a house where they would spend the night. The weather was freezing, and the snow was knee-deep. The road disappeared into a mountain pass. Every step was an effort. Every step felt that much further from safety.

The mountain pass stretched out for what looked like miles. The group tried to stay together, but those who were slow encouraged the others to go ahead. With three young children, Arian's family were among the slowest of the group. Within a few minutes on the trail, Shayan was crying from fear and shaking from the cold. He could not continue walking. A young man named Ahmad offered to carry Jamal so that Arian could carry Shayan. The young man held out his arms and told Arian he would meet them at the end of the mountain pass. Arian had no choice. He handed Jamal to Ahmad, knowing he might never see his baby again. Ahmad waited while Arian held Jamal's head in his hands and kissed him goodbye. Arian hoisted Shayan onto Ahmad shoulders. Rana buried her face in her hands as Jamal and Ahmad disappeared around the bend along the mountainside.

After an hour of slow progress, the pass opened out to a gorge, and the path narrowed. On one side, the steep face of the snow-covered mountain. On the other, a drop-off into the deep gorge. Knowing the danger, Arian gestured to one of the older men behind him to take Amir from Rana. Rana complained that her legs were growing numb. With each step, her feet slid on the ice along the precipice. Her flimsy shoes were not designed for such conditions and were by now almost completely shapeless. Arian wondered with a feeling of despair whether she would make it. Remembering an episode of *Man vs. Wild* on the Discovery Channel, Arian removed his socks and slipped his bare feet back into his wet shoes. He gestured for Rana to sit on a rock beside the trail and pulled the socks over the outside of her shoes. The socks would keep her from slipping on the ice. At the end of a seven-hour hike, Arian and Rana found Ahmad and Jamal waiting outside the house where they would spend the night. The water in the bottle attached to Arian's belt had frozen.

The next morning, the smugglers picked up those who remained, arriving at the edge of town in battered SUVs for the 1200-mile drive to Izmir. Several days later, they arrived at a small dingy hotel in the city of Izmir along Turkey's southwestern coast. There, they waited to hear from the smugglers about when they would make the six-mile boat trip to the Greek island of Chios. The boats left from the small coastal community of Cesme, an hour's drive to the west. On their first attempt to get on a boat, the family, along with several others, spent the night in the forest along the beach. The sole on Shayan's shoe had fallen off. Rana found a small pink shoe in the underbrush and slipped it on to Shayan's cold, damp foot. Arian created a small shelter for Rana and the children with a black plastic garbage bag. Arian stood in the rain all night.

In the morning, the Turkish police came to the makeshift encampment and sent the families back to Izmir on a bus. Arian sent a message to the smugglers, who sent a taxi to take them back to Cesme. The police caught them again and told them to board the bus to Izmir. This time, Arian told the police he had no money to pay for the bus. The police told him to "disappear."

Later that day, the smugglers sent Arian a message saying their boat would leave that night from a Cesme hotel. A few hours later, the family boarded a rubber dinghy with 80 others. The boat was designed to hold no more than 30, and, as they left the coastline, the sea grew angry. Large waves were overtaking the boat. The people on the dinghy were screaming and crying. As the boat seemed ready to capsize, Arian spotted tiny lights in the water perhaps a mile away. It appeared to be a Greek Coast Guard boat. Arian flashed the light on his cell phone toward the boat. Three of the other men on the boat did the same. The Coast Guard arrived and loaded them onto rescue vessels. Arian felt sick as he realized their rescuers were the Turkish Coast Guard. An hour later, they landed on the dock at Cesme, where the police sent them back to Izmir.

The next day, the smugglers drove the families back to Cesme for a fourth attempt. They gave each passenger a choice. They could board a wooden boat for $2,500 for each adult or a rubber dinghy for $1,000 for each adult. Arian no longer had enough cash for passage on the safer wooden boat. He didn't have cash for life jackets, either. Arian had purchased life jackets on each of the three previous attempts. Each time, the life jackets were confiscated and burned by Turkish police. The family would have to make this trip without them. He also had to leave without his daypack, which contained his phone and food for the children, because, as Arian boarded the rubber boat, one of the smugglers threw his pack into the water. The extra space would permit another passenger to board the boat.

Arian knew the dinghy the family had boarded was designed to carry twenty passengers. It left the shore with sixty. Within moments of leaving shore, some of its passengers cried and screamed as the dinghy moved out into whitecaps on open water. Arian prepared himself for the chance they would all drown. Rana clutched Jamal and buried her head in his neck. Near the back of the dinghy, a baby slipped out of his mother's arms and onto the bottom of the boat. The baby's mother screamed and began to lurch toward the baby, causing the dinghy to pitch abruptly to one side. More screams. A man next to the baby's mother grabbed her before she had a chance to dive to the floor of the dinghy to pick up the baby. Another man in the boat's stern yelled, "No one move!" He spoke in Arabic, but his words were clear to everyone. Rana was crying. Arian put his hand on her shoulder. He felt his fists and jaw stiffen. Shayan and Amir were still on his lap, shaking uncontrollably, soaked and making tiny whining noises into his chest. Jamal was only slightly better off, buried under his mother's sweater.

A few minutes later, Arian saw the lights on the island of Chios, and then he saw the lights of another Coast Guard boat. The boat flashed its lights toward the dinghy. The distant purr of the engines grew to a growl. As the boat approached, Arian could see that boat was Greek. He sat paralyzed in disbelief. They had made it into Greek waters. They could not be sent back. They were in Europe.

As the Coast Guard boat approached, two members of the crew yelled something in Greek and waved their arms to direct the passengers to remain seated. Holding Shayan and Amir close, Arian put his arm around Rana and Jamal. Arian laughed with joy. One of the men on the ship dropped a rope ladder and held out his arm to a squealing baby who had been lifted into the freezing air. One by one, the passengers on the dinghy boarded the Coast Guard boat. Ten minutes later, the Coast Guard boat bumped up along the dock in

Chios. Except for the baby who had fallen to the bottom of the boat, everyone arrived safely. Dozens of people waited on the dock with blankets and open boxes full of warm clothes. A young man in a bright green vest approached Arian and held out his arms, "Welcome to Greece, my friend."

II
ELPIDA
Hope

Chapter 4

December 2015

The Shortest Distance Between Two Points

THE GREEK ISLAND OF LESVOS is closer to Turkey than any other part of Greece. For that reason, Lesvos has been the first place of safety after a journey from Turkey which, for Armenians, Kurds, and Greeks, has historically been a place of danger. For the refugees of the 21st century, Lesvos might be the first place of refuge after journeys through Turkey involving thousands of miles of dangerous travel.

The first time I saw a map of Lesvos, I wondered how it could be Greek. It is almost 300 miles from the Greek mainland and less than five miles from Turkey. I later learned the island had been part of Greece off and on for about a thousand years until the Ottoman Empire claimed it in 1462. The Greeks got it back in 1923 under the terms of the Treaty of Lausanne, which dismantled the Ottoman Empire and had remained a source of indignation for Turkey. In 2016, Turkey's president, Recep Tayyip Erdogan, publicly claimed that Lesvos and the other islands in the Aegean Sea belonged to Turkey. A few weeks later, he dispatched a pair of fighter jets into Greek air space over Lesvos.

In other ways, Turkey had figured prominently in Greece's troubles that year. But in December 2015, I wasn't following the evolution of international politics between Turkey and Greece. I was on my way to Lesvos to volunteer with a small NGO in its efforts to support refugees coming to the island.

My one-hour flight to Lesvos left Athens on a clear, cold day. The plane, owned and operated by Astra Airlines, was small and pitched unpredictably in the winter winds. On any other flight, I might have felt anxious or nauseous. That day, I didn't have the capacity for such worries. Something about this particular journey felt special. In spite of my analytical nature, I was preoccupied with finding or manufacturing metaphysical connections that day. "Astra" meant "star"; surely a reference to the refugees. The cookie the flight attendants served was good, I thought, nothing like the airplane snacks I had come to expect. Another sign. Of something. Half of the seats on the plane were empty. Did that mean everyone had already arrived or that no one cared? On that day, there seemed to be nothing in the world but Lesvos.

The plane landed without incident, and, as I waited for my suitcase at the baggage carousel, I saw a young man holding a cardboard sign with my name written on it under a logo that said "Billy's." This is an airport welcome normally reserved for moneyed travelers who have engaged high-end services. Billy's was a cheap car-rental agency, probably not Greek because of its name (which was possibly a reference to my first boyfriend or my second horse). The smiling young man holding the cardboard with my name on it escorted me to a tiny white car parked in a red zone outside the terminal doors. He spent a little time showing me how his paperwork acknowledged the car's dents and scrapes. I thanked him, climbed in the car and, after three tries, jammed the reverse gear into position.

The drive to Molyvos was 42 miles from the airport in Mytilene, on the island's northern coast. I had chosen to stay in Molyvos because of its proximity to the boat arrivals on the beaches called "Limantziki" and "Eftalou." I thought I knew what to expect from the articles I had read, which described the town as idyllic and historic, with umbrellas of wisteria covering cobblestone streets winding up the hillside to a Byzantine castle. It was a place where cats sat along the sea wall waiting for the fishing boats to arrive with the day's catch, and Greeks danced in the *tavernas* after a few glasses of *ouzo*. Molyvos wasn't just a place to volunteer on the beaches — it was a paradise.

I drove through Mytilene along the harbor road lined with cafes and government buildings; then I headed north, where the road opened into small valleys beneath craggy hillsides of olive trees and grazing sheep. A few miles out of town, I saw a sign for the island's largest refugee camp, Moria. I had read about Moria, a former Greek prison that was being used as a "transit camp." There, refugees registered with the Greek government before they could continue their journey to Northern Europe through Athens.

Impulsively, I turned onto the road toward the camp and pulled over near the entrance gate at the bottom of a barren hillside. There, I could see rows of cement barracks surrounded by a 12-foot-tall chain link fence topped with barbed wire. A cement wall along the front perimeter had been spray painted with the word for "hope" in French, Spanish, and English. I assumed the other words on the wall were Arabic and Farsi and also said "hope." None looked Greek. The smell of sewage was prominent, and plastic bags in the gutter flapped quietly in the breeze. Small groups of people I assumed to be refugees were standing quietly along the roadside and in lines in front of some of the cement buildings. They were wearing heavy, dark clothes. Most of the men were wearing watch caps or had hoods pulled over their foreheads. None of them seemed to be wearing enough to stay warm in the December weather. Members of the Greek military stood restless outside the fence around a large, blue government bus. I could hear a drone of generators but not much else. Even the children were quiet.

As I got out of my car on the side of the rutted road, a blond-haired, blue-eyed 20-something greeted me with a smile. She was wearing a bright-green vest with a logo on it. The vest identified her as a volunteer, although that would have been obvious enough without the vest. Besides being blond, she was wearing clean, expensive winter gear. As I put my key into the door lock, she said I didn't need to bother locking my car. When I inquired about the suggestion that the camp is a safe place, she responded that the only disruptive behavior occurred when local police showed up. The Greek police, she said, were "openly antagonistic."

I walked to the gate made of chain link fencing. It was closed, and no one seemed responsible for opening it. Since my mission was to get a sense of things rather than make an immediate commitment to anything, I walked back out into the road toward a hillside of tents in an area that was not fenced. I learned later that this was "Afghan Hill," so named because Afghan and Pakistani men were not provided shelter or services by the Greek government or the large NGOs. Shelter and services were reserved for Syrians and people with children. Afghan Hill had been created by a group of young volunteers calling themselves "Better Days for Moria" to support those who were denied services on the basis of their nationality.

Afghan Hill was dirt brown except for the white octagonal tents that crawled up the hillside, creating the ironic effect of a small-town circus. A brightly colored homemade banner was hanging between two poles to designate a sort of camp entry. The banner said "Safe Passage" in Arabic, Farsi, and English. I walked toward the banner. Candy wrappers and empty plastic cups lined mud pathways. The feeling was quiet and controlled. Young men stood or sat in small groups near the tents or around a bonfire on a few low benches made of rough planks. There was a tree that might provide a little shade in summer. The men were speaking in low tones.

At different sites around the perimeter of the camp, hundreds of young men were standing in lines for tea or dry clothes or a few minutes with a nurse. The young men were wearing what already appeared to be standard attire — dark sweatshirts and watch caps, faded, fitted blue jeans, and shoes called "trainers." There were a few older men, mostly with beards and looser layers of clothes. A group of young boys played soccer with a beach ball on a small patch of flat asphalt. I smiled at the boys, and they waved. I was conscious of wanting to feel comfortable enough to feel empathy. Instead, I just felt confusion about what these people must be feeling besides the effects of the biting cold. Were they glad to be in Europe? Afraid of the future? Miserable in this depressing camp? Exhausted from the journey they had completed so far?

Doubting my capacity for understanding my feelings or anything else in those moments, I walked around looking for an assignment. I found a tent with a sign that said "Volunteer Center" and walked inside, where a half-dozen young Europeans sat on small wooden stools talking and drinking tea. I asked one of the young men whether I could help. He said he didn't know. I asked whether he knew who would know. He said he didn't know. The volunteer center didn't know how to deploy volunteers. I didn't really want to know this. I wanted to know that everyone was working together to alleviate the suffering of the hundreds of people here waiting in the cold and mud, thousands of miles from their families and communities.

I moved on to another tent perched on a 10-foot hill along the road and 100 feet down a slippery mud path. The tent had a large Red Cross sign attached to a post next to the tent door. A young woman watched me approach. I knew she was a physician by the white lab coat she was wearing, and I asked her whether I could help with anything. She introduced herself, but I wasn't present enough to hear her name or give her mine. Her way of speaking suggested she was American. She said a very-pregnant Afghan woman and her family needed a ride up the hill to the processing center. I nodded, and she whispered something to someone inside the tent flap. My pregnant family came out of the tent with two volunteers, tall, handsome English 20-somethings in oversized hiking boots and with bushy heads of hair.

I led the family and volunteers back down the path to my car. The pregnant woman lifted her billowing black skirt as she waddled through the mud. She wore a brown *hijab* and a sweatshirt that hung in folds everywhere except over her belly. The man who accompanied her was thin and deferential. He was carrying a crying three-year-old boy.

As they climbed into the back seat of my car, the man and woman were waving their arms and speaking with agitation in Farsi. One of the volunteers said he would go back up to the camp to find a Farsi-speaker and bounded back up the dirt path. He returned a few minutes later with a young man who was still wet and shivering from his dangerous journey across the Aegean Sea. After some back-and-forth, he explained that the man in my car was the brother of the husband, not the husband. The little boy was wailing. The pregnant woman raised her hand in his direction, threatening to hit him. Startled, I almost intervened and stopped myself. My gesture would not relieve the stress of the situation. The volunteers left with the man in the wet clothes to find the husband. When the husband arrived ten minutes later, the three-year-old stopped crying. A three-year-old who understood the fear of losing his father.

I dropped off the family at the registration center, which was located inside another chain-link fence, and watched them walk slowly toward a very long line of shivering people. A police officer at the gate gestured me to turn around.

I drove back down to the road, unsure whether the buzz in my ears and my inability to think in whole sentences were signs of exhaustion or exhilaration. I stopped the car a hundred yards later, without thinking, after passing a couple of young men. I waited while the men approached the car. When they were within earshot, I rolled down my window. "Ride?" They nodded and smiled. They were dressed in the regulation woolen watch caps and layers of dark sweaters, but they were shaking when they settled into the car seats. I cranked up the heater. They didn't speak English, and I didn't speak Arabic, but we managed to share a few words in French. As I assumed, they had set out to walk five miles to Mytilene in the freezing wind. They were going to pick up funds wired to Greece by a relative in Syria. As we neared the center of town, one of them said, "*Nous le trouverons.*" I stopped in front of a tourist hotel and said, "*Bon chance, mes amis.*" The young man in the seat next to me grabbed my hands and kissed them with his head bowed. After the young men got out of the car, I drove a few blocks and pulled the car into an empty parking space and rested my head on the steering wheel.

The second time I left Mytilene that day, I drove straight past the turnoff for Moria so I could get to Molyvos before dark. The narrow, bumpy road snaked through the hills, straightened out through flat, pastured valleys, and then crawled up the hillsides again. I dodged a couple of goats nibbling underbrush and an old man on a donkey packing baskets of produce.

The road passed a beach town called Petra and climbed a large hill over the expanse of the sea. Rounding a corner, I saw the Molyvos castle, big and square and gray, hovering over a hillside draped with red-tiled roofs. A few minutes later, I arrived at my hotel, perched on a ridge overlooking the sea just east of Molyvos Hill.

After I checked in and slipped my bags into the room, I got back in the car and headed to nearby Eftalou, a three-mile stretch of coastline just east of Molyvos. My first NGO assignment was to meet with Eric and Philippa Kempson, celebrities among those who were following the drama on Lesvos. The Kempsons had been featured in many of the news articles I had read, which usually featured a photo of Eric looking out over the water with a pair of binoculars or leading a woman with a baby, waist deep in the water.

The Kempsons had moved to Lesvos from England in 1999 and lived a simple life until February 2015, when Eric committed himself to helping the refugees after seeing a baby's life jacket lying next to a doll on the beach in front of his land. Thereafter, they were always at the center of the island's relief work, which meant steering boats onto the land, pulling people out of the water, handing out clothes and water or, in the case of the Kempsons, advocating for more help.

I drove along the one-lane road to the Kempsons', which followed the coastline to a narrow gravel drive lined with four-foot stone walls. Their one-story house sat at the base of a small hillside covered with olive trees and grazing brown sheep. The setting might have been right out of a travelog if it had not been for the makeshift plastic-walled storeroom jutting out from the side of the house. Behind the plastic storeroom, 4x4 bales wrapped in plastic were balanced on wooden pallets. The plastic was stamped with United Nations High Command for Refugees' (UNHCR) logo. Behind the pallets, a dozen wetsuits were hanging in a door-less closet.

Eric and Philippa seemed to appear out of nowhere when I got out of the car. Eric, blond and weather-worn, nodded and disappeared behind the house. Philippa held out her hand and pulled at her long, brownish curls. She was wearing layers of tired sweats and t-shirts. She smiled politely, and we chatted briefly. Although I had a thousand questions and a dozen ways to compliment the Kempsons' work, I felt at a loss for words. I followed Philippa to the storeroom, where dozens of plastic boxes of clothes were stacked to the ceiling. Each box had a strip of masking tape on the front with handwritten descriptions of what was inside. "Boys winter jackets." "Women's jumpers." "Men's sweatpants." Women's underpants were identified as "knickers." Large suitcases were piled just inside the door, holding donations of clothing from around the world. Philippa suggested I attend a meeting with "Drop in the Ocean" that evening to get on the roster of volunteer assignments. She thanked me for coming and unceremoniously resumed her work in the storeroom.

Drop in the Ocean was a tiny Norwegian NGO created by a Norwegian woman who had come to Lesvos the previous September. Like most of the small NGOs on Lesvos at the time, Drop in the Ocean deployed its meager resources to helping refugees on the beaches of the island's northern coast. It didn't pay employees, and all of the volunteers paid their own expenses. I went to the meeting that night, where a dozen volunteers talked about cleaning up the life jackets and deflated rubber boats left on the beaches and navigating the treacherous coast road after a hard rain. The group conversation was in English. Although most of the volunteers were Norwegian, the NGO culture was said to be inclusive, and, in that time of the world, English was inclusive.

The next morning, I got into my car to begin my first assignment, which was to patrol Eftalou for incoming boats. Most arrived before daylight to avoid detection by the Coast Guard, both Turkish and Greek. I was supposed to be joined by another volunteer who'd apparently left for the mainland at the last minute. I wasn't glad to be on my own, but I tried to console myself with the hope that my experience would be deeper, more reflective, if I were alone. "Hope" was already a theme on this journey — the hope the refugees needed to survive the challenges they faced and my own hope that there would be something about my own journey to connect me to something bigger, something important.

For three hours before dawn, I drove up and down the tiny coastal road that had first connected me to the Kempsons' farm. Heater blasting, I listened to podcasts of "This American Life." This American life for me that day was waiting for people to arrive who could drown if I weren't there to text for lifeguards and medics. During the previous 32 years, my other jobs had involved analyzing problems that had no immediacy at all.

As the sun rose that first surreal morning, a late-model SUV pulled up alongside my car. It was full of young, dark-haired, olive-skinned men smiling and leaning over to greet me. The sign on the car door identified them as working for Islamic Relief. The young man in the driver's seat asked how I was doing. Looking at those young men smiling and engaged, I felt lonely. I smiled and replied that I was fine. Just fine. The driver paused for a few seconds and then put the car into gear. He nodded and slowly gestured with his hand, "You *look* like you are alone, but you are not. God is with you." The car pulled away while I was still in a fog. Why didn't I say something? What should I have said? I hadn't thought about God that morning or most mornings before that one, but their greeting left me with a feeling of safety and comfort.

No boats arrived during my watch that day and, after the sun came up, I didn't go to the Kempsons' to sort clothes. I was exhausted and cold and something else that I didn't understand. I felt a pressure in my chest that seemed like sorrow and a kind of loneliness that I didn't want to disturb with small talk or box labels. How did people do this for months at a time? Nothing had happened to me — what had I done that had evoked so much emotion? I pointed the car in the direction of my hotel.

Back in my hotel room, I didn't need to feel strong, but it wasn't exactly a place to relax, either. Although it was clean and perfectly pleasant, it was designed for summer visitors. The floor was shiny white tile, and the beds were made with single cotton blankets. The only heater in my room was an air conditioner with a heating function that would have been perfect for a cool September evening. But in January, what little heat the air conditioner produced seemed to float stubbornly in a shallow pocket near the ceiling. The night before, I had complained about my room being cold, and the hotel owners brought in a space heater.

By now, the room was slightly warmer than outside from the work of the space heater and the radiant heat of the sun through the windows. I sat on the bed, holding back tears, and unzipped my boots. The floor-to-ceiling windows were foggy and dripping with condensation. I parted the gauzy white drapes, opened the sliding glass door, and stepped out onto the tiny balcony. Across the sea in Turkey, the coast was lined with abandoned resorts and forest, where thousands of refugees waited out the weather and the Coast Guard before crossing. I stood shivering in the cold and imagined what it must be like to live in those forests — sometimes for days — without shelter.

As I stood there, I wondered whether my grandfather had come across from that coast. Whatever the truth, what had happened on Lesvos that day had somehow connected me with him as if he were with me. Just as Lesvos was a first place of refuge for people escaping war, Lesvos was becoming for me a first place of discovering something special and new in my life.

Chapter 5

January 2016

Two Boats

F OR THE REST OF THE WEEK, I was assigned to stand watch for boats to arrive. My assignment was at a beach called "Limantziki," which means "tiny harbor" in Greek. Limantziki was nestled at the bottom of a windswept hill just east of Molyvos. English-speaking volunteers called the beach "Lighthouse" because of its proximity to one of the island's four lighthouses. No one seemed to know why the volunteers called it "Lighthouse" instead of "Limantziki," and renaming the beach had caused some practical problems. "Lighthouse" was the name of another beach a few miles east. Both beaches were destinations for refugee boats, so volunteers occasionally ended up at the wrong beach.

The lighthouse at Limantziki couldn't be seen from the beach, but it was still operating. It had guided hundreds of refugee boats to safety when they crossed at night. Sometimes refugee boats headed straight for the rocks at the base of Limantziki lighthouse. Refugees from landlocked countries had become temporary seafarers without even the most rudimentary knowledge of navigation. For them, it was easy to assume a lighthouse was a destination rather than an indication of potential danger.

The refugees on the boats that arrived at Limantziki were from Syria, Iraq, and Afghanistan. The boats were rubber rafts, rotting fishing crafts, leaking wooden ferries — anything to get them across the water. The refugees paid Turkish smugglers large sums for the passage, as much as $2,000 for an 8-kilometer sail that cost about $17 on a government ferry. Refugees of war were not permitted on government ferries, which required visas. The refugees did not have visas, and most could not get them. The countries of Europe didn't issue visas to foreign nationals whose countries were at war.

I arrived at Limantziki before dawn and took a seat on a large rotting beam. A piebald cat took the seat next to me and then leaned up against me a little. She let me run my hand down the back of her neck. Three of us had been assigned to Limantziki that morning, but the other two volunteers had medical skills and were called to the refugee camp at Moria.

In the dark, I could see tiny whitecaps on the water and the layer of snow that had settled the night before on Mount Olympus to the east. The temperature on the beach was below freezing. Having lived most of my life in warm California climates, it was cold for me, but I felt exhilarated by the sea wind, protected by several layers of borrowed clothes. My jacket had been donated to the refugee efforts by Norwegians, who knew a few things about winter clothes. It was made of black Polar Tec and fitted through the middle for a 20-something skier. It was stretchy enough that I had managed to zip it closed.

The air was silent except for the hum of a small generator lighting the white canvas tents and piles of bright-orange life jackets, left there to guide refugee boats like little lighthouses during daylight hours. I watched the sun edge up over the hill and turn the life jackets fluorescent.

Limantziki had some of the best facilities of the landing sites on the north part of the island. "Best" was not much — a couple of tents where arrivals could change into dry clothes and a couple of storage rooms that doubled as tiny medical facilities for the injured. No bathrooms, no place to provide medical care, no facilities for making tea or food.

The beach was also the site of a makeshift lifeguard station. That morning, two members of Lifeguards Hellas, a Greek organization, were sleeping in a tiny tent on the shore next to a bright-red rescue boat. I knew from the news articles I had read that the lifeguards were volunteers who had left their families and jobs to pull desperate people out of the sea or, preferably, to tell them they must not jump out of a leaking boat into freezing water. Sometimes they used a few words of Arabic, although many of the refugees spoke only Farsi. Most communications also involved arm waving.

The only evidence of the rest of the world that morning at Limantziki were large logos on the tents in block letters: "UNHCR," the acronym for United Nations High Command for Refugees. I later learned that the UNHCR had donated a lot of logo supplies but, by necessity, relied on island residents and volunteers to take care of the people.

The lifeguard on watch came out of his tent. Isadore, dark and handsome, with the physicality of Apollo. The day before, a photographer named Alex had taken dozens of pictures of Isadore coming out of the water after a swim. He was dripping and shiny wet against the backdrop of a rusty-orange wooden boat, abandoned by refugees and rotting, one plank at a time. One of Isadore's colleagues, Nikos, playfully called him "modelo" later in the day. Isadore didn't dignify the comment with a reaction. Nikos reminded me of the Greeks described in tour books. He was handsome, effusive, and full of life. The night before, while a group of us sat around a campfire on the beach, Nikos and Alex entertained the rest of us by openly competing for the attention of the women lifeguards. The women seemed to have the upper hand. Alex later told me Nikos was "not Mr. Right. He is Mr. *Right Now*."

Isadore nodded at me through the part-light and then took a few steps toward the soft, jagged line where the water meets the sand. He stretched his arms and scanned the sea with large binoculars. I watched him.

"A boat. It will arrive in 20 minutes."

For the briefest moment, I wondered what Isadore meant by "boat." After waiting months for this moment, the boats had become something not quite real. On my first three days of watch, I hadn't seen a boat, and some illogical, narcissistic voice in my head wondered whether this was another indicator that my life of privilege was keeping me from seeing this reality. I didn't know where this thought came from, but it reminded me of the times I laughed at my father for blaming "God" for his bad cards in bridge, as if God was taking time out for that kind of mischief. I knew the boat arrivals had slowed to a near stop because of the high winds and freezing temperatures. Even smugglers have a little humanity.

Isadore was waiting for a reaction from me. I felt a surge of adrenalin and noticed my ears were cold. I remembered that my instructions were to text my volunteer coordinator, Maria, for help. The people in the boat would be wet, and the supply of dry clothing was low because a boat of 250 refugees had come into Limantziki the night before. People who are cold and wet must get out of wet clothes or risk hypothermia. In addition to more dry clothes, we needed a medic and a pair of arms for each baby. I paced as I tapped my phone, anxious and unsure. "Boat coming to lighthouse in yen minited. Www need clothes." The spelling errors didn't matter, and I knew from my short orientation earlier in the week that I didn't need to tell her we needed people.

I paced along the water, to the tent, back to the water. I was thinking that I was not a very nurturing person. I worried that I would not know what to do, what to say, how to be the person who was practical enough to take action but sensitive enough to understand what the people on the boat really needed from me.

A few minutes later, a half-dozen cars rolled down the dirt road toward the beach, and a dozen Norwegian and American volunteers poured out, wearing lime-green vests and red jackets — a medic, more lifeguards, and a lot of youthful arms for babies.

I stared at the water and adjusted my eyes to the soft, gray expanse dotted with morning light. A boat came into sight, green and wooden on the bottom, topped with the bright orange of life jackets. As it approached, it looked like a crude fishing boat, maybe twenty feet long. The boat would have been overloaded with twenty passengers, but

I guessed that it was carrying more than forty. Still, this was one of the safer vessels that arrived on this beach — it had plenty of freeboard (the distance between the water level and the upper edge of the boat's side), which meant the passengers were probably Syrians, who tended to have more resources than Afghans and Kurds. More resources meant safer passage.

A few minutes later, the boat neared the shore. A couple of the young men in the boat positioned themselves to jump into the water. The red-vested lifeguards were wading out to the boat, by then knee-deep in the icy water. They yelled something in Greek, or maybe Arabic. They gestured to the men to remain inside. Because the boat had a keel, it might capsize if it were to hit the sand. People on a boat for the first time might not know that. Two of the lifeguards swam to the boat to guide it toward shore, while two others rowed to the boat in a bright-orange rescue raft.

Those of us onshore waved and cheered. A young man in the boat's stern stood and raised his arms in triumph. Others waved back, and I could hear what could have been laughter or crying, probably both. I felt tears running down my face and quickly moved with purpose to check my emotions.

A lot of the passengers on the boat were babies and children. The rest were mostly young adults. Under the bright-orange life jackets, the men were wearing blue jeans, black sweatshirts, dark jackets, and navy watch caps, like the men at Moria. The women were wearing headscarves, dark skirts, and woolen coats, like the women at Moria. Two of the women appeared to be seven or eight months pregnant. There was no luggage, although a few had small backpacks.

The lifeguards began taking babies from the green boat into the orange rescue boat and then rowing it 40 feet to the shore. A dozen volunteers formed a line from the rescue boat's bow 30 feet up the shore and handed sea-soaked infants and toddlers from one pair of arms to another. Someone stuffed a baby into my outstretched arms. My baby was about a year old, shaking and immobilized by fear and a stiff, oversized life jacket. I took off my hat and put it on her wet head. I peeled off the life jacket and wrapped her in a silver reflective thermal blanket that I knew would not be effective over wet clothes, but it was better than nothing. I scanned the boat and the shore for a mother who might be watching me. I had been warned to keep family members together. How could I do that? The women who looked like mothers were helping other children. Someone trusted me with this baby.

I didn't understand it. These people, who had just narrowly escaped drowning, were quiet and calm as they stepped onto shore. They hugged us, and they smiled. Watching them, I stood numb. Then my foot slid down the side of the large rock I was using to steady myself. I realized I was holding someone who needed me to be more careful.

Lifeguards pulled older children off the boat and left them on the sand. Those of us still there at the shoreline gestured to them, hugged them. Still holding my baby, I took one of the children by the hand and headed for the women's changing tent, where, in an area the size of a large bathroom, 20 wet women and children were already rummaging through 30 bins of clothes. The air was steamy. Some of the babies howled as volunteers pulled off sopping clothes and diapers and their clammy skin hit the near-freezing air. Some of the babies didn't cry because the drugs hadn't worn off. Many babies were drugged before they were taken across the water so their cries wouldn't alert the Coast Guard boats that might keep them from entering into Greek waters.

The child at the end of my arm recognized one of the older children and left me. Inside the tent, I exchanged half-smiles with people who believed for the previous three hours that they might die hearing the screams of their children, their wives, their husbands. They weren't talking about it. They were quietly changing their clothes. It didn't make sense.

I paused with my baby just inside the tent flap to find a path to the stacks of clothes bins. The inside of the tent was too crowded to move around. A young woman in a green headscarf and clammy bare feet touched me on the shoulder and put her arms out. She smiled at my baby, who leaned toward her and away from me. The woman disappeared with my baby into a warmer corner of the tent. I felt conflicted, glad for the reunion of the mother with her baby but sorry for my loss.

Two teenage girls standing wet in the tent saw me idle and asked me to find them skinny jeans. They didn't use English. They pointed to their legs and pushed their hands together to suggest "smaller." I nodded and gestured that I would return. I walked to the storage tent and dug through several unpacked boxes of unsorted clothes. Most were summer clothes. Some were suitable for a cocktail party. I tried not to feel relieved to escape the intensity of the women's tent. I felt alone again. Where were the young men from Islamic Relief? I grabbed several pairs of what looked like girls' jeans, probably too big but small enough to make the point that I had honored their request for the adolescent equivalent of dignity. When I returned to the women's tent, they grabbed the jeans and grinned at me.

The delivery of the skinny jeans ended another short period of usefulness. I noticed that the other volunteers seemed to know what they were doing. An older volunteer in the women's tent was standing behind a large table, handing out sanitary pads and bottles of water. She was holding a two-year-old with a sucker in his mouth. Two young men from a group called "Four Brothers and a Friend" were standing in front of the tent, handing out protein bars to some of the older children. A five-year-old girl in a hoodie was sitting near the door in the women's tent and smiled at me as she comforted a newborn. Someone stuffed a pair of dry socks in my hand and gestured for me to put them on the girl's feet. I removed the wet ones, which I hadn't noticed earlier, and tossed them in a pile. I took her damp feet one at a time between my hands, hoping to warm them up a little before I put the dry socks on. "*Shukran*," she said.

Left again without a clear path for how to be useful, I kept moving. I returned to the storage tent to get more diapers. I shuttled between the men's and women's tents, delivering gloves to one and hats to another. I pulled a pile of wet blue jeans and sweatshirts away from the tent flap and slipped on a small rubber boot. A medic looked my way and advised "*Shway, shway*" — Arabic for "Slow down."

After an hour, a large white van arrived to take the refugees to Moria. I watched as men quietly escorted women and children into the van. The men waited for a second van. An older woman lumbered out of the tent and stopped to hug me. I felt her substantial weight softly engulfing me as I wrapped my arms around her and rubbed her back. She began sobbing, as if the horror and hardship had finally caught up with her once she had changed into dry clothes. Several young men made a point to thank us as they gathered up toddlers in knitted hats and the Protec ski jackets of affluence once worn by Norwegian children. Some of them tapped on cell phones, reporting to loved ones left behind that they had arrived safely in Europe. Volunteers positioned themselves for photographs next to the children and adults who had become something like extended family in the previous hour. As the people in dry clothes climbed into the vans, we threw extra blankets onto the laps of the children and pregnant women before the doors pulled shut.

We waved to the vans. The people in them, lucky to be alive, were on their way to more danger and uncertainty. If we had helped them at all, we couldn't help them now. I felt sick.

Those of us left behind didn't look at each other. We moved back to the tents to begin cleaning up the piles of abandoned clothes and restocking the clothing bins. When we did speak, sentences were short and unanswered, and then abandoned. We pushed wet, sandy handfuls of dark clothes into large, black plastic bags. At the end of the day, volunteers from a new organization on Lesvos called "Dirty Girls" would pick them up, launder and sort them, and then put them into boxes marked "Women's small pants" and "Boys' socks" and "Toddler hats." They might return here or to one of a dozen other places on the island.

I left the tent and returned, holding back tears, to the large, rotting beam. The people from the boats were gone, but I felt a love for them that would stay with me. I felt they had connected me to every human being in the world. My love for them did not require me to know them or to even understand anything about them except their need to be free from fear. It required nothing but acceptance.

Isadore was standing, facing the water in front of me with his binoculars.

"Another boat! Ten minutes."

Chapter 6

January 2016

Lesvos Friends

FREEZING TEMPERATURES and unpredictable winds made boat crossings too dangerous, and only two boats arrived that week during my watch. But the emotional drama of the boats and the feelings of connectedness they left with me enriched my experiences with the more prosaic waiting periods.

I spent most of the week with volunteers at Limantziki, folding and sorting recently laundered clothes for the next batch of boats, restocking the rickety shelves with diapers and Mylar blankets, and just hanging out waiting. Some of the volunteers were naturally attuned to these kinds of maternal tasks. I was not, and yet here, these tasks felt precious and important somehow.

The Hellenic Lifeguards and two English photographers were there that week as well, waiting, as we were, for boats to come in. At times, my beach watch was a little like a colder version of spring break. There were soccer games with cheap, undersized balls. Occasionally someone pulled a car down

to the water and played music from *Zorba the Greek* on the
car speakers. We danced, as if no one had thought of doing
that before on a Greek beach. The (male) photographers
and (male) lifeguards would compete for the attentions of
(female) lifeguards all day and into the bonfire-lit evenings.
The men called each other *malaka* (in Greek, something
worse than "jerk") and then giggled like naughty children.
The photographers practiced photography, and the lifeguards
conducted training exercises. One of the lifeguards posed
along the shore in the freezing wind wearing only her bikini.
The photographers had a drone named "Atlas" that crawled
along the sand like a large spider and then sailed through the
sky to monitor the frontiers of the Greek waters. Those of us
who were neither athletic nor especially courageous sat on the
shore laughing as the bright-red rescue boat bounded through
the whitecaps, pulling surfboards of wetsuited lifeguards.

A group of German rescue workers built a couch from
pieces of broken boats and then hauled it to the top of the hill
west of the beach. We complimented their work as an example
of German engineering made from imported materials.

In the evenings, I joined eight or ten of the volunteers
from Drop in the Ocean for dinners at one of the family-
owned *tavernas*, drinking carafes of cheap Greek wine. The
tavernas served up platters of a garlicky eggplant dish called
imam, shrimp *saganaki*, and Greek salads topped with fat
bricks of feta cheese made from the milk of the island's sheep.
The conversations focused on debriefings and the kind of
chatter that follows introductions.

Most of the island's volunteers were young people using
their vacation time or school breaks to help, so they were only

around for a week or two. I enjoyed the company of these young people and admired them for spending their limited free time helping others. They were having an experience that would affect them for the rest of their lives. Toward me, they were polite, but most of them were more interested in each other than someone who looked like their mothers.

I hoped to get to know someone who understood why I didn't go out with the crowd for a party that started at 11 p.m., so I was grateful for Anne-Lene, a blond, blue-eyed 50-year-old from Oslo. Anne-Lene had the optimism of Pollyanna and, unlike me, an extraordinary amount of patience for nonsense. We had been assigned on beach watch together with another older volunteer. While Anne-Lene and I acted as captive audience on long car rides, our colleague jabbered in long, rambling paragraphs, and helped me with decision-making on the smallest of matters. In the context of all the humanity and goodness of our little north-coast-of-Lesvos world, she was the sound of fingernails across a blackboard. I tried to tune her out, but I occasionally interrupted to say something like, "Well, you know, we all have different ways of doing things." Anne-Lene sat silently in the back of the car. One day, our colleague was not assigned to work with us. When I met Anne-Lene at the hotel that morning, she looked out from under her horn-rimmed glasses with an impish smile and said, "Well, well. It looks like it is just the two of us today!"

At home in Oslo, Anne-Lene worked as a payroll manager in city government. She had a husband and two grown children. She said she had heard of Drop in the Ocean from a news article and began following its Facebook page. She didn't know whether she would volunteer on Lesvos until she saw a posting of a three-year-old refugee who looked like her son when he was the same age. In the photo, the little boy was raising his arms in surrender, believing the camera pointed at him was a gun.

The hours at Limantziki were always full of anticipation and camaraderie, but they didn't feel very useful, so one afternoon we filled the car with warm donated clothes and oranges, and headed for Mytilene. The temperatures were near freezing, and we had heard that refugees were waiting on the dock for the ferry to the mainland for hours and sometimes days. It was up to small NGOs and independent volunteers to make sure the refugees had food and clothing.

The ferry dock in Mytilene was not much more than an asphalt staging area adjacent to a parking lot. When we arrived, we found about 100 people sitting in the rain. A giant ferry had been sitting at the dock since that morning, empty. The ferry companies did not allow anyone on the ships for more time than was necessary to get them to Athens, and they made no special accommodation for people who were stuck in the cold. I had heard they were also making a tidy profit filling the ships with thousands more people than normal during the winter months. They offered no discounts to the refugees, many of whom would have to wait for tickets from small, underfunded NGOs. Sometimes the ferries were delayed for days when union employees went on strike. One of the volunteers told me that, during the previous summer, some refugees had waited for days to board the ferries because tourists had been given priority ahead of them.

On the dock, a few volunteers from a small NGO were passing out granola bars and bananas. Others were distributing raincoats made of plastic that was just slightly more durable than Saran Wrap. The people waiting on the dock politely expressed interest in the Norwegian jackets we had. I had never seen a group of people with so little have so much patience. Maybe compared to what they had been through, this didn't seem so bad, although I eventually concluded that this graciousness was cultural.

On the dock, I noticed a handful of people selling snack foods from tiny carts. They wanted jackets as well. Most were Roma (also called "gypsies"), who were treated with suspicion by many of the island's Greek residents. Their children were standing in front of us with their arms wrapped around their shoulders, shivering, and I am sure they were cold. I felt conflicted. On the one hand, these people needed support. On the other, I suspected they would sell the jackets to the same people we were there to support. I left the decision-making to Anne-Lene, who did not hesitate to say the jackets had been donated to help refugees, so that was how we had to distribute them.

The rain and wind were fierce that night. People were still on the dock when we started back to Molyvos. I hated to leave, but there was nothing we could do. As we started back, I was disappointed to find out that the headlights on my Billy's car produced about the same amount of light as a large flashlight. As we left town, I leaned bare-knuckled over the steering wheel. The road back to Molyvos did not have streetlights or striping, and the rain further reduced visibility. As we crawled over the first hill out of town, Anne-Lene announced, "I am going to talk your ear off for the next hour so you won't have to worry about driving off a cliff. We will be home before you know it!" And she did.

My time on Lesvos passed too quickly. The drama of my days on the beach and helping people whose lives had been pushed to the very edge of their existence connected me to something bigger than myself and filled me with a sense of humanity. Every minute seemed filled with meaning, or maybe it awoke something in me that inferred meaning or transcended logic.

The night before I left Lesvos, I felt anxious and profoundly alone. Looking for some music to pack to, I inadvertently came across an online video of Michael Jackson singing "Heal the World" at the 1993 Super Bowl and, like a heartsick teenager, watched it 20 times while I cried.

The next morning, I headed back to Mytilene to board the overnight ferry back to Athens, where I planned to stay a couple of days before flying home. I assumed the ferry ride would help me understand a little about the journey of the refugees. I also anticipated that I would be joining large numbers of refugees that evening. I was wrong about both. There were no refugees on the ferry I rode. Because of the weather, the boats had not been coming to the island beaches in a steady stream, so the ferries were not carrying a steady stream of refugees to Athens. And the refugees did not usually ride the ferry the way I did. I had a large berth with a private bathroom, crisp cotton sheets, and a lot of privacy. Most of the refugees traveled to Athens sleeping on chairs in a common area with the lights on, uncomfortable but probably a lot better than their sleeping arrangements of the previous weeks or months.

In Athens, I stayed in the neighborhood called Monastiraki, near the Acropolis, and Plaka, one of the few Athens neighborhoods where developers had not been permitted to tear down the city's historic buildings in the 1950s and '60s. I wanted to see the city that tourists see. As it turned out, I had no interest in the historic, the artistic, or the beautiful. The Benaki Art Museum, which I would have loved at another time, felt uninspired. The Archeological Museum required too much focus. I loved the Acropolis, partly because it provided a quiet place where I could stare into an expanse of open sky and cry.

I needed to reconnect with the refugees before I left Greece and had heard about an organization called "Soup-Port" that worked in the Port of Piraeus, where my ferry had docked a few days before. Soup-Port was a group of Swiss volunteers with a truck and some mobile cooking equipment. They fed refugees getting off the ferries, most of whom did not have opportunities or money to buy food before their departure on the buses that would await them at the terminal. I sent a message through the Soup-Port Facebook page and a few hours later got a response inviting me to join the team at Piraeus in the morning. Christian suggested meeting at 5:30 am on the ferry dock called "E1."

I woke before dawn to the barking-dogs ring tone on my phone and pulled on several layers of cottons that were not well-suited for Athens in winter. My borrowed Norwegian ski jacket was on Lesvos. After a 20-minute taxi ride from my hotel, I arrived at E1 in the dark. It was deserted and silent.

In other circumstances, I might have felt nervous. My taxi driver waited until Christian waved me down from the other side of the parking lot and then jogged out to meet me. He led me to a single-story building behind the terminal ticket office, where a half-dozen Soup-Port volunteers were in a tiny kitchen, preparing food and tea for the estimated 2,000 refugees who would arrive two hours later.

As soon as I arrived, a young woman led me to a trolley loaded with two giant metal pots. She asked me to fill them with hot water from the tap in the showers, for the tea we planned to distribute at the dock. Still in a bit of an early-morning fog, I rolled the trolley to the showers behind the kitchen and found the hose coming from the hot water tap. I turned on the tap, and the hose jumped, spraying me with very hot water from the waist down. It smarted, and I gritted my teeth to stifle a scream, but I was thinking about spending the next few hours in the freezing weather wearing wet jeans. After filling the pots, I rolled them, slowly, back to the kitchen and joined three others on a production line spreading pita bread with hummus. Preparing food for the refugees dampened my own feeling of hunger. Christian returned with a cardboard container holding six large paper cups of hot coffee and passed them around.

It was still dark and silent outside when we loaded the truck with dozens of crates of sandwiches and fresh fruit. The truck was the kind that might deliver a new washing machine, usually called a "box truck." It was painted bright orange — like life jackets — with tasteful black lettering on the bottom corner of the "box" that read "Soup Port."

We arrived at Terminal E3, where two Lesvos ferries were scheduled to dock a few minutes later. Christian parked the truck strategically to attract refugees who would be heading toward the buses that would take them to the Macedonian border or a transit camp. The truck would serve hot tea and the foods we had prepared, and distribute diapers to people with babies. To accommodate refugees who would not be able to stop before getting on buses, we would hand out packages of food just outside the terminal gate.

As we set up the boxes of food outside the gate, an older man on the other side of the metal gate yelled at us in a thick Greek accent, "You are making it hard for me to sell anything! I am poor, too!" He was standing at a portable kiosk with stacks of cellophane-wrapped sandwiches and bags of cheap potato chips. I felt bad for him. So many Greeks were scrambling to make ends meet. Since I was only a few feet from him, I replied, "I am sorry, but, sir, most of the refugees don't have money to buy anything." One of the other volunteers put his hand on my shoulder and said, "It's OK — don't worry about him."

The ferry arrived as the sun rose. My jeans were still wet, and I was cold. We watched as trucks and cars crept off the ferry ramp and drove past us at the gate. The passengers were slower to arrive at the gate, and then they were a steady stream for more than an hour. We handed small bags and pieces of fruit to the people who walked by us. Most took the time to thank us. A few asked for extras. When this happened, the other volunteers politely explained that giving extras to one family would mean none for another. It was harder for me to say "No." I wanted to say, "I'm sorry but it's only a piece of pita bread with a spoon of hummus — I wish I could change this whole screwed-up world for you!" They all seemed to expect us to be there. Perhaps they were accustomed to small gestures of support, or maybe they had worked with the smugglers who charged them extra, claiming to have paid people like us to provide services in Greece. I had heard many stories of refugees who were surprised to learn that the volunteers were not paid to help.

The bags and the fruit were gone before the last groups of refugees arrived at the gate. I saw many expressions of quiet disappointment. One of the men approached me and politely asked whether we didn't have something left to share with his children. They were hungry, he said, but I had nothing, not even a euro in my pocket. I didn't know what to say. I said that I was sorry. He paused. "It is OK. Thank you. How are you doing? You look tired." A man with hungry children living in a constant state of trauma was worried about me. I thanked him and said I wished him well on his journey.

I left Greece the next day. A few days later, I read that the Greek Coast Guard arrested three Spanish firefighters for rescuing a boat full of refugees off the coast of Lesvos. They were charged with human smuggling. The firefighters had professional skills, and they belonged to an NGO that had registered with the Greek government. In the previous months, they had been cooperating with the same Coast Guard unit that arrested them. This event, which was decried by every large humanitarian organization, signaled a new kind of trouble.

Chapter 7

February 2016

Return to Lesvos

BEING BACK IN SAN FRANCISCO was wonderful and painful. The air sparkled like glitter. Warm houses. Thai food. People who talked about books and film. Still, I longed to return to Greece. I cried every day during the week after I arrived home and, unexpectedly, in the weeks that followed. Crying became a part of me. Me — the strong, the self-reliant, the one who was always able to just move on. I don't know why I cried, whether for joy or sorrow or gratitude. Maybe I was allowing myself to grieve for the people I had lost in my life — my brother, my parents, my aunt. Maybe my experience on Lesvos was a reminder that I was not needed in California — Gabe was on his own, and I was without a partner. For whatever reasons, Lesvos unleashed a torrent of emotion. What I found in Lesvos satisfied one longing as it created another.

My experience on Lesvos also changed the way I viewed my work as a consultant for several nonprofit organizations in the energy industry. My career had worn down something inside me, and my experiences in Greece forced me to question whether I wanted to fight another futile battle against the construction of a dirty power plant or help innocent people in trauma. I wondered whether I could leave my career work behind and live on my pension to return to Greece and tolerate a lot of unknowns.

I had asked myself before what I was missing in my life that motivated me to travel and eventually decided I was asking myself the wrong question. It wasn't so much that I was missing something at home but that my life at home empowered me. The security I felt in my life with family and friends, and the life I had led, gave me confidence to look over a few of the fences in my life. Travel had made me feel connected and free. And occasionally something small would happen that felt revelatory. In India, local children sat on my lap and draped over my shoulders during a fire ceremony on the banks of the River Ganges. In Cambodia, an impoverished young man from a rural village explained his dream to be governor of his province. In Egypt, I rode a stallion at a gallop I couldn't control along the Pyramids. These kinds of experiences were addictive. It was selfish, but I needed to accomplish or understand something, some things, that required unfamiliarity.

So maybe Greece was just the next logical step. And everything seemed to be pointing in the right direction. The week after I arrived home, I went to a friend's 70th birthday party at a San Francisco restaurant. Me'irah was a rabbi I had known since we were hippies raising goats and spinning wool in the Oregon countryside. For her party, she had engaged a local poet to write a poem for each of her 40 guests. When it was my turn, I sat down next to the poet, a petite young woman sitting behind a 60-year-old typewriter. She asked, "What is important to you this year?" I responded, "I want to go back to Greece to work with refugees." As I watched, she typed a short poem on a small piece of stationery:

> your heart
> will travel
> over water,
> into stories that must be told.
> you will find
> refuge in justice,
> the kind that
> saves families
> from hunger, war
> and teaches every
> human breath
> about the
> sanctity and
> sacredness of
> human kindness.

Later that week, on a walk through a modest Berkeley neighborhood, I passed by a parked truck with a very large bumper sticker plastered to the tailgate:

> *"Where love rules, there is no will to power;*
> *and where power predominates, there love is*
> *lacking. The one is the shadow of the other."*
> — Carl Jung

For me, these were signposts on a road to Greece. I knew
that I could have just as easily found messages pointing me
in another direction, but I was not looking for those messages. Two weeks after I arrived home, I told my clients I was
terminating my consulting work and began the process of
planning my departure — buying travel insurance, packing
boxes for storage, researching accommodations. I couldn't
describe what compelled me. It was more than being able to
help. I had opportunities to help everywhere in the world,
and I didn't have any illusions about the limited effects of
my individual contributions. Something about Lesvos was
different, emotional, and a voice inside me was saying, "You
are going to miss out on something very important in your
life if you don't go back."

One day while I was still in the Bay Area, I got an email
from a friend introducing me to someone who was on her
way to Lesvos in a few weeks. Would I be willing to talk to
her about my experience there? A couple of days later, I met
Nanci Clifton at a high-end bakery near my apartment in
Marin County. Nanci showed up in black yoga pants and a
hiking vest. Her thin build was topped with a striking gray
bob of thick hair that tended to fall in her face. She was
friendly and focused.

By the time we met, Nanci already knew more than I
did about some of the ins and outs of the volunteer world on
Lesvos. Drop in the Ocean was on her short list of NGOs.
She wanted suggestions for where to live, what to expect, and
what to avoid. My advice was to start with a plan that she
could easily change. She would learn from her time there how

to contribute and what was important to her. We promised to connect again in Greece.

Six weeks later, I arrived in Mytilene on the ferry from Athens. I planned to stay on the island for what remained of the 90 days I could spend in the Schengen area, according to the rules for non-resident visits. This time, I didn't sign up to be a volunteer with an NGO. I had never been much of a joiner, and my first trip to Lesvos had made me a little leery of NGO culture, even though I myself had been director of two in California and on the boards of several others. The large ones were, by necessity, bureaucratic and slow to adapt. They were fundraising machines, and some of them would ultimately have a stake in the status quo as a result of contracts with the Greek government. In an extreme example, one of the largest reportedly spent millions on an isolated transit camp that would hardly be used after negotiating the abandonment of another transit camp at a much more practical location.

The small NGOs were adaptable and altruistic, but my work with them was too limiting. They operated (well) on a shoestring, usually with volunteers and inexperienced leadership. But I didn't want the routine of folding clothes or sitting on a beach day after day.

I also parted company with some of the NGO volunteers. I assumed all were well-intentioned, but some seemed to have surprisingly little capacity for empathy. On my first trip to Lesvos, I had too often heard phrases like "Beggars can't be choosers" or "She has to take what we give her." I understood that time and resources did not always permit attending to personal preferences when we distributed clothes or food. But, to my mind, such comments were demeaning and out of place. The people coming in on the beaches needed dignity and to know we cared about them as much as they needed a dry pair of shoes. I also questioned whether some of the volunteers focused too much on affirming their own goodness. A ritual that accompanied every boat arrival was the selfies with shivering refugees on the beach. Many of the photos were later posted on Facebook pages or in local newspapers accompanying "local hero" articles. I myself had been guilty of taking photos on the beach until I was reminded by another volunteer that many of the refugees might be uncomfortable having their pictures published because they were religious or escaping persecution.

Like many longer-term volunteers, I planned to work *with* but not *for* NGOs so that I could help with whatever seemed most useful. There were many individual needs that NGOs might not be able to address. I also wanted to learn at least a little about everything, including the communities of Lesvos that had been so overwhelmed for the past year and the residents who did so much for so many people.

After picking up a rental car, I met Panagiotis Mariola-Vati, who owned a modest resort called "Villas Elpiniki," where I had rented a cottage for this visit. My cottage sat with several others in a tiny valley between a sheep pasture and the community football (soccer) field on the road from Molyvos to Eftalou. When I arrived, half a dozen Rhode Island Reds were grazing for bugs and seeds near the parking area, and the sun was setting. Panagiotis showed me the cottage, which was comfortable and modern — a single large room with a small kitchen and a sleeping loft. He encouraged me to call him with any problems and waved as he walked down the stone path to his car. I opened the French doors for a view of the coastal hills and a field of native grasses and wildflowers. I unpacked while I ate a gyro sandwich with a glass of minerally Greek red wine. I had brought a couple of handwoven wall hangings from home that I'd originally purchased in Viet Nam. I balanced them on the picture hangers that had held a couple of prints of sailboats and felt satisfied that these beloved small treasures transformed the cottage into my own.

The next morning, I awoke to sheep bells clanging from the pasture in the farm across the small valley. When I opened the door, several scrawny cats were perched on the stone patio, politely staring at me in expectation. I rifled around in the kitchen and found a small, half-full bag of cat food under the sink. I poured handfuls into little piles on the patio as the cats scrambled for spots. Later that day, Panagiotis laughed when I told him about feeding the cats. "Yes, it's OK. But remember that, when you feed the cats, they stop eating the snakes and the mice, and then who knows what kind of ecological disaster we will have on our hands!"

I headed out the door and, on the way to my car in the parking area, met Elpiniki, Panagiotis's mother. She wore a flowered cotton dress underneath a large apron. She was round, with short, gray hair, and her eyes suggested a life-time of laughter. "*Kalimera! Ti Kanis?*" I returned her smile and extended my hand, which she grabbed to pull me in for a hug. Before I could reply, she responded "Good! Good!" Elpiniki greeted me this way almost daily for the next two months. Her greetings often included a container of roasted eggplant and tomatoes, eggs from the hens, homemade olive oil, or fresh cookies. She ignored my requests that she stop cleaning my apartment. I thought that kind of work was an indignity for someone her age, but she appeared to consider it something to look forward to.

My first stop that morning was a truck on the edge of town I had seen the day before, piled high with bags of bright navel oranges from the island's orchards. I asked the man in the truck for 50 kilos, which I would take to Afghan Hill, where produce was scarce. According to the sign on the truck, 50 kilos should have cost 50 euro. But my purchase involved what I would learn was a typical Greek negotiation: Without asking for any special consideration, I received a significant discount and two free bags of oranges. I loaded up the back of my ramshackle rental car and headed out of town, tuned into one of the only radio stations available, which played Turkish music — reflecting the proximity of Lesvos to the Turkish coast.

I hadn't eaten breakfast that morning, so, after about half an hour, I stopped in the unremarkable town of Kolloni for a spinach pie at a corner bakery. Spinach pies — made with a hearty variety of spinach, feta cheese, and filo dough — are a staple on Lesvos. At the Kolloni bakery, I chatted with the man behind the counter, who introduced himself as Michael. When I told Michael I was visiting from San Francisco, he lit up, sensing that I might be the kind of person who would enjoy talking about rock music from the 1960s. After we did a lot of name dropping — Jim Morrison, Joni Mitchell, the Grateful Dead, the Jefferson Airplane — I told him I was on my way to Afghan Hill. He paused and then said he missed the refugees who, until a few months before, had walked through town in droves on their way to the ferry dock in Mytilene. As he spoke, he filled three very large flour bags full of bread "for the refugees" and shook his head when I offered him 20 euros. He asked me to stop the next time I was on my way to the camp.

At Afghan Hill, the mood was peaceful. Young men were sitting in groups under the trees and in the shade of the tents. Others were standing in two long lines at the clothing tent. I didn't see many women, and those I did see avoided eye contact. Volunteers were in abundance, serving tea in one tent and preparing meals in another. Small groups of them congregated inside and outside the volunteer tent. I asked one of them about distributing the oranges and bread and was directed to the meal tent. A young woman there suggested I give her the oranges and bread, to be distributed "later." Well, no. I selfishly wanted the connection with the people in the camp, and I wanted to know the food got to the people who were hungry. So I hauled the bags up the hill and quietly handed them out to people congregating outside the center of the camp, hoping to avoid a stampede. The woman at the meal tent was correct that this distribution wasn't completely fair because some would be left out. But nothing was fair about the situation here, and things were about to become less fair.

By this time, the international community was coalescing around ways to stop people from entering Europe. Macedonia had announced that Afghans were no longer permitted entry at the border along northern Greece, leaving thousands stranded without shelter or services. The other Balkan

States — Slovakia, Slovenia, and Bulgaria — were threatening to close their borders as well, which would cut off the path to the Northern European countries that had been most willing to accept refugees — Germany, Sweden, Denmark, and Norway.

On Lesvos, the weather was keeping the boats in Turkey. But the number of refugee boats had dwindled also because of intensified patrolling by NATO and Frontex, the European Union's border patrol, in the sea between Turkey and the northern part of the island. Predictably, the smugglers responded by moving their operations south, along the Turkish coast, where the boats crossed to the beaches near Mytilene. Among the volunteers, rumors spread that the Turkish government had agreed to step up its monitoring along the beaches and had scared away some of the smugglers and arrested others. Politicians issued statements justifying efforts to clamp down on refugee migrations by claiming they were efforts to catch smugglers who were exploiting people wanting to get to Europe.

Of course, the smugglers were not the refugees' problem. They were the refugees' solution. The smugglers offered a service made possible only by wars and political decisions, and they were getting rich as a result. With every barrier erected by government, smuggler prices went up. The only good news was that the Coast Guard and Frontex were picking up most of the refugees who had managed to cross into Greek waters and dropping them off at the harbor, improving their chances for survival.

The week after I arrived on Lesvos, Nanci arrived from Oakland, and my 24-year-old nephew, Devin, arrived from his family's home north of San Francisco. Nanci was going to work with Drop in the Ocean, patrolling the beaches. Devin had signed up to work as a lifeguard with Life Guards Hellas. Both Nanci and Devin had come to help with the arrival of boats that were no longer landing on the northern coast. Since Nanci was assigned to patrolling the beaches on the northern coast, she quickly became frustrated. We all wanted to feel useful, and something about the boat arrivals felt extremely useful and, strangely, almost metaphysical. The boats were still arriving on the coast below Mytilene, so we occasionally drove to that part of the island to patrol the coastal road or hang out on the beaches. We combined these journeys with a stop at Afghan Hill with oranges from the truck in Molyvos. Usually, we would make a stop at a grocery store or the Chinese store to buy whatever was most needed at the camp, like shavers, soaps, shampoos, flip-flops, and tiny tents. We paid for these supplies with cash donated by friends and family.

Our buying sprees felt deceptively useful and satisfying. People were genuinely hungry and genuinely appreciative. But I knew that we were among dozens of people who brought in carloads of food and supplies every day and that people like us were not reliable sources of sustenance for the people staying on Afghan Hill. On one of our visits, I apologized to an NGO coordinator that I had only 10 tents for 30 people. He replied, "Well, then you will make 10 people very happy." This encouraged more buying.

On one of our first visits to Afghan Hill, Nanci was interested in talking to some of the young men. We walked through the central area of the camp. Several well-groomed young men were looking at a map of Europe at a kiosk where various kinds of information had been posted. Nanci approached one of them, and I watched the two of them speaking to each other out of the corner of my eye while I handed out shavers to men standing in line at the clothing tent.

When we got in the car a while later, Nanci described her conversation with the young man. He had arrived with his teenaged brother from Afghanistan the previous day. He had been in college and worked part time as a translator for a contractor to the US military. Members of the Taliban had threatened him and eventually took a gash out of his side with a knife. He and his brother were told if they did not join the Taliban, they would not be safe in Afghanistan. A short time later, they left their families, their jobs, and their homes, and they spent most of the family's savings to get to Greece.

A little while later, we left the camp to run errands in Mytilene. As we drove toward town, Nanci became more animated in her description of the young man and his situation. By the time we arrived in Mytilene, she was eager to turn around, regretting that she had not gotten his contact information. Maybe she could help him and his young brother. At least, she could provide him with some emotional support.

When we returned to Afghan Hill a couple of hours later, the young man Nanci had met was no longer at the information kiosk. We walked around the common areas of the camp looking for him and then to the meal tent, where dozens of young Afghan men were watching a handful of others dancing. They laughed and clapped to the Afghan music coming out of an iPhone perched on the meal counter. This kind of brotherly love — the touching and playfulness and sharing — had become familiar to me during visits to Muslim communities in places like Morocco, Jordan, and Egypt. Perhaps the restrictions on relationships with women in conservative Islamic communities drew men closer to each other.

Nanci pulled one of the clapping men aside and asked him whether he knew a young Afghan man in a red sweater who could speak English. He replied, "That's my brother, Muzamil. He's in our tent." The young man introduced himself as Modaser and returned a few minutes later with Muzamil. Since we didn't expect to find Muzamil among the hundreds of young men in the camp, Nanci interpreted stumbling upon Modaser as a sign that her second meeting with Muzamil was meant to be. We stood in the clearing sharing stories and contact information, knowing there was not much we could do to help these young men. We heard from them months later that they had arrived safely in Germany. We never heard whether they were granted asylum there.

Afghans are famous for kite-flying, and there seemed to be few opportunities at the camp for enjoyment. One day we saw a display of large kites outside a small store in Kolloni and bought a dozen of them to take to the camp. When we arrived, I asked one of the volunteers whether she had a suggestion for how to distribute the kites, not nearly enough for the hundreds of people at the camp. She responded that she would put the kites in the warehouse and they would be distributed "later."

By now, I knew that a lot of what went to the warehouses got stuck there while people lived in desperate need of what was in the warehouses. The week before, a toy-store owner in Mytilene told me about the time she donated 20 boxes of new toys to an NGO coordinator who promised to distribute them to the children in Moria. Several months later, a friend of the toy-store owner saw the toys still packed in their logo boxes in a warehouse on the other side of the island. This seemed to be a common circumstance all over Greece. Each time I asked about this, NGO workers explained that they didn't have enough people to sort and distribute the donations, which I believed. But instead of recruiting refugees to support their own services, NGOs allowed donations to pile up in warehouses, believing that some refugees might "play favorites" if they had access to supplies. I didn't understand this logic. The volunteers themselves played favorites, and I wondered why so many NGOs seemed to resist empowering the people they were trying to support. I raised this with several independent volunteers, all of whom told me that the patronization of the refugees expressed the difference between "humanitarian relief work" and "solidarity." "Humanitarian relief" suggested an unequal relationship between those in need and those helping. "Solidarity" emphasized that the refugees and those there to support them were committed to a common purpose and assumed responsibility for each other as part of a global community. Solidarity was a little bit like the less-political principle of *philotimo*, the Greek value of generosity toward community and humanity.

I told the volunteer I would distribute the kites that day because this was "Clean Monday," a religious holiday in Greece with a tradition of kite-flying. I sat down on a bench outside the tea tent with the kites and string at my feet. Within about 15 minutes, a dozen young men approached me one at a time to ask about the kites. "Will you fly them?" "What are they for?" "Are they real kites?" Not one of the young men asked me directly for a kite, but each had a look of longing. As soon as I handed one of them a kite, he would gesture to other boys and men to join him. That afternoon, the sky was dotted with red kites, while dozens of young men on the dusty ground looked toward the sky.

Nanci never saw a boat come in, and she expressed frustration with her assignments on long, uneventful beach watches. She had heard that there was a desperate need for volunteers on the mainland and proposed that we go to the port at Piraeus. The northern border to Macedonia had closed, leaving more than 5,000 people on the docks at Piraeus without government services or anywhere to go. Drop in the Ocean was setting up shop there, literally. It had purchased a blue metal container to store and distribute non-food items.

We arrived at Piraeus a few days later and rented a couple of hotel rooms in the busy commercial neighborhood near the docks. Like all commercial ports, there was nothing warm or fuzzy about Piraeus. The air had an acidy chemical smell that hovered over vast concrete terminals. Large freight trucks growled up and down service roads along the docks, spewing diesel fumes. Piraeus sat exposed to the sea and the sun and the wind. And there they were: hundreds of flimsy tents clustered around tired service buildings on top of filthy, diesel-stained concrete. Turquoise porta-potties lined the perimeters of the tent villages, some of them within a few feet of living spaces. At any time of the day, people were standing in long lines for small meals, soap, baby milk, a used pair of shoes. The lines. *Someday, when these people remember Greece,* I thought, *they will remember the lines.*

A large shipping-company waiting room had been converted to shelter for people identified as "vulnerable," mostly women and children traveling alone. The Greek government had contracted with a private company to serve evening meals, which were mostly white starches, including, at times, dinners of moldy potatoes. We wondered how we could be in Europe, the continent of social welfare and good governance and all things refined.

The campsites were segregated by nationality which, as always, created suspicions and jealousies. Government agencies and NGOs continued to discriminate in favor of Syrians. Somehow, well-meaning people justified treating a seven-year-old Kurd with less dignity than a seven-year-old Syrian. The discrimination in the camps reflected the discrimination in how the refugees' asylum applications were considered. Syrians were almost automatically granted asylum, which made sense in light of the ongoing violence in so much of the country. But it did not make sense to assume that refugees of other nationalities were safe to return home, and international law provided that asylum seekers were to be treated according to their circumstances and without reference to nationality. However, even the UNHCR declined to help those who were not Syrian, because Syrians were "the priority," and the agency didn't have enough resources to help everyone. The kids felt this bias. A 15-year-old girl at Piraeus asked Anne-Lene, "Why doesn't anyone want Afghans?"

For a few days, I helped at the Drops container in the afternoons when we opened shop to hand out items like shampoo, shavers, and toothpaste. Baby formula was in especially high demand. Most new mothers were unable to breastfeed because of the extraordinary stresses in their lives and lack of calories. The Greek Ministry and the NGOs never distributed enough baby formula, which was extremely expensive, so Drops provided that, too.

The lines at the Drops Shop were long but mostly calm. A chart of pictures was hanging on the wall to show what we had inside so that our "customers" could point out what they needed. We had interpreters, too. Affable, easy-going Rafiq was one, an Arabic-speaking Algerian who worked in customer service for an Apple contractor. He volunteered dozens of hours of his time on the weekends and evenings, and eventually became a member of our extended family.

Young children loitered near the shop, hoping for snacks and hugs. Sometimes one or two of the volunteers danced with them or played ball or led an art session on the filthy concrete roadbed. When the Drops asked the adults to clean up the garbage around the tents before the dinner hour, the children did the work. Not surprisingly, so many of the adults were depressed and listless, fearing for their futures, without work or purpose or the communities they had always known. The children, on the other hand, seemed able to remain in the moment and looked for emotional connections. They followed us everywhere, holding our hands, hugging us, trying to speak a little English.

After the first couple of days at Piraeus, I came down with what felt like pneumonia and stayed in my hotel room, feeling imprisoned and frustrated. Anne-Lene and Nanci included me in their work by sending photos during the day and debriefing me every night at dinner. Their days usually began at Jumbo, Greece's answer to Walmart, where they filled shopping carts with goodies for the Drops Shop. In addition to essential items like soap and baby formula, they splurged on tiny pocket mirrors. brightly colored combs, and cheap underwear. These small luxuries were intended to send a message — *We know you need more than two meals a day.*

Anne-Lene and Nanci stayed on at Piraeus for several weeks. I returned to the beauty of Lesvos and odds and ends of noncommittal helping. I was on my own, but I could usually find company at one of the cafes or by showing up for a dinner with the Drops. I got to know one of the Drops volunteers who, unlike most of the younger people who had come to the island, had developed a deep and longer-term commitment to working with refugees. Sofie was an 18-year-old Norwegian from the Lofoten Islands in the far north, where her parents ran a hotel for tourists who came to see the Northern Lights. Her father was a celebrated photographer. She rode horses and, before her experience on Lesvos, had planned to learn farming.

Sofie attached herself to me, probably, at first, because I had a car, and she didn't. And I liked dogs. Sofie had rescued a young dog at Afghan Hill, where the dogs were competing with hungry humans for scraps of food. Sofie named the dog "Jungle," in honor of the camp at Calais. Jungle looked like a small German Shepherd, but she was as nervous as a squirrel, especially when Sofie wasn't with her. Jungle once chewed her way out through a hotel room door when she was left alone. The first time the three of us drove to Mytilene together, Jungle threw up in the back seat while Sofie snacked on soda and cheap candy.

I liked hanging out with Sofie because she was always full of stories about her Norwegian life and shared insights about the drama on Lesvos that I did not expect from an 18-year-old. On a few occasions, Sofie asked me to join her and her friends for drinks at a *taverna* called "Pirates" in Molyvos. I felt flattered to be included in a group of people younger than my son. Each time, I accepted the invitation and later declined it after learning the get-together began at 11 p.m. Occasionally, she called to see whether I was planning a drive to Mytilene "tomorrow," and I almost always said "Yes." On these field trips, I took the opportunity to deliver oranges or shavers and shampoo to Afghan Hill.

Sofie called me one afternoon. I expected her to invite me to drive her to town. Instead she said, "We are getting tattoos tomorrow in Mytilene. Are you in?" Well, of course, I was. One of the privileges of this time of my life was doing a few things I didn't do during my career in mainstream organizations. Sofie said she didn't need a ride this time, and I suggested I meet the group at Phoenix Tattoo Parlor at 2 p.m. The next day I arrived at Phoenix Tattoo according to schedule and took a seat on the wooden bench in the black-walled, street-level waiting room. It was otherwise empty. I checked my phone every few minutes for a message saying the girls would be late. Nothing. Sofie was always on time, so I suspected I had been snookered. If the girls were testing me, I was not going to back out. I started up the stairs where the tattooing was performed, and there they were. Two were lying on tables, and a third was watching from a strategically placed stool. Sofie got a tattoo of the island of Lesvos covering her right shoulder. I left with a tastefully small word in Arabic letters on the outside of my left wrist. It said *amal* — Arabic for "hope." "Hope" had been a theme during my time on Lesvos. It seemed to be the word of the moment, and I learned that hope was ultimately more important to the welfare of the refugees than food or water. It was the real function of so many of the volunteers — to lend a sense of hope to people in trauma, to show them that they were not alone at this most difficult time of their lives.

I also learned that I had my own hopes. I hoped to see the world in a kinder light through the efforts of the people on Lesvos and to feel that I was contributing to human welfare in some small way. I hoped to find something on Lesvos, something both universal and personal.

Chapter 8
March and April 2016
Here Am I

"The arc of the moral universe is long but bends toward justice."

— Martin Luther King, Jr.

I WENT TO LESVOS TO understand *philotimo* and how a community of hotel owners, farmers, and fishermen could help so many people in crisis — without expectation of reward or recognition — people who didn't have backgrounds in managing crises or large numbers of people, who weren't rich, and who were already struggling with the collapse of the Greek economy. My time on Lesvos was a daily lesson in human generosity, courage, and solidarity. I felt privileged to be a small part of it even when I was only an observer.

More importantly, I felt some kind of deep connection to something outside myself that I had never experienced — a communal innocence, a simple commitment to kindness. I felt a sense of purpose according to an uncomplicated formula:

finding a smaller pair of jeans for a teenager, handing out oranges to hungry children, returning a smile.

But the ad hoc nature of the humanitarian response didn't last. By March, the mood of the international community was changing. Refugees who had been treated as innocent victims of war and persecution were increasingly being portrayed as a political problem. Sweden, which had done so much to support refugees from Syria and Afghanistan, announced a plan to "send back" 80,000 asylum seekers. Bulgaria closed its borders. Some EU countries proposed to kick Greece out of the Schengen area for allowing refugees to land safely on its shores. NATO boats were deployed to the Aegean Sea to "deter smugglers." Thugs bombed the homes of refugees, and the news media reported on a plan by the European Union to criminalize the acts of people helping other people in the Greek Islands.

All of this found official expression on March 8, when the EU announced a "deal" with Turkey designed to end the "flow" of human beings into Europe. Turkey would be considered a "safe" state under international law, which would permit the EU to send back refugees who had come to the continent by way of Turkey. In consideration for Turkey's assistance, the EU agreed to pay $6 billion to "support" refugees in Turkey. The EU in turn agreed to accelerate discussions regarding Turkey's membership in the EU and open its borders to Turkish nationals, who would be able to travel in Europe without visas.

The international humanitarian agencies immediately rejected the agreement as violating international law and humanitarian principles. Turkey was not a safe state for refugees, and it offered virtually no rights to them. Moreover, Turkey's president Erdogan was on a path to turn his democracy into a dictatorship. He had shut down any media critical of him. He defined "terrorists" as just about anyone who disagreed with him, which gave him license to persecute almost anyone and harshly — and he had already used that authority to prosecute even journalists.

The deal suited Erdogan's political objectives in various ways, including a provision that could potentially rid him of dissenters — that is, Turkish citizens who feared him and those Erdogan considered a problem for him would be able to enter Europe without restriction. And they would probably not return. The people with limited rights under Turkish law — refugees and other migrants — would be stuck in Turkey. Europe would still get refugees, but they would be Turkish and Kurdish instead of Syrian, Afghan, and Iraqi. Part of the March 8 deal required Erdogan to change his definition of "terrorist" to avoid this outcome. Erdogan decided to ignore this part of the bargain, which became a subject of controversy throughout 2016. The EU responded by refusing to suspend removal of visa restrictions to Turkish citizens and other aspects of the agreement.

Somehow, Germany's Chancellor, Angela Merkel — once a champion of humanitarian relief — became Erdogan's champion. She dodged questions about Erdogan's human-rights record, gave Erdogan the right to prosecute a comedian who referred to Erdogan and goats in the same poem, and defended Turkey as a safe state for refugees. We watched in disbelief the news reports showing Europe's most privileged elites congratulating themselves for supporting all of this.

Amnesty International described the announcement as a "dark day in Europe," and Oxfam called the deal "a further step down the path of inhumanity."

Overnight, Lesvos was transformed from a place of peace with a humanitarian mission to a place of sorrow and anger and exhaustion. Lesvos became a sort of prison for the refugees who had arrived on the island after March 20. For the first time, refugees were not permitted off the island. Thousands of refugees on Lesvos who had been living peacefully outside the camps were rounded up like sheep and taken from the people and infrastructures that had been supporting them with food, medical, clothes, blankets. Compliant people were handcuffed and threatened with deportation. Young men announced they would die rather than return to Turkey, and there were reports of suicide attempts. The municipality bulldozed No Borders Kitchen, where dozens of refugees had lived quietly in tents north of the ferry dock in Mytilene. Eventually, Afghan Hill closed as well because the Greek government would not permit refugees to live in unofficial camps.

The refugees who remained on Lesvos were confined behind razor wire, managed by the military and guarded by riot police. Moria — once a transit station where refugees might need to stay for a day or two — became permanent accommodation for thousands. The large NGOs, like Save the Children, The International Rescue Committee, and Oxfam, refused to support the camp because of its new status as a virtual prison, in violation of international law. The aid that had once been provided to supplement what little the Greek government had provided was now gone or almost gone, and independent volunteers were no longer welcome. The impact of these changes was dramatic.

The camp became dangerously overcrowded, and many of the refugees lived in the dirt in makeshift tents. The food served by the Greek Ministry was almost inedible, and the camp was filthy, unfit for farm animals. Medical care was lacking, and there were reports of abuse by Greek police. The living spaces were blistering hot that summer and would later become unbearably cold. Eventually, frustrated inhabitants would riot and light the camp on fire. Before that, the half-million refugees who'd arrived on Lesvos had never been arrested for a single criminal offense.

In April, after 28 days as prisoners, the refugees at Moria were permitted to come and go. However, there was nothing outside the gate for miles except kiosks selling falafels and fruit. For the few who had money, shopping for food required traveling miles to a grocery store, and there were no cooking facilities inside the camp. Because they could not work with the refugees, volunteers began moving to the mainland to support the 50,000 refugees scattered around the country, some living in the streets, others in substandard government camps. The volunteers who remained on Lesvos were dismantling the infrastructure they created and trying to find small ways to help, knowing that the intervention of government would change things permanently.

In the name of hope and in response to the outcry from humanitarian organizations all over the world, Pope Francis announced his plan to visit Moria on April 16. This announcement created a lot of optimism among the refugees and their advocates. I had gotten a copy of the Pope's itinerary, which

I assumed would provide an opportunity to see the Pope. I would not have assumed this in my own country. I asked my nephew Devin whether he wanted to drive to Moria.

We set out toward Moria early, because we thought the Pope's visit would create traffic and crowds. For some reason, we found none along the way. When we arrived at the turnoff to Moria, a Greek police officer stopped us and, after a brief conversation, advised us to park our car illegally on what he referred to as "the national highway." This seemed very Greek in a couple of ways. The road he referred to as "the national highway" was mostly a two-lane road with potholes and no center line. The other thing that was Greek was the assumption that parking on a national highway was permitted, even encouraged by the police. Something else was strange — there was only one other car parked within view, and we didn't see anyone walking to Moria for this highly publicized visit by one of the world's most celebrated religious figures.

But we parked illegally on the national highway at the suggestion of the police officer and walked a mile to the camp, where we found almost no one. A handful of volunteers were holding protest signs above the road where Afghan Hill camp had been. Across the road, a reporter was being filmed and pretending to be right in the middle of the excitement. Like us, he had the Pope's itinerary but not the details of the Pope's security protocols. We knew he was inside of Moria because of the official vehicles we could see from Afghan Hill, but it seemed everyone else on the island knew that it was futile to hope to get a view of the Pope at Moria.

After hanging around outside Moria for an hour, we realized the police weren't going to let us get close enough to see the Pope, so we walked a mile back to the illegally parked car on the national highway. We drove to Mytilene, where the Pope was scheduled to lead a convocation in prayer on a stage set up behind a 10-foot wall. By the time we arrived, the streets were packed with volunteers and residents. We joined a group of volunteers in a peaceful demonstration opposing the "deal" between EU and Turkey. There were no reporters taking photos, and it seemed the Pope would never see the banners or signs we were holding. We never actually saw the Pope, but we saw a dozen of our volunteer friends from Molyvos. After about an hour, the demonstration wound down, and Devin took off with a couple of the Norwegian women. I drove back to Molyvos.

The next day, the media reported that the Pope joined the residents at Moria for a lunch of rice, olives, mushrooms, and halvah. Subsequent reports that the Pope had eaten "what the refugees eat" was a verbal sleight of hand. The Pope and the residents ate the same food that day, but, when the Pope wasn't visiting, the residents at Moria ate not much more than macaroni or potatoes.

The Pope's visit didn't change anything on Lesvos except that the walls around Moria had a fresh coat of paint that covered over the graffiti expressing solidarity. Within hours after the Pope's visit, the military re-installed the razor wire it had removed for the Pope's visit from the top of the fence surrounding the camp. We all felt sick about this deception, but we were beginning to understand that it was the new paradigm.

After the gates closed at Moria and Afghan Hill shut down, I wanted to help get supplies to the refugees in Moria because, as we all knew, the situation inside would be dire with the departure of organizations like Oxfam and the Red Cross. But with the strict security at the gate, the only way to get in was through one of the few remaining NGOs inside, and I didn't have a connection.

As things happened on Lesvos, I made a connection to a Moria volunteer by giving a ride to a stranger. Shaman had been helping the Kempsons at Hotel Elpis and needed to get to Mytilene one day. During our 40-minute drive to town, the conversation naturally involved the frustrations of the evolving situation on the island. When I mentioned that I had supplies for Moria, Shaman jotted down the name of a volunteer inside the camp. The same day, I called Brent, a blond, blue-eyed wholesome American. For the next month or so, Brent let me know what was most needed at the camp. Often, what was most needed were the very things you would expect government caretakers to provide — tents, soap, basic clothes items, and shoes. Toys and shavers and oranges were arguably not essential, but they were equally appreciated. Ironically, perhaps, most of what I delivered came from the warehouses of the very NGOs who refused to help at Moria. It was an open secret that those NGOs were helping — they just didn't want their names attached to the militarization of the camp.

One day, I bought 20 soccer balls at the Chinese store and asked Brent whether I could help distribute them inside the camp. He agreed to meet me at the gate, where the guards waved me through. Inside, I was shocked at what I saw.

Dozens of men were sitting in the dirt along the roadside to take advantage of a bit of shade below a stand of trees outside the camp. Others poked their heads out of tiny plastic tents. Children with matted hair in tattered clothes played with rocks and sticks. As I followed Brent to a place to park, a large garbage truck came barreling down a narrow road without regard for whatever or whomever was in its path. The air smelled sour, like water that collects at the bottom of a garbage bin. Plastic bags lined the roadside and hugged the chain-link fence.

As soon as I was inside the gate, children who saw my car began following it, surely hoping for some kind of gift or a distraction from the gray tedium of their lives. By the time I stopped, a dozen had surrounded the car and welcomed me out of it with huge smiles. A couple of little ones threw their arms around my legs. A girl who was probably 11 or 12 touched my arm and then my cheek. These children needed so much more than soccer balls. When I opened the trunk, it was clear they all knew at least two English words. "FOOTBALL! FOOTBALL!" "Me! Me!" Brent put up his hands to get their attention. I asked him, "How do I do this?" He replied, "It doesn't matter. Just do the best you can." I tossed the balls into open arms, trying to distribute them to a cross-section that included girls. The more aggressive kids got most of the balls, but they all felt the excitement of this brief moment. I cursed myself for not buying more balls.

As we walked through the camp, I asked Brent about his work. He was a full-time employee of an NGO called "I-58," which was an affiliate of a larger organization called "Euro Relief." I had heard that both organizations were

Christian, and I noticed that many of the women volunteering at the camp were wearing attire that was much like the Mennonites of the United States — modest cotton blouses, headscarves, and long skirts, even in the heat of the summer. They presented a stark contrast to European and American volunteers, who typically wore yoga pants, tight tank tops, and flip-flops. I asked Brent about his organization's mission and the meaning of its name. He explained that his NGO differed from organizations like MSF and Oxfam because it did not involve itself in the political aspects of humanitarian relief. Its mission was to help people in need as a way to honor Christ's teachings. "I-58" was a reference to the Book of Isaiah, Verse 58.

When I arrived home that night, I looked up the passage that had inspired Brent and his colleagues:

> Is it not to share your food with the hungry
> and to provide the poor wanderer with shelter —
> when you see the naked, to clothe them,
> and not to turn away from your own flesh and blood?
> Then your light will break forth like the dawn,
> and your healing will quickly appear;
> then your righteousness will go before you,
> and the glory of the LORD will be your rear guard.
> Then you will call, and the LORD will answer;
> you will cry for help, and he will say: Here am I.

I was not and would never be Christian, but these words moved me deeply. I understood that what I was feeling on Lesvos as a non-believer was like the religious inspiration of believers, an essential feeling of empathy and concern. I understood for the first time what I had heard in church as a child: When you open your heart, you are rewarded with gifts you could never expect. I was beginning to feel what I already knew intellectually — that the world is a constant fight between the best in us and the worst and that one will never fully overtake the other. We each have only the power of one, and we focus on the riches of working for what we believe is good.

III
PHILOTIMO
2012–2016
Friend of Honor

Chapter 9
Spring 2016
Learning Greek

BY THE TIME I FIRST arrived on Lesvos in the winter of 2015, dozens of NGOs and thousands of volunteers were providing food and water, temporary shelter, and transportation across the island. They were everywhere — driving medic vans, hauling clothes in white rental compact cars, hanging out at all hours in the *tavernas* and cafes. They sat on beaches in lime-green hi-vis vests and red-vested wetsuits, and sorted clothes in abandoned buildings.

In contrast, Lesvos residents seemed to be going about their usual routines. They acknowledged the volunteers with discounts and friendly conversation. There were occasional complaints about careless drivers and young people who partied too much. At the time, however, I did not see many Greeks pulling refugees out of the water or driving vans between Molyvos and Mytilene. This motivated a view by some of the volunteers that "If all of the volunteers went home tonight, there would be nothing left but empty tents and dead bodies."

In fact, the residents of Lesvos already had done so much. By winter 2015, many were suffering from a sort of exhaustion after nine months of saving lives and providing moral support to more than 300,000 people who came into Lesvos on boats before October 2015 — that is, before the island was swarming with NGOs and volunteers. Many of them had extended themselves when they could have looked away. Some were on the beaches. Some were cleaning up the predictable messes or hauling bottles of water and clothes. Some risked arrest by transporting pregnant or disabled people across the island. Some sailed their boats out into dangerous waters to save lives. Many did not have the choice, either practically or morally, to conduct their lives as they normally would have. Even those who did not actively help were affected by the stress of the circumstances.

Some Lesvos residents committed themselves to the cause of the refugees even after the volunteers and NGOs arrived, the Kempsons and Melinda McRostie among them. Alison Terry-Evans was another resident who had thrown herself into the work by creating a nonprofit called "Dirty Girls," which laundered and re-deployed clothes the refugees had shed when they arrived on the beaches.

But there were other residents who had complicated lives and, in some cases, full-time responsibilities with jobs and families when the refugees began arriving on Lesvos. They did not volunteer to help — the task came to them, and they accepted it. Their support of the refugees was not a political act or a cause but a responsibility to their human neighbors in trouble. Lesvos residents did not want to be identified as part of the effort or especially as "heroes." I heard it many times: "It was nothing. It was just what we had to do." When the subject of the previous year came up in conversation, one of the residents looked out into the distance as if he were trying to hear another voice help him explain what they had seen and done.

I spent several months on Lesvos hoping to understand more about what the residents of Lesvos had done before I arrived and how it had affected their lives. I learned the stories of a few.

Chapter 10
December 2012
Baba Nur

I MET MICHALIS IN MY SEARCH to learn something about Papa Stratis, who had died three months before, in October 2015. Papa Stratis was a Greek Orthodox priest who had spent the last years of his life dedicating himself to supporting the refugees on Lesvos. Michalis was his son. The first time I met Michalis, he was standing in front of the Coast Guard office in Molyvos, tall and athletic, dark-eyed, dark-haired, olive-skinned. His manner was friendly but modest like so many of the people I'd met on Lesvos. He was single — a distinction for a 36-year-old man in this traditional Greek community.

As a member of the island's Coast Guard, Michalis was very familiar with the boats coming to the island and had been a part of many rescues. Michalis lived in Kolloni, about 20 minutes from the Coast Guard Station in the harbor at Molyvos. Beginning in early 2015, on his drive to work, he passed lines of young men walking along the road toward Kolloni. Most were thin and dark-skinned with a mop of black hair, wearing blue jeans and fitted jackets. Most were carrying small backpacks. They were not Greek.

Although the sight was strange for the island, Michalis did not think of the men as strangers. He may have picked up some of these men in his Coast Guard boat as they struggled to reach shore in rubber rafts or tiny fishing boats along the northern part of the island. The vessels were never seaworthy, and they were always overloaded. Worse, the smugglers facilitating these crossings sent the boats out at night to avoid detection. Night crossings were dangerous. The people on the boats lacked navigation skills. There were no lights on Molyvos beaches to identify safe landing places, and the boats were not equipped with searchlights.

The Coast Guard command in Athens reported to the national government, which Michalis knew had directed the island Coast Guard patrol to discourage the boats from coming into Greek waters. The island command followed orders by blocking the refugee boats before they crossed over into Greek water and radioing the Turkish Coast Guard to pick them up, an open secret and arguably a violation of international law. Once the boats arrived in Greek waters, they could not be turned back, according to international law. Unless the Greek authorities or Frontex notified the Turkish Coast Guard of the boats in Turkish waters, the Turks looked the other way. Refugees from Afghanistan, Syria, and Iraq were pouring into Turkey across the land borders with Syria and Iran, and Turkey was not going to force them to stay.

Most of the boats that landed near Molyvos were coming from sites along the Turkish coast near Konunevi where the hills ran down to the water and where abandoned resort hotels and forests scattered the shore. Turkish smugglers there had a steady business selling seats in small boats to people hoping to reach Europe. Most of the men were from Afghanistan and Iraq. Because they did not enter Europe legally when they arrived on Lesvos, transporting them on land was also illegal, tantamount to smuggling, until they were registered with the police in Mytilene. The law applied to public transportation as well as private, paid or unpaid. So these refugees walked from their landing sites on the north part of the island to Mytilene. There they would register with the police and take the ferry to Athens.

The walk for the people off the boats was 40 miles along a road that is steep in places, hot in summer, cold in winter. Except for Kolloni, there were few villages along the way and few prospects for shelter, water, or food for these men, especially if they had used the last of their cash paying smugglers.

Michalis also knew these men and their situation well because his father had become consumed with the task of helping them survive the part of their journey that had them crossing the island of Lesvos on their way to the mainland. Ordained Father Estratrious Dimou, "Papa Stratis" led a small congregation in the little village of Parakolia outside Kolloni. The Syrian refugees waiting in Turkey called him "Baba Nur," Arabic for "Father Light."

Except for the chain smoking, Papa Stratis looked every bit the part of a Greek Orthodox priest. He was large, bearded, with kind eyes and long black hair. He laughed easily, but he was dead serious when it came to his commitment to the refugees, which had begun five years earlier after he had seen a group of refugees sitting by the roadside, exhausted and frayed. He detoured to the local bakery and purchased cheese pies for them. The gesture soon evolved into a way of life. He would find the refugees, feed them, sit with them, and, in a language they did not understand, offer them encouragement.

In 2009, Papa Stratis started a small NGO called *Agkalia*, Greek for "embrace," and began soliciting donations wherever he could find them. Although Michalis could not remember a time when his father wasn't helping someone in the community, this more-recent group of people coming to Lesvos on boats seemed to have a more-profound effect on him. Perhaps his compulsion was connected to his grandparents' escape from Smyrna in Anatolia in 1922, when the Turkish government burned down most of the city and killed most of its Greek and Armenian residents.

Michalis understood his father's obsession and referred to it as "our historic duty," as his father did. And history did not stop for the celebration of Christmas, which, for followers of the Greek Orthodox church, was sacred, a time for reflection and communion. Following services at the church that morning, Papa Stratis and his family gathered for the traditional meal of roasted lamb, spinach pies, and baked eggplant. At the table, the cell phone rang, by then a frequent occurrence without regard for the hour of the day, the day of the year, or illness. Papa Stratis answered and listened for a moment. He put the phone down and picked up the napkin from his lap. "A boat of 60 people at Skala Sykamania," he said. The local fishermen had hauled it to shore after pulling many out of the water. They would need clothing, shoes, food. Michalis looked at his mother, whose eyes were lowered. "Father, please don't go. We need you here today. They will get help from others."

His father pulled his heavy wool coat over his robes and reached for his *kamillavka*, the black conical hat of the Greek Orthodox priesthood. "My food will wait for me. These people cannot wait." He left.

Chapter 11

March 2015

Aphrodite and Panagiotis

"Thank you. This is the first time in two months anyone has smiled at me."
— Refugee arriving at Aphrodite Beach, Lesvos.

I FIRST MET Panagiotis Vati-Mariola on my second visit to Lesvos. My cottage at Villas Elpiniki belonged to his family, and he was my landlord. When I arrived on Lesvos that February, Panagiotis met me at the ferry dock. He did not look very Greek — more like a 40-year-old professor at a Midwestern college. He was blue-eyed, fair-haired, and fair-skinned. He wore khaki pants and a button-down shirt and worked as an accountant at the Port Authority. Panagiotis invited me to have coffee at a cafe a few blocks away on the waterfront road and seemed eager to talk about the past year on Lesvos. It had been an emotional and challenging time. Hundreds of boats had arrived on tiny Aphrodite Beach, where his family owned and operated a large resort hotel. At first, the arrivals presented problems to be solved. Eventually, they became so routine that they were just another part of hotel operations. His voice had a cadence of ease, and the way he told his story suggested affection for the people his family helped. "We were not philanthropists. But this has changed us. It has changed everything on the island."

Panagiotis suggested there were tensions in Molyvos. Not everyone appreciated the assistance some were providing the refugees, among them, some of the community's business owners and members of a right-wing populist movement called "Golden Dawn." Others, like the Kempsons, thought Lesvos residents were not doing enough. Panagiotis understood both. He was more of a pragmatist than an advocate.

Panagiotis was married to Aphrodite, who taught English to the community's children. Aphrodite was a dark-eyed Greek with a full mane of black hair that was cut and colored in a way that seemed suited to her personality — energetic, easy, and a little dramatic. She laughed a lot, and she was comfortable taking the lead, whether in front of her classroom or at a community event. Although she was Greek, Aphrodite spoke English like an American because she'd been born in Texas. After moving to Lesvos with her family at age 11, she returned to the US to attend college at the University of Texas. Aphrodite and Panagiotis lived with their two children in a large stone house near the top of the hill in Molyvos. The house had a view of the harbor in Molyvos and had been remodeled with wooden floors, large, insulated windows, and a modern kitchen.

In spite of the flailing Greek economy, the Vati-Mariola family had successfully built their hotel business, partly by working with tour companies in Germany and Norway that chartered direct flights to Lesvos. In addition to Villas Elpiniki, the family owned the Aphrodite Hotel, a modern resort nestled below the hills between Eftalou and the promontory of Molyvos that was once the ancient city of Mithimna. The hotel sat at the intersection of two one-lane dirt roads, flanked by sweeping hillsides speckled with the island's brown and black sheep. Its two-story pink stucco buildings had simple rooms with tiled floors, Wi-Fi, and satellite television. The hotel perimeter was lined with mature date palms and bushy pine trees and was one of the only hotels on the northern part of the island that had its own "level in" beach, also called Aphrodite, small but protected by thirty-foot bluffs on either side of the tiny cove.

By early 2015, the Aphrodite was almost completely booked for the summer season. Bird watchers were scheduled to arrive in April and May for the migrations of dozens of species, including herons, flamingos, and egrets. Later in the summer, families and couples would spend their holidays lounging by the pool, kayaking, and hiking. It promised to be a busy and lucrative year.

Aphrodite and Panagiotis had plenty of work to do in spring to prepare for reopening the hotel in early April. Winters in Molyvos were quiet except for the weather. That winter, fierce winds had blown down trees and left debris in every corner. The rains left ponds of brownish-green algae in the sea-blue swimming pool. Walls needed painting. Shrubs needed trimming. By late February, the family had engaged a handful of their regular employees to begin this work.

On his frequent visits to the hotel after work on the weekdays, Panagiotis found evidence that small boats were arriving at Aphrodite Beach. Bright-orange life jackets and black inner tubes were piled in a corner of the beach, usually next to a deflated rubber raft. Balloons and wet socks were scattered among the rocks. Panagiotis knew the boats carried Syrian and Afghan refugees from the Turkish coast just a few miles across the water. This was not new. Most Molyvos residents had seen them, the young men off the boats, tired but determined as they walked in small groups from the beaches and through town to the main road. They were easy to identify, most in fitted blue jeans and dark jackets, carrying smart phones and small backpacks. Many would stop at Theodosius' market for food and water. They were quiet and polite. They came, and they left.

In past years, the boats had been infrequent, maybe one or two a week over the entire island. The Hellenic Coast Guard had been patrolling the waters in recent years to discourage these crossings. This would change after January 26, 2015, when the people of Greece elected Alexis Tsipras to be its prime minister. Tsipras was a member of the nation's socialist party, SYRIZ, and had promised to put the Greek people ahead of non-Greek investment bankers, who were banging on Greece's door for repayment of 316 billion euros — considerably more than the country's annual gross national product. The Tsipras government would have an unexpected impact on the people of Molyvos. Someone in some corner of the government's ministry offices directed the Hellenic Coast Guard to change its procedures. In patrolling the Aegean Sea on the island's north coast, the Coast Guard stopped blocking boats from entering Greek waters. Instead, it watched for boats in trouble. The smugglers responded. By March, the number of boats arriving on Lesvos had increased dramatically, and many were beginning to arrive at the Aphrodite Hotel.

The work to prepare the Aphrodite Hotel for opening in early April was steady by the middle of March. One afternoon, Aphrodite's father, Dmitri, took a break from the paperwork in the hotel and walked down to the beach. He pulled a cigarette pack out of his pocket and fumbled in his front pocket for a lighter. As he looked out over the water, he saw something approaching the beach. He waited to light the cigarette, squinting. A small flock of terns flapped along the horizon against the hills on the Turkish coast. He picked up a rock and skimmed it across the glassy sea water. As his eyes followed the rock to the end of its dance on top of the water, Dmitri saw something approaching the beach. Walking closer to the water's edge, he saw a tiny boat, bobbing and lurching, black rubber with a blur of bright-orange life jackets barely above the water line. He could hear its weak motor, sputtering through the muffled clanging of the sheep's bells on the hillside above the cove.

Dmitri yelled up the hill toward the hotel. "Aphrodite, there is a boat approaching the beach! Bring dry clothes and blankets!"

When she heard her father call, Aphrodite was cleaning glasses in the restaurant 50 feet from the beach. She had heard that refugees were starting to arrive during daylight hours, but, because the boats had arrived only after dark, she had never seen a boat land or the people who crossed the hotel property on their way to town.

Aphrodite ran to a hotel room where she kept extra clothes for her own children and stuffed what she could find into a plastic bag covering a trash bin under the dressing table. She grabbed blankets off the beds and threw them over her shoulder. On her way down the path toward the pool, she passed the hotel bookkeeper — "Despina, please bring bottled water and whatever food you can find to the beach!"

As Dmitri watched, the boat reached the shelter of the cliffs forming the tiny beach cove. He waved and tried to smile in welcome. From the beach, he could see the boat held twenty passengers. It was not large enough to carry more than eight safely. Twelve men, three women, five children. Two of the men jumped into knee-deep water, pulling the boat to shore. They were tall and fit with stylish haircuts and recently purchased shoes called "trainers." One of the men in the boat raised his arms and yelled *"Allahu Akbar!"*

The two in the water extended their arms to two women who slowly and gracefully climbed over the side of the dingy and waded through the cold water to the pebbled beach, where they collapsed on the stone retaining wall separating the beach from the hotel lawn. One woman in a brown headscarf and ankle-length skirt was carrying a baby. The baby was soaked from head to toe and swaddled in a light plastic life jacket that would not have been much help in a swimming pool. The woman, wet and exhausted, walked toward Dmitri and pushed the child into his arms. Unprepared, he fumbled as he steadied his hold on the infant and managed to say, "Welcome to Europe, my friend." The woman nodded and smiled as she looked toward the water's edge, where a young boy was shaking and moaning in the cold air.

Dmitri stood with the baby, immobilized. He pulled off the flimsy life jacket that had been tied on to the baby and then peeled off his sweater and wrapped it around the baby. Her lips were turning blue, so he walked toward the pile of clothing on the sea wall as he scanned the area for the baby's mother. One of the men from the boat reached into his pocket and pulled out a large hunting knife. He raised the knife over the boat and plunged it into the black rubber again and again. Dmitri instinctively shivered at the sight, even though he was aware that the gesture was intended to ensure no one would fill the boat with its former passengers and drag it back into Turkish waters. The boat's tiny engine fell over onto its side as the boat collapsed into a flat mass.

Aphrodite's heart was pounding. Running down the lawn adjacent to the pool, she could see her father and the people who had come in on the boat. Dropping the clothes and blankets onto the retaining wall, she held her arms out to take a toddler from the arms of a teenaged boy who was shaking uncontrollably. She began peeling off the cold, wet plastic tied onto the toddler as she gestured to the people on the beach to help themselves to the pile of blankets and clothes she had brought. The baby in her arms began crying, a good sign because it meant she was not in shock. Mothers were helping older children remove wet clothes and get into those Aphrodite had brought from the hotel. She pulled the baby under her sweater and felt cold skin pressing against her neck. The baby's mouth found a fold of skin on Aphrodite's neck, and Aphrodite heard the familiar sucking sound of hunger.

Aphrodite looked up. A tiny Afghan girl was smiling at her. She was wearing Sofie's pink sweater with the duck sewn onto the pocket and the red sweatpants Sofie wore to dance class. An older boy next to her was wearing Pavlos' blue jeans and hooded green sweatshirt. Aphrodite fought back tears, realizing these children could be her own.

The following morning, another boat arrived, a blue wooden fishing boat with 40 Syrians. It was a Saturday, so Sofie and Pavlos were at the hotel. Sofie followed her mother down to the beach and kept an eye on her. Sofie watched the children get off the boat and change into dry clothes and shoes as Despina handed out oranges and bags of chips. Sofie had brought a bag of popcorn down to the beach. A girl off the boat stood quietly 10 feet from Sofie. Her thick black hair was still wet, and she was wearing an oversized sweatshirt from one of the plastic bins Despina had brought down to the beach. Sofie took a few steps and held out her bag of popcorn toward the girl. The girl nodded her head slightly and smiled, reaching her hand into Sofie's paper bag. Sofie nudged the bag into the girl's hand. Pavlos sat above the retaining wall on the beach, watching in silence.

Sofie watched as the little girl and her family headed for the van that would take them to the village. Sofie followed. As the girl approached the van, she handed Sofie her own bag of chips. Sofie watched the van pull away, a tiny hand extending from a window, waving goodbye.

Chapter 12
April 2015
Natasha

LESVOS WAS A SMALL community, and Molyvos was much smaller. After living there for only a couple of weeks, it became almost impossible for me to go two blocks without running into someone I knew. Partly for this reason, it always felt safe, and I got into the habit of picking up people walking on the long stretches of road between the town and the beaches.

One day, I stopped the car when I saw a woman walking in the direction of the beach roads and asked her whether she wanted a ride. She hopped into the car and introduced herself as Laura. Laura was American, mid-thirties, with cropped blond hair and blue eyes. She was on her way to Donkey Warehouse, so named because of its proximity to the sign for Michalis' Donkey Farm. At Donkey Warehouse, Laura helped manage boxes of clothes and medical supplies donated for the people coming in on the beaches and at the camps. Laura subsequently boasted that she had enjoyed a Valentine's Day date with a Lesbian. The Lesbian was her co-worker at the warehouse, a sheepherder named Stellios, who invited her to help round up the herd on the back of his motorbike. The boast and the timing of the roundup turned out to be providential. Several months later, Stellios became Laura's sweetheart.

Laura was a volunteer and had been on the island for only a couple of weeks, but she knew some of the residents, and she thought I would like to meet Natasha, who worked for Starfish. And to find Natasha who worked for Starfish, I should go to the Captain's Table.

The Captain's Table was a small, modest cafe with a large and sweeping view of the harbor in Molyvos. It served traditional Greek food that was just slightly healthier and occasionally a little more inventive than what was served in the other cafes in town. Patrons could order off the menu, but Avram might discourage diners from the menu and describe whatever came in on the fishing boat or from the farms in the central part of the island. It was one of the only places on Lesvos that didn't permit smoking.

The Captain's Table sat just inside the tip of a promontory that looks out to a site on the Turkish coast the volunteers called "Three Hotels." Formerly a stretch of popular resorts, Three Hotels was abandoned except for the smugglers' operations and the dozens of refugees waiting to cross the water in the forest, sometimes for days if the weather was poor or the delivery of rubber dinghies was delayed. When they set sail, it was often for Molyvos harbor, in front of Captain's Table.

The owner of Captain's Table, Melinda McRostie, began supporting the refugees coming in on the boats early. Melinda was English, in her 50s, a strawberry-blonde, *zoftig*. She grew up mostly on Lesvos after her mother, Jennifer, divorced Melinda's father and married a Lesvos fisherman. Melinda herself married a Greek man, Stergious, and settled into her life in Molyvos. In some ways, though, Melinda remained decidedly English — reserved, private, self-assured, and careful with her words.

At first, Melinda helped the people coming in on the boats with sandwiches and tea. They arrived at night and slept in the harbor until sunrise. Until 2015, the number of people arriving in front of the restaurant was small — about 100 every week. She could manage providing them a little support without organization or outside resources. That was changing by early 2015, when hundreds might arrive in a single day.

As the numbers of refugees increased, the cost of helping them became overwhelming. Feeling a responsibility that was draining her resources, Melinda created a nonprofit organization to facilitate fundraising and recruiting volunteers. She called it "Starfish," in honor of a story by anthropologist and author Loren Eisely, that provided a beautiful metaphor for her efforts:

> While wandering a deserted beach at dawn…I saw a man in the distance bending and throwing as he walked the endless stretch toward me. As he came near, I could see that he was throwing starfish, abandoned on the sand by the tide, back into the sea. When he was close enough I asked him why he was working so hard at this strange task. He said that the sun would dry the starfish and they would die.

> I said to him that I thought he was foolish. There were
> thousands of starfish on miles and miles of beach.
> One man alone could never make a difference. He
> smiled as he picked up the next starfish. Hurling it
> far into the sea he said, "It makes a difference for
> this one."

Because, at the time, no one was providing the refugees transportation to the ferry dock in Mytilene, they needed a way station after their treacherous sea crossing. By March, Melinda and Starfish had created a transit camp designed to provide refugees arriving in the Molyvos area a place to change clothes, get food, and rest before walking to Mytilene. Melinda moved the clothes from the small restaurant storeroom to her sister's empty house on the hill and recruited a half-dozen local residents to help make 100 or more sandwiches every day.

Natasha was one of the Starfish volunteers. By the time I met her, she had worked part time for Melinda for almost a year. Natasha lived with her son and a horse and a lot of cats on the piece of land adjacent to my Villas Elpiniki. She was short and thin, with a huge mane of grey curls and weathered skin. She usually wore a black beret and scarves. She smiled easily, but there was sorrow behind the smile.

Natasha had been injured in a motorcycle accident in 2012. The local hospital checked her for broken bones and concussion and sent her home. When she awoke the next day in her bed, she couldn't speak or walk. Natasha couldn't afford medical care, so for the next year, she spent every day teaching herself how to get out of bed, how to nod her head, how to tell her teenaged children she loved them. During that year, she could not work. Natasha and her children had been poor during the good times. Without savings or work or family support, food was scarce for Natasha and her children that year except on the days neighbors dropped off a pot of stuffed tomatoes or a roasted chicken.

By early 2015, Natasha's health had improved enough that she was able to plant a large garden in the pasture behind her house and reopen her gift shop on the harbor road in Molyvos. The shop was the size of a large closet. There, Natasha and her daughter, Anastasia, sold fragrant massage oils, handmade bags, and locally made soaps during the tourist season. The walls were draped with silk and cotton scarves to soften the whitewashed walls and make the most of the small space. Natasha sold small paintings her father-in-law painted, simple depictions of saints painted in white on the driftwood he found on local beaches. They sold well because tourists could buy original art for 10 or 15 euros. Considering the tourist season had only started, the shop had been busy.

Natasha's modest farmhouse was on the road from the beaches where the refugee boats were coming in. By March, the refugees were walking past her property at all hours of the day and night on their way to Mytilene. Sometimes she went out to the road and talked to them. Even when they had been provided dry clothes by the Kempsons or the hotels, the people were always hungry. She was able to give them apples and oranges she had stored and extra tomatoes from her garden. When she was at work, she left bottles of water outside the gate for them. Shortly after she began helping this way, she was always distracted from the routine of her life, always hoping for an opportunity to see the refugees, feed them, give them water. They brought her deep sorrow and great joy. They had become such a part of the community that no one could talk of anything else. Often in quiet moments, Natasha broke into tears.

Chapter 13
May 2015
Khabez Dawle

By May, boats were landing every day on Aphrodite Beach, and most of their passengers were women and children. The hotel had become a transit center. A first-floor guest room housed dozens of boxes of clothes, sorted and marked. Some had been donated by local residents, and some had come from Starfish, which, following Melinda's appeals to European media, was getting donations of clothing in large weekly shipments from Norway and England. Panagiotis bought hundreds of extra cases of bottled water and deployed the kitchen staff to help make sandwiches and snack bags for boat arrivals. Almost daily, members of the family and hotel staff cleaned up hundreds of life jackets on the beach, washed hundreds of pounds of clothes, and restocked bins of clothing and water. Aphrodite briefed the hotel employees about how to handle the boat arrivals and assigned the hotel's assistant manager, Kostas, to oversee them.

Panagiotis and Aphrodite were conflicted about the boat arrivals. The family did not fear the people on the boats, who were always kind and grateful. Still, they could not help feeling invaded. Strangers were arriving on their beach and walking through the hotel property all hours of the day, every day, and, even after several months, they received no help or protection from their government.

And there were the business risks. Although Aphrodite and Panagiotis felt compelled to help, they worried about how the island's reputation might change in a way that would affect tourism. The arrival of exhausted, sea-soaked refugees speaking Arabic and Farsi would surely scare off some visitors who were reading the papers. The issue was more immediate for the Vati-Mariola family than for most other hotel owners in Molyvos because of the proximity of their hotel to a beach that had become a key landing site. Hotel guests sitting at poolside or at tavern tables could not ignore the boat landings and the drama that followed as exhausted refugees shed life jackets and changed into dry clothes.

Easter is an important holiday on Lesvos, as it is throughout Greece. Greeks observe Lent by eliminating meat and dairy from their diets, and church services are held every night during the week preceding Easter. Churches organize candlelit processions through town on the evening of Good Friday, with chanting and an effigy of Jesus. On the Saturday before Easter, churches celebrate a midnight liturgy, and families break their Lenten fast in the early hours of Easter Sunday with a soup called *magiritsa*, made from lamb offal. On Easter Sunday, families and friends gather for lamb barbeques and celebrate with dancing, egg-breaking contests, and special baked delicacies.

Taking advantage of the Easter-week vacation and accommodating guests who would visit to enjoy the Greek Easter traditions, the Vati-Mariolas opened the Aphrodite Hotel as planned on April 4. Forty-eight guests checked into 22 rooms and, by mid-afternoon, the *taverna* was serving beer, *ouzo*, and *mezes* to guests at tables and deck chairs around the pool. Some guests left for hikes to Eftalou Beach over the hill or walks into town. Aphrodite had hoped but not expected that this first week would be quiet so that the hotel employees could get back into the rhythm of managing the hotel. Some of them had helped with boat arrivals but not with the added complication of hotel guests. Aphrodite was relieved that the hotel's opening day felt unusually normal.

Easter Sunday was different. Just after dawn, one of the German guests, Herrick, was swimming in the cove and spotted a small boat that appeared to be headed straight for Aphrodite Beach. Herrick had heard about refugee boats coming onto the island from his tour company, but he wasn't prepared to be startled by the sight. The dinghy was low in the water and packed with people in bright-orange vests. A couple of them waved their arms when they saw him. He waved back. In such moments, they felt oddly familiar, almost like friends. He knew they needed help. He swam to shore, grabbed his towel, and headed for the hotel lobby.

Aphrodite was ready for this. She thanked Herrick and sent Kostas to the beach. He knew the steps. He unlocked the bins of clothes and bottled water lined up along the stone retaining wall and laid out several large blankets on a dry corner of the beach, where people could rest and change into dry clothes. Despina walked down to the beach carrying two large bags of oranges and boxes of biscuits. As the boat approached, two hotel guests — German women in their 60s — were standing on the retaining wall, curious. Aphrodite never asked the guests to help, but, because the boats were now carrying babies and young children, there were never too many hands on the beach. Mothers often arrived too traumatized to care for more than a single child, and most arrived with several.

The black rubber dinghy appeared to be carrying about 40 passengers. It was, as usual, gravely overloaded but not in any danger at this point. The water was calm, and the boat would be able to pull up right onto the beach. Kostas waved his arms and shouted, "Welcome to Europe, my friends!" Young men on the boat waved their arms. He could hear a few of them yelling, "Hello, Greece!"

Just before the boat hit the beach, Aphrodite noticed that one of the young men on the boat was videotaping the boat's landing with his cell phone. In spite of the bright-orange life jacket he was wearing, she could tell that he and several others were well dressed. They were probably from Syria. As the boat approached the shore, the young man with the camera caught Aphrodite's eye. He jumped from the boat and extended his arm toward her. "Hello Madam! We are a special boat!" Aphrodite laughed at his joy and his enthusiasm. She was grateful that this was one of the easy landings. "I know that! All of the boats are special!" she replied. "Yes ma'am, but we are *very* special. We are Khebez Dawle. We are a rock band from Syria. You will see — we will be famous!"

All of the others were by now helping two older people and lifting children onto shore and directing them to the fruit and dry clothes. Everyone was safe, unharmed, quiet. The hotel staff were pulling blue jeans and socks out of the bins. Sometimes there were these special moments when the boats came in, and Aphrodite did not want to pass up the opportunity to know more about the young man. "I am Aphrodite, and you have arrived at my family's hotel. You must promise to send me a CD of your recordings when you are famous." "Yes, mother. I am Anas, and I can do better than that." He reached into the backpack he had dropped at his feet and pull out a small stack of CDs. "Here you are, ma'am. We are on our way to Germany, and we will return someday to Lesvos to sing for you." "I will be waiting for you, Anas!" replied Aphrodite.

After the people on the boat changed into dry clothes, Panagiotis invited them to ride in the hotel van to town. Earlier in the year, he had risked arrest as a smuggler when he drove refugees to Molyvos. But he had made an arrangement with the island police. They would leave him alone if he called them in advance to say he was driving unregistered refugees to town. That morning, he made six trips up the hill.

Later in the afternoon, Kostas yelled toward the tavern where he knew Panagiotis was sitting at coffee. "Panagiotis, a boat is coming!" "How far out is it, Kostas?" "15 minutes!" "OK. The clothes bins on the beach are full. I will join you after I finish my coffee!" The boats had already become a routine part of managing the hotel.

The second boat was like most of them — dangerously overloaded with wet, scared passengers. It pulled up to the beach easily. After the children were safely on shore, Aphrodite noticed two of the men pulling a wheelchair off the boat.

She scanned the arrivals for its owner and saw a legless man on shore, pulling pants over his hips. She could hear two of refugees speaking Greek to Kostas, which surprised her. Later that day, Kostas told her the men were Pakistanis who had lived in Greece as refugees ten years before. They had returned home and were displaced again when extremists retook parts of northern Pakistan. At the pool, two blue-eyed blondes in bikinis were sipping a Greek beer called "Mythos."

The scene repeated itself all summer in one way or another. Most of the hotel guests were understanding, and some wanted to help when the boats came in. Those who felt comfortable with the people on the boats seemed to feel good about their contributions, and it drew the family closer to their guests. Aphrodite remembered an 80-year-old Belgian man who never spoke to her during his week-long stay but left his suitcase full of clothes for the refugees. But some were fearful and did not know what to expect when men in dark clothes arrived on the shore. Occasionally, a man on a boat pulled out a knife and stabbed the boat, yelling *"Allahu Akbar!"* In the first week after opening, the hotel issued a refund to one family who admitted to knowing in advance about the boats coming into the hotel beach but justified a refund on the basis that they "didn't think there would be so many."

Panagiotis attended a town meeting to plead for help. He explained that the hotel and restaurant owners were concerned that the tourist industry was going to suffer. They needed help cleaning the beaches and the roads. They needed help moving the refugees from the beaches to the ferries. But there was no offer of help that night and no prospects for help. The residents were left to figure it out.

Later that week, Aphrodite got a call from a tour operator in Germany saying he had cancelled reservations for more than 300 hotel guests scheduled to arrive in July and August. The travel agent explained that his clients did not want to spend their vacations on a beach where refugee boats might arrive.

Chapter 14

July 2015

Platis Gialos

A S THE NUMBER OF boat landings increased that summer, so did the boat engines piling up on Aphrodite Beach. Local men in tired t-shirts and greasy blue jeans crept down to the beach at dawn or dusk to take the engines before the island police traveled over the hill to haul the contraband away in trucks bearing official seals. Some of the village residents referred to the men who scavenged the engines as *korakia*, meaning "crows."

The engines were cheaply made in Chinese factories. Although they weren't worth much, even after a single use, $50 was a substantial sum for those on the island who had lost income with the collapse of the Greek economy. It could feed a family for a week when the summer gardens of Molyvos were producing peppers and tomatoes and beans. But even small outboard engines were heavy and large, and Aphrodite

Beach was not a place for any kind of stealth. Tourists lounged with cocktails at the pool overlooking the beach, and hotel staff were on watch for boats most of the day and night.

Strangely, several large piles of neon-orange life jackets found their way to a neighboring beach called Platis Gialos where, as far as anyone knew, no boats had landed in recent months. Intended or not, the life jackets guided future refugee boats there, which for now was still the shore of a beach where tourists and hotel staff would not notice the disappearance of the engines or the comings and goings at dawn and dusk of people looking for engines.

Sixteen years before, Natasha had discovered Platis Gialos, a tiny cove between Molyvos' harbor and the hill of the town's tiny lighthouse. Sitting at the base of an expanse of meadow lined with olive trees, the narrow beach was a carpet of large and small pebbles in grays and browns. The water was calm, and the trees on the shoreline provided shelter from the glaring summer sun. In 500 BCE, the cove had been a small harbor for the ancient town of Mithimna, and the pottery shards of ancient Mithimna hid in the layers of rocks and sand that comprised the tiny bluff where the beach meets the hillside.

When Natasha told her friends about her discovery, they laughed. "No, Natasha, you can't swim there, you stupid girl." The beach had once been the terminus of a large clay pipe that spewed Molyvos sewage into the turquoise Mediterranean. The beach carried the stigma of sewage even after the island's sewage was treated and disposed of elsewhere, and the beach and the water lapping onto it were clean. So Natasha swam alone at Platis Gialos. It became a place of refuge — "my father, with my name all over it" — where Natasha could escape the anxiety of raising two children alone, wondering whether she could pay the month's electric bill, find enough wood to heat her cottage, or pay for the medication needed for her son's heart condition. It was a place of poetry and Greek history and, for sixteen years, hers alone.

In 2017, poetry and history and overdue bills were overwhelmed by the endless sorting of dry clothes, hauling of wet clothes, and crying. Natasha no longer went out at night to share a bottle of *ouzo* with neighbors who danced and passed platters of *souvlaki* around the room. Eating, drinking, and sleeping were not much more than lifelines that allowed her to continue to cry for the refugees and pretend she could do something that would make a difference to them — offer a bottle of water, a bunch of grapes, a pair of tired socks.

After a long day at work, Natasha put on her bathing suit and tied her hair into a knot on her head. She walked up the hill past the castle road toward her beach, past the sign for Michalis' Donkey Farm, three whitewashed hotels, and fields of brown and beige sheep. The sky was bright blue, and the air was still and hot.

Arriving at the top of the cove's tiny bluff, she breathed in the sea air and scanned the horizon before reminding herself that she had not come to watch for boats. She carefully climbed down the bluff, aiming for small trees and roots to stop her from sliding on the loose soil and dead leaves. Looking down at the beach, she scanned hundreds of life jackets, dozens of inner tubes, and two rubber rafts. She felt her face flush and fought back tears of conflicting feelings, wanting a place of peace, hurting for people of courage and sorrow, her refuge no longer her own.

She sat on the beach for a few minutes and then started organizing life jackets into piles along the bluff. A tiny, clear-plastic inner tube had "Barbie" designs printed on it. It was made for swimming in a place of safety, where an athletic father or vigilant mother would be close. Natasha hauled the two rubber rafts to the outcropping on the east side of the cove and stuffed an old sack with plastic water bottles and sandy, wet socks and balloons that had once held passports and cell phones. There were no engines.

She wiped the sweaty grime from her forehead and let her hands fall over her eyes. She sat down on a black, partly wet, slippery inner tube at the intersection of water and stone, and cried, thinking about the people who had landed on the beach. She needed the sea and pulled the inner tube up around her waist. This artifact of refuge for some Syrian woman or Afghan man would hold her, too. She slipped off her flip-flops and walked slowly into the clear water on this tiny corner of the Aegean Sea. She kept walking until her feet no longer touched the pebbles of the wet earth and let herself float away from the secluded cove and out toward the rocky bluffs. As the water made her weightless, she turned her face upward toward the sun and took a deep breath. She could feel the ends of her long, graying locks lap the water around the outside of the inner tube.

As she let herself float with the slow rhythm of the tide, she heard quiet, heavy footsteps on the leaves and sand above the beach, interrupting her release of care and emotion. She wished she didn't have to open her eyes. As she did, she saw a large man in a dark shirt, dark pants, dark hat. He stood motionless, with his hands on his hips. He watched her, unsmiling, without any gesture of acknowledgement. Like her, he seemed locked in a moment of paralysis. She sensed he knew something about her that he either shared or feared. He tipped his police cap with his right forefinger and turned around. She heard the footsteps again, getting softer, softer.

Later in the week, Natasha returned to Platis Gialos and founds hundreds more life jackets on the beach and more boats, more plastic bags. She didn't clean them up or swim. She returned home. Platis Gialos had become a place of sorrow and unease, haunted by the ghosts of war.

Chapter 15

Fall 2015

Another Way Station

Fall arrived, and the sea that surrounded Molyvos had lost its horizon line, its sunsets and smells and meaning. It had become a flat expanse that carried dots of orange and black, something to watch and fear and thank. Roads were described according to which landing sites they passed. The winds and the weather were either deadly or helpful. For many residents, every conversation, glance, plan, and gathering seemed to be about refugees. The word was as common as air, taken for granted, like water.

Throughout the summer, Papa Stratis had been out on the beaches and roads patrolling for boats and providing water and clothing to the people who had landed on shore. His emphysema was literally killing him, and he often went through two or three oxygen tanks before he arrived home at night. He did not stop smoking. One day, on the drive home to Kolloni, an ember from his cigarette came into contact with the oxygen from the tank. His nose caught on fire. When Papa Stratis arrived home, he was bleeding and too weak to climb the steps to the front door.

A few days later, Papa Stratis lay in the hospital, struggling for air in an oxygen tent and negotiating on his cell phone for a donation of 10,000 diapers to be delivered to Skala Sykamania. Now he did not smoke. Michalis and the family stayed with him as he faded. On September 4, 2015, Papa Stratis died at age 57. He left the family in debt from the purchases of food, water, clothing, shoes. Papa Stratis was buried in the vestments he had worn until they were rags.

Part of the community mourned. Others didn't notice. The boats kept arriving on Aphrodite Beach, now as many as seven a day — 400 people and 30 trips to town in the van. The work was overwhelming on top of managing the hotel. The costs of providing even inadequate amounts of food and water cut into the hotel's profits that year, and hotel employees were having to work harder. Many stayed after their shifts to help with cleaning up debris on the beach or finishing the laundry or restocking the bins of clothing and shoes. The guests at Aphrodite Hotel had become a routine part of the operation by July as well. The family provided each a short description of what they could expect. Most expressed support for what the hotel was doing and made the best of things when they heard Panagiotis yell, "The restaurant is self-service for the next hour!"

Over the entire north coast of the island, as many as 4,000 people were arriving every day in five locations. Most were directed to the Starfish transit camp on the hill in old Mythimna above Platos Gialis, behind Molyvos village. The location was convenient for people who had arrived near the harbor and for those working at the Captain's Table making sandwiches and organizing dry clothes. But the camp was increasingly causing stress in Molyvos as throngs of refugees walked through the village to get to the camp and back through the village when they were ready to board buses. Tourists at the café tables along the harbor road watched the processions with concern, some with alarm. Sanitation was a big problem. Many of the town's residents had objected to installing porta-potties in public view.

Panagiotis was still hoping to find ways to balance the community's humanitarian instincts with the community's need to protect the local economy. Minimizing the distractions from other of life's commitments was virtually impossible for those who lived or worked near the beaches or in the harbor. Still, he wanted to protect the local tourist economy.

One evening, Dimitri and Panagiotis sat at the Aphrodite Hotel's *taverna* overlooking the beach. Panagiotis was fed up with all of the back and forth in the community about where to provide a safe but discreet stopping place for the refugees. The community, so far, had been pragmatic about how to support the refugees and had changed as circumstances changed. This problem should be no different.

Panagiotis looked up from his beer. "Dimitri, let's talk to Dirk about using Oxy. He has always been supportive of the community, and I suspect he will consider it if we can draw up a business plan and get UNHCR to sign off."

Oxy was the nightclub on the main road between Molyvos and Petra. Unlike anything else on Lesvos, its architecture had been inspired by spaceship design. It lit up at night with lavender neon against a backdrop of olive groves and overlooking a vast expanse of the Aegean. It was an ironic candidate for sheltering thousands of weary Muslim families, but its visitors would be away from the village in a clean, central place to rest, eat, and change into clean, dry clothes.

The next day, Dirk agreed to the conversion of Oxy from nightclub to refugee transit camp. Things moved quickly from there. A few days later, on September 14, Panagiotis saw Starfish volunteers setting up tents in Oxy's parking lot. By October, Oxy had become a short-term refuge for as many as 6,000 people a day. The tents and tin storage rooms had UNHCR's logo on them. UNHCR committed funds for buses to transfer refugees to Oxy from the beaches and then to Mytilene.

Oxy did have a sanitation problem. Every day, the toilets backed up. They were not designed to accommodate the hygiene needs of two or three thousand people a day, and the people using them did not understand the damage they were doing by throwing paper into the Greek plumbing system. When the toilets backed up, the refugees used quiet corners of the hillside behind the disco, but the rain washed what they left on the hillside down to areas where people were camping and children were playing.

Melinda needed help with this, and she knew that Natasha had closed her gift shop for the winter. Melinda asked Natasha to work for Starfish cleaning the toilets at Oxy. Melinda apologized but said she was desperate, worried about the health risks and the potential for new rounds of controversy in the community. Natasha knew the job was beneath her, but she agreed. She missed being around the refugees now that they were no longer walking by her house along the road to Eftalou.

The job turned out to be better than Natasha had expected. When she helped the refugees, her life had purpose and, for now, no other purpose filled the need in her. And she didn't clean the toilets very often. The young Muslim men visiting the transit camp saw in Natasha their own mothers, and they did not want their mother to clean the toilets. They took her equipment from her and cleaned the toilets themselves.

At about the same time Oxy opened, things were changing at Aphrodite Beach. The number of boats arriving every day was tapering off. One afternoon, a young woman arrived at the hotel lobby in a bright-green high-visibility vest. Aphrodite knew that a handful of volunteers were starting to arrive on the island, and, apparently, this one knew something about the boat arrivals on Aphrodite Beach. The young woman extended her hand to Aphrodite and smiled. "Hi. I bet you are Aphrodite. I'm Chantel. I work for Drop in the Ocean, and we have just started patrolling Limantziki Beach for boats. We have run out of bottled water today, and we have seen several boats on their way into Limantziki. Can we buy some water from you?"

Limantziki Beach was just over the hill from the hotel. The UNHCR had provided two tents that stored clothes and were used as dressing rooms, one for men and the other for women and children. Volunteers sat on the beach with bottled water and disposable diapers and snacks. The smugglers knew when circumstances changed on the island and managed their operations accordingly. They had begun directing boats toward the piles of bright-orange vests and the searchlight that lit up the tiny cove at Limantziki every night.

Aphrodite was happy to provide several cases of water and asked Kostas to bring it up from storage. She was interested in this NGO that had taken on beach patrols. "Could we talk about your work on the other beaches? We could use some help here."

By the following week, Drop in the Ocean was sending volunteers to Aphrodite Beach whenever someone from the hotel sent a text to Charly, the volunteer coordinator. As long as she had 15 minutes' notice, Charly sent volunteers down in cars loaded with clothes and water and blankets, depending on how many passengers were estimated to be on the boats. A few weeks later, the number of boats arriving at the hotel tapered off to almost zero.

Exhausted, Aphrodite and Panagiotis closed the hotel for the season, as they usually did. Fall and winter were normally a quiet time on Lesvos for most of the other hotel and restaurant owners as well. When the tourists left, the cost of remaining open couldn't be recovered. That winter, however, some of the hotels and *tavernas* remained open, hoping to compensate for lost tourist business by serving the volunteers, who were beginning to be a large presence on the island.

Pirates was one of the businesses that remained open. Pirates was a small *taverna* that overlooked the Aegean Sea on the road to Molyvos Harbor. The space was small and dark and, whether full or empty, had the sour, vinegary smell of stale beer. The bartender got the best view of the harbor, stationed next to the room's only window. Janos owned Pirates. He was a quiet man in his 60s, with a head of black thinning hair and thirty extra pounds. His complexion was sallow, probably from the cigarette smoke the filled the bar every night.

Janos was not the kind of person to indulge in his political views and, for him, there was nothing political about feeding people who were hungry. All summer, he had brought sandwiches and bread from his bakery on the hill to people walking along the harbor road. He had kicked out the members of the right-wing group called Golden Dawn, who picked fights with Pirates customers who helped refugees. By September, this loss of business was more than compensated when hundreds of international volunteers began arriving on Lesvos. Pirates was a favorite watering hole, packed every night with affluent Norwegians, Germans, and Americans, who had plenty of cash to spend on partying. Some said Janos was among the biggest beneficiaries of the refugee crisis. But Janos carried a lot of worry in his smile, and he predicted that the welcome the refugees had received for the previous year was about to end.

Chapter 16

October 2015

Taxia and Giannis

The Tropicana was my favorite restaurant on Lesvos. It had the best stuffed mushrooms and the best grilled fish. Its outdoor tables dotted a tiny plaza under a canopy of two mature plane trees, and tiny white lights crisscrossed the plaza above the tables. The people at the tables always seemed especially friendly, and sometimes the village children were there, swinging at the end of a long rope attached to one of the largest tree branches. But the best thing about the Tropicana was Taxia, the owner of the Tropicana. Taxia was probably 40, energetic and engaging. She was always there, usually with a glass of wine in her hand, and she was one of those people who made everyone else feel special. If the food at the Tropicana had been mediocre, I would have eaten there anyway.

Taxia had two cousins who were fisherman. They had pulled a lot of people out of the water that year. Because the Tropicana was on the hill and the restaurant took up so much of their time, Taxia and her husband, Giannis, had not had many experiences with the refugees. But one afternoon in early October, she learned how the refugees elicited such a deep emotional response for so many on the island. The weather was near freezing that day, so Taxia had closed the doors of the tiny restaurant. With the tourist season over and the weather too cold for outdoor dining, the plaza was quiet. A couple of English tourists sat inside, sharing dishes of hummus and *dolmas* over a bottle of *ouzo*. After serving them, Taxia sat down at a table by the door.

Looking across the plaza down the cobblestone road, she saw a group of three adults and a young child walking up from the harbor, obviously wet and cold off a boat. She grabbed her coat and walked out the door. As she neared them, one yelled in English, "Help, please! People in water!" She moved toward them and motioned for them to come to the restaurant. When they were inside, Taxia removed her sweater and wrapped it around one of the women. In broken English, the woman described the beach where a boat was stuck on the rocks.

Taxia called her husband, who was cleaning the grill in the kitchen. "Giannis! Call Kostas — there are refugees who need help at Platis Gialos!" Giannis grabbed his knee-high rubber boots and foul-weather gear by the door as he punched his cell phone. In October, there was still no one to call in these situations but other neighbors. He couldn't rely on the Coast Guard, which could help boats in distress outside the harbor, but the draft on the Coast Guard boat was too deep to get near shore, and the Coast Guard was not permitted to help on the beaches. Something about jurisdiction.

Taxia called a friend with a shop in the harbor, Ilektra, on her cell phone and asked her to bring dry clothes to the restaurant. She pulled a pile of old blankets out of the storage room and carried them in piles to the back of her car.

Giannis and Kostas arrived at Platis Gialos a few minutes later and found a black rubber dinghy that had been hurled onto the rock cliff on the west side of the cove. It was bumping up against the cliff each time a wave hit it. Nine people were in the dinghy, screaming, crying, waving their arms. Giannis and Kostas waded out toward them and threw a heavy rope toward the dinghy. On the third try, an older man caught it and tied it to what might have been an oar lock. The easiest way to bring people onto shore would have been to pull the boat in, but the dinghy did not budge. The only way to get the passengers on land would be to drag them with the rope along the rocks.

Giannis directed each passenger to grab on to the rope and climb along the rocks toward him. Kostas positioned himself on the sea side of the rope in case someone lost his grip. Giannis and Kostas were soaked from head to toe and nearly numb with cold even before they could help a single person to shore.

The effort required hours in the freezing wind and turbulent water. Slowly, one at a time, each of the boat's passengers grabbed the rope hand over hand for 20 meters until they collapsed on the shore. Giannis watched as an aging woman in yards of black struggled to make it to shore. Two of the younger men placed themselves in front of her and behind her. Giannis thought of his own grandmother, and warm tears streamed down his cheeks as she walked onto shore, turning blue with the cold.

Taxia and Ilektra arrived at the top of the hill overlooking the beach with the car full of dry clothes, energy bars, and bottled water. With the car heater blasting, they shuttled the boat's passengers to Oxy, four at a time. With gashes in their legs and arms, hypothermia, and in shock, they all made it to Oxy. They all survived. That night, Giannis could not forget the woman who might have been his beloved grandmother and cried himself to sleep.

Chapter 17
October 28, 2015
Oxi

O N OCTOBER 28, 1940, Greek Prime Minister Iannis Metaxi told Benito Mussolini that Greece would not cooperate with the fascists. He gave Mussolini notice that the Italian troops would be met with resistance at the border. Mussolini sent his troops anyway, and Greece lost the battle at the border. The fascists occupied Greece until the end of World War II. But the Greeks have remained proud of their defiance of the Axis powers ever since. They celebrate their moral victory every year on October 28. Their holiday is called *Oxi*, which means "No."

Like most Greek communities, Molyvos celebrated *Oxi* with modest parades and speeches that emphasize the meaning of patriotism and Greek values. But in 2015, the meaning of *Oxi* changed for the people of Molyvos.

At 7 a.m. on October 28, Panagiotis was making coffee when his cell phone rang. It was Giannis. Panagiotis could barely hear him over the sound of the wind. Giannis asked him come to Limantziki beach with the hotel van and plenty of warm blankets and clothes. He should also bring whatever heavy rope he had. A big boat had landed on the rocks. The only way to get the passengers to shore was to tie them to lines between the boat and the shore and help guide them in one at a time. Panagiotis made his way to the hotel, where he could load his truck with boxes of clothes and rope from the storeroom. He spent the next couple of hours at Limantziki helping bring refugees onto the beach, getting them dry clothes, and then driving them to the bus stop near the school.

When he arrived home later that morning, Sofie and Pavlos were watching cartoons on the couch, cradling bowls of cereal. For them, the morning was like many holiday mornings, slow and easy. Panagiotis made a point to avoid talking about the ordeal that morning in their presence. He didn't want it to interfere with the children's enjoyment of *Oxi* that day.

Aphrodite made a cup of coffee and gulped it down. Then she left for the village to help organize the day's events with her sister, Gabriella. They would need to pull the Greek flags out of storage, help organize refreshments, and set up tables, the podium, and PA system for the speakers. Panagiotis would stay behind with Sofie and Pavlos and make sure they were in the square by noon. Both children would be marching in the parade through the village.

With some urging, Pavlos and Sofie got dressed, Pavlos in his Boy Scout uniform with yellow shirt, navy shorts and blue tie. Sofie wore the traditional dress of the Molyvos *Oxi* parade — white dress shirt, navy skirt, and white stockings. Panagiotis led the children down the cobblestone road of Molyvos Hill, toward the village road above the harbor, and then down the path to the tree-lined square just above the water.

All but the youngest children in town had walked in this parade in previous years, and it didn't take much to get them organized. Since Molyvos residents numbered fewer than 2,000, the parade was more of a short march, but it was attended by almost everyone in the village and a handful of tourists. The high school band played the Greek national anthem, and the marching children carried blue-and-white Greek flags.

Afterward, the community gathered in the square. Gabriella handed out small cheese pies and sugar cookies. The mayor spoke about honoring Greek independence and described the community's commitment to *philotimo*, the Greek value of generosity toward the community and humanity. The village dogs attended and afterwards cleaned the grounds. The Vati-Mariolas left for the hotel to join Aphrodite's parents for the afternoon meal.

Down in the harbor, locals and tourists were sitting at outdoor café tables and sampling plates of *dolmas* and hummus. Most were celebrating the day with a glass of *ouzo* or beer. The intense autumn sun was dropping, leaving long shadows along the road and tiny diamonds of light on the quiet water inside the harbor. Beyond the breakwater, small waves built to whitecaps, and a cool wind was gathering strength, as it often did in fall afternoons.

Stergious was sitting at his usual chair on the patio at Captain's Table near the end of the harbor road. He was at the end of a long day. Refugee boats had been coming in all day long around the island. He had shuttled food, water, and clothing to and from the beaches at Eftalou and Chapel, east of Molyvos along the north coast. A large boat had come into Molyvos as well. As he drew on his cigarette, he noticed a fishing boat coming into the harbor at full speed. It was Panos, waving his arms to get the attention of the people in the harbor.

Stergious stood up from his chair at the Captain's Table and moved toward the slip, where Panos would pull in. The people at the tables stood as well, straining to hear Panos, who was yelling as he approached. "A large boat is sinking outside the harbor! We need the Coast Guard boats and lifeguards and medics. There are hundreds of people onboard! I am going out now!"

Three other fishermen working on nets next to the harbor road rushed to their boats and started their engines. Stergious ran to the Coast Guard office next to the Captain's Table and shared Panos' message with Marious, the captain on duty. Theofilos, who was normally in charge, was on vacation. Marious had come to Lesvos from Athens to cover for Theofilos and did not know the local waters well. He would have to rely on the crews. Neither his boat nor the fishing boats in Molyvos harbor were large enough to carry more than a handful of passengers. If Panos was correct about the numbers, there would need to be many more vessels to rescue passengers. Marious called the Harbor Police and Proactiva, the Spanish lifeguards who were on call on the northern part of the island. Between them, they might be able to deploy six more small boats, but none were designed for this type of crisis. He notified Frontex, which would take an hour or more to arrive but had a larger boat and rescue vessels onboard.

Ilektra was in her souvenir shop halfway up the harbor road when she heard ambulance sirens in the distance. Nadia called to tell her something horrible had happened outside the harbor. Did she know what? Ilektra did not, but she worried as the ambulances flew by the shop. She could see people she knew running toward the end of the harbor road. Her cell phone rang again. Someone asked her to bring all of the cups and glasses she could carry to the Captain's Table. Whoever called hung up before she could inquire about anything else. Ilektra grabbed a couple of large canvas bags, stuffed them with bags of plastic cups and ceramic mugs off the shelves, and headed down the road.

Halfway to the harbor, Melinda was carrying a box of dry clothes and approached Ilektra. "A boat carrying 300 people. It broke apart outside the harbor. Many have died. We will be here all night."

Ilektra had been working with Starfish for months by October 28. She had seen plenty of traumatized people coming off boats, and she had seen death. But nothing prepared her for what she saw at the harbor. Friends and strangers were rushing in different directions, some leading children or women, all wet, some bleeding or sobbing. Volunteers from the IRC and MSF scurried between their vans and the people on the pavement. Stergious carried a limp toddler toward an ambulance, where medics were trying to revive several young children lying on blankets in the road. Passing by the tiny chapel in the harbor parking lot, Ilektra saw dozens of wet women and children lying on towels and blankets. Some were motionless. Some were slowly trying to change into dry clothes. Ilektra heard crying and moaning and screams.

The scenes repeated themselves as she walked past the cafés and restaurants to Captain's Table, where several Starfish volunteers were passing out cups of tea and energy bars. Ilektra gestured to one of the volunteers that her bag had additional cups and dropped the bag inside the café door.

While she stood there, Georgious' fishing boat came in with eight more victims of the shipwreck. A medic was standing beside the boat, whispering *Shway, shway* — "Slow, slow" in Arabic — as he helped them onto shore. Two Proactiva lifeguards lifted two sobbing children into the arms of two young women Ilektra didn't know. As soon as his passengers were on shore, Georgios pulled away from the dock and headed back toward the open sea.

From the Tropicana, Taxia had heard the sirens. But the sirens stopped after a while, and she didn't think much about it. There had been so many crises on the island in recent months that it was hard to know when to investigate and when to hope for the best. She left the restaurant to pick up her eight-year-old son, Kostas, at a friend's house on the other side of the hill. When she arrived, the two boys were alone, and she asked Kostas where Panos' parents were. It was not like them to leave the children alone.

"They are saving people in the harbor. A big boat sank." She held out her hand to Kostas and said she needed to go to the harbor to help. Kostas shook his head. He would not go. "I don't want to see dead children." So she left the boys and headed back to the restaurant to pick up clothes and shoes to take to the harbor. At the restaurant, Giannis joined her, and, together, they hurried down the hill on foot, balancing boxes and black plastic bags.

When Taxia and Giannis arrived at the harbor, they found hundreds of locals and volunteers engaged. Those who were not medical professionals were carrying blankets or hot tea to traumatized victims. Many had assigned themselves individuals or what was left of families, hoping to calm them and reassure them.

Taxia went to the chapel, which was full of women and children, some crying, some motionless, some helping each other into dry clothes. Virginia, a local who had helped Starfish tirelessly for the past eight months, was carrying a three-year-old girl wrapped in a wool blanket. Now in her 70s, she barely had enough to eat herself, and she moved with some difficulty, but she showed up to make sandwiches every day. Virginia looked at Taxia and explained, "She is without parents now. I want to keep her." As she spoke, the baby turned her head toward a man 50 yards down the walkway coming toward them. Taxia walked over and put her arms around Virginia. "It looks like this man might be her father, Virginia." Virginia stroked the little girl's head as she leaned out to the man who was now jogging. "No, I am not giving her to this man. Who is he? I am not sure."

Melinda was busy managing resources and trying to identify shelter for those who needed it that night in Molyvos. Many of the building owners had already offered space in floors above restaurants and shops along the harbor. When she saw Stergious, she asked him whether he could comfort a man who had lost his wife and four children. She led him to a corner of the patio of Café Mistral and motioned him to sit with a man who was sobbing uncontrollably. Stergious thought about what he himself would need in such a moment and realized it was a tragedy that was impossible and too horrifying to imagine. He sat down and put his hand on the man's shoulder He let his body align with the sobbing man until he felt his warmth transfer to the man's cold skin.

The sun was setting beneath the sea's horizon, the sky striped with orange and purple. Panagiotis and Aphrodite could hear helicopters from the hotel and went down to the beach. From there, they didn't see anything and didn't think much more about it until Maria called. Maria was Panagiotis' co-worker at the Port Authority. "There is a terrible shipwreck. There are hundreds of people here helping. Stay with your children tonight. We will all need our strength tomorrow."

By the time the sun had set, Marious had confirmed that at least 300 refugees had been passengers on the boat. The small wooden ferry had been so overloaded that the top level had collapsed on to the lower level, crushing many and causing the boat to capsize. By the time his crew arrived at the site, the boat was below the water's surface. Hundreds of desperate people were floating in the water, some for hours, as the small boats from the harbor shuttled back and forth. The lifeguards used jet skis that were agile and could pick up people who were floating away from the larger vessels. People off the shipwreck were dispersed for hundreds of yards, clinging to inner tubes. Lifeguards had to make impossibly difficult choices about who to rescue. A child? A woman? The strong? The weak? Those who were closest or those who were farthest out? By nightfall, the rescuers had brought in 11 lifeless bodies. Marious knew there would be many more.

Although no one would ever know for sure, the Coast Guard estimated 200 deaths from the shipwreck on

October 28. The *Oxi* shipwreck united the community. Many of those who had dissented or who had tried to ignore the refugee migrations across the island realized the issue was not a political one but one that was personal. This shipwreck was international news and finally mobilized a community of NGOs and volunteers.

Chapter 18

November 2015

Remembering Papa

"Philotimo, *to the Greek, is like breathing.*
A Greek is not a Greek without it. He might
as well not be alive."
— Thales of Miletus (c. 624–546 BCE)

THE WEATHER AND THE SEA were unpredictable
that day, as they always were in November. The morning
had been quiet, but the wind was picking up as Michalis and
Theofilos made their way outside the harbor for the afternoon
patrol. Michalis scanned the water toward the Turkish coast
for boats. They were coming into Lesvos' north coast in large
numbers now, often 15 or 20 a day. None were designed to
carry the weight of the people in them. Many were dinghies
made in China, with glued seams that were coming apart by
the time they arrived on land two hours after the beginning
of their maiden voyage. Some of the motors were cheaply
made in China as well, probably for the express purpose of

getting one dinghy across the water from Turkey to one of the Greek Islands.

Michalis noticed, too, that many of the life jackets the passengers were wearing were not made according to international specifications. Although they looked like regulation life jackets, they'd been stuffed with hay or upholstery batting. These materials were more likely to cause a drowning than to prevent one. Ironically, many of the life jackets had been sewn together by the very people who would use them. The smugglers hired Syrian refugees who needed funds to get across the water, and, since they were not legally permitted to work in Turkey, the smugglers paid them little. Some of the refugees sewing together the life jackets were children.

The life jackets typically identified the refugees according to nationality. So many of the Syrians were affluent, professional, able to pay for a little more safety and comfort. Iraqis, Afghans, and Pakistanis usually came with less. When Michalis was patrolling for refugee boats, he knew that the passengers wearing bright-orange jackets were most likely to be Syrians. Those with fewer resources paid for black life jackets, harder to see, inferior quality, and sometimes worse than useless.

The Hellenic Coast Guard's job had become increasingly difficult and more dangerous. The numbers had not only increased, but the Turkish Coast Guard was obviously looking the other way. Michalis knew when to expect the boats to arrive in Greek waters by checking his navigation equipment for the location of the Turkish Coast Guard boats — when they were some distance from the path to Lesvos, the refugee boats would begin arriving.

The refugee boats may have had the biggest effect on the local fishermen, who had been saving lives all year. They couldn't go out to fish without coming upon boats in trouble, and none of them were able to turn away. They were losing their livelihood because they were spending so much time attending to refugee boats. By November, many had stopped setting nets in most of the places they normally fished, worried that the refugee boats would cut the nets, or worse, that the propellers on the boat engines might catch in the nets and leave the boats floundering at sea without power.

Michalis saw a dinghy in the distance. It was overloaded, balancing precariously between swells, with almost no freeboard. No sound from an engine. The dinghy was in Greek waters, and he saw a couple of the men frantically waving their arms. He ducked his head into the navigation room and told Theofilos he was going to lower the rescue vessels. Theofilos clicked on his ship-to-shore radio and requested assistance.

Michalis lowered himself on the ship's rope ladder, carrying the loudspeaker. Waving to the dinghy, now about 200 yards out, he yelled, "Remain seated and calm. *Shway, shway.*" The passengers were sitting quietly, but Michalis could see that the dinghy was quickly being overtaken by small waves and the sheer weight it was carrying. He could hear screams and crying. They knew their time was short if something didn't change within moments. Michalis saw three small fishing boats headed toward them.

The Coast Guard ship moved slowly toward the dinghy to avoid swamping it, but the dinghy was lurching back and forth in the choppy sea. A young man in the bow was holding on to two toddlers as the ship approached. Michalis reached for them and, one at a time, handed them to Theofilos on the deck. One more child, then another. Screams, crying. The dinghy had only an inch or two left of freeboard. One at a time, Michalis pulled nine women onto the ship, heavy with the yards of wet clothing that covered them. Two were carrying infants in scarves wound around their chests. The dinghy was sinking. Theofilos was throwing lifesaving rings to the dozen men remaining in the boat, knowing their life jackets might not be functional.

All of the men managed to get onto the Coast Guard ship except for three, who were now fighting to stay afloat. Michalis jumped into the sea toward the man who was closest to the ship and pulled him toward the ladder. He was strong enough to climb it without help. Another was frantically dog-paddling toward the ship on top of two lifesaving rings, but the tide was impeding his progress. Michalis reached him and pulled him to the ladder.

Michalis swam toward the third man, who was without a life jacket and clinging to a small black inner tube that was barely buoyant enough to keep the man's head above water. He was struggling, as if climbing out of the water by grabbing at the insubstantial wind. Michalis saw the man's head bob to the surface while he gasped for air and then disappear. Michalis knew the man was close to death.

Michalis was working off of adrenalin. He reached the man with the inner tube. The man yelled something he didn't understand and grabbed at Michalis's shoulders and head. The man's arms were waving through the air, without strength to do anything else that would keep him afloat. Michalis wasn't sure if his own strength would hold out.

He grabbed the man by his shirt and moved toward the rescue boat; then he lost his grip as a wave plunged them both underwater. By now, the man was deadweight, and Michalis's own exhaustion was overtaking him. He pictured his father and thought about what it would be like for one or both to drown now. He thought about how his love for his father turned on this moment. A dozen pictures of his father appeared before him, sitting with a group of young refugees on the road, negotiating on the phone for a case of baby formula or men's shoes, dying in the hospital, smoking one of his last, lethal cigarettes.

Michalis gathered up one final bit of strength, grabbed the drowning man again, and pulled him toward the ship. Theofilos grabbed the man, hoisted him onto the ladder, and pulled him onto the deck. Michalis let his exhausted body float on the indifferent sea. He turned his face into the sun as a hot tear fell to the corner of his eye, and he gratefully inhaled the salty sea air.

IV

PETALOUDES

Butterflies

Chapter 19

January 2017

Auntie Dawn

EVERYONE IN MY FAMILY called my father's sister "Auntie Dawn," and I was still calling her that when she died the week I returned home from Greece in January. Although she had been a sort of no-nonsense professional woman, she never stopped being the kind of person a grown-up niece would call "Auntie."

Auntie Dawn grew up in a small house in Pasadena, California, the daughter of my Armenian refugee grandfather. She had an unremarkable post-World War II childhood and graduated from UCLA with a degree in music theory. Then she did something that was very remarkable for a woman of her era: She packed her bags and moved to Kabul, Afghanistan, to teach at a small Christian elementary school. This was in 1961, when Afghanistan was a mostly poor but safe country. Women voted and attended university. The rural economy did not rely on the opium trade. The Taliban did not terrorize people for their values, and foreign troops were not driving tanks down city streets. Still, it was an exotic outpost at a time when international travel was a novelty for the American middle class. Whenever Auntie Dawn traveled to or from "overseas," her whole family drove 50 miles to take her to or meet her at the airport.

After her year in Kabul, Auntie Dawn returned to the United States to attend medical school. She practiced family medicine at a Kaiser hospital in the Los Angeles area for more than 30 years. During that time, she helped me through college, joined my family on holidays, and sent my son See's chocolates and a check every year at Christmas. She sang in her church choir and learned Armenian so she could serve Kaiser patients who had immigrated from the old country.

Because of Auntie Dawn's independence and professional career, I grew up understanding that women had choices. Women could travel alone, and women could have demanding, important careers. Women didn't have to do what was expected of them. She didn't make a big deal about it. She just followed her instincts and her intuition. I made these points when I spoke at her funeral, as if I were speaking to myself instead of an audience full of mild-mannered churchgoers.

Shortly after Auntie Dawn's funeral, my sisters determined that Auntie Dawn had returned to the world as a butterfly, just as my grandfather had returned as a dolphin. Because my sisters had asserted so confidently that my aunt had become a butterfly, I didn't feel so foolish a couple of months later, when I told them I had adopted an adult son. And the Butterfly must have had something to do with it, because my new son was Afghan.

Chapter 20
May 2016
Arian Joon

UNTIL MID-2016, most of the people in my life were people like me — middle class, educated, comfortably situated Americans. People who never had a gun pointed at them and never had been persecuted for their beliefs or their job choice. And then in Greece, someone inexplicably came into my life who didn't fit any of these categories.

I was living on Lesvos during the spring of 2016. Some days I hiked through the hills or visited an historic town, often with other volunteers or local residents. Other days, I packed sandwiches for one of the camps or delivered food and clothing to another. I learned about needs at the camps from other volunteers or from postings on social media, which had been used extensively over the previous six months to connect people with information and resources.

Checking social media one day, I read a posting by a Danish volunteer named Anette, who was soliciting a small amount of cash to buy medication for a disabled child. I had money from donations that I was using for such short-term emergencies, so I got the contact information from Anette and contacted the child's father, whose name was Arian. When I contacted Arian a few hours later, he said he had gotten the medication for his son from Doctors Without Borders. He thanked me for my offer and said he was not comfortable taking my money. He could have accepted my offer without telling me he had already obtained the medicine. I asked him to stay in touch.

I heard from Arian a couple of times over the coming weeks. He was living in a camp in Athens with his wife and three young sons. The son who had needed the medication had cerebral palsy. The family had arrived in Greece in February after a treacherous journey from Afghanistan that included a boat crossing to the Greek island of Chios. The borders closed the day they arrived in Greece, so the family could not continue to Sweden, where his uncle lived. Arian wanted to find a job, but, since he could not work legally, he had spent many of his days visiting NGO offices in Athens to find resources for his family and others at the camp. He was the oldest son in his Afghan family, and he was not accustomed to getting help from strangers — or anyone else. After some nagging, he accepted some cash from me, which I sent by way of a volunteer in Athens. He later sent me a message to say he had used the money to buy cans of tuna to add to the gluey macaroni the Greek government served every day at the camp. He used a little of it to pay for a bus ride to the beach with his sons.

I had to leave Greece in early May because I had been in the Schengen Area for almost 90 days, and I would not be able to return for three months. I wasn't ready to leave

Lesvos, so I consulted with the local police about whether I could get an extension of time. The answer was "yes" but only if I could provide evidence that I was hospitalized. I didn't want to stay that badly. I realized in the moment how my privileged status was so much a part of my thinking — I felt indignant that Europe would not allow me to work as a volunteer on one of Greece's biggest problems while I was spending my money in Greece's failing economy. But I got 90 days. Afghans, Syrians, and Iraqis (and most others who were not white) got no days unless they risked their lives to sneak in.

Before leaving Greece, I wanted to spend a few days in Athens with Nanci, who was still working at Piraeus Port, where thousands of refugees still lived in tents on the cement along the waterfront. Nanci was happy to get together, so I booked a hotel in the center of the city. And then I sent a text message to Arian, asking him whether I could meet him in Athens. He replied that he was eager to meet me. I suggested getting together somewhere convenient for a meal with his family, and he sent me the address of a small Afghan restaurant.

For all of my work on Lesvos, I had never had more than a handful of brief conversations with refugees. The refugees were transient, and I am often a better observer than participant. I had admired the volunteers at Moria and on the beaches who so comfortably engaged people they might not know for more than an hour or a day. So I anticipated my meeting with Arian as a sort of novelty. Here was someone I might actually get to know and understand. From my first communication with Arian, something about him felt special — maybe the lyricism of his brief messages or his eagerness to share the frustrations of his life and what remained of his dreams. He had trusted me with his feelings.

We agreed to meet outside of the metro stop on the street in a corner of Athens that was typical — block after block of uninspired '50s-era cement apartment buildings where street vendors sold cheap umbrellas and shopping bags and crates of produce. Plastic wrappers and grimy dirt lined the gutters, and everything felt covered in a layer of gray soot. The feeling was tired, like most of Athens.

Breaking the dreary Athens landscape, Arian appeared from across the street sparkling with physical and emotional energy. He approached me with a soft smile and held out his hand. He seemed to be in his late 20s. He was handsome and edgy in blue jeans and a black t-shirt. He had a distinct haircut and moved with an easy confidence. Unlike many of the young men I had met at the camps and on the beaches, Arian was a full-grown man with a sense of himself and his world. His face expressed intelligence and discernment, and there were signs of anger and playfulness.

Arian's wife, Rana, was behind him, pushing two-year-old Jamal in a stroller, flanked by their two other sons, Shayan and Amir. Rana was wearing a pink *hijab* and a skirt. She wore no makeup and lowered her head slightly when she smiled at me. Arian helped her with the stroller and lifted the toddler onto his shoulders. He was solicitous. I sensed that his family was a responsibility he had assumed according to his culture but perhaps not according to his soul. I reminded myself that all of them were living under tremendous strain.

Rana and Arian were joined by a married couple, Asgar and Samin, and their seven-year-old daughter, Amena. The two families shared a "caravan" (trailer) at the camp. Samin was made up and fashionable, with manicured nails. The hair poking out of her *hijab* had been highlighted, and she was wearing a new pair of delicate beige shoes. Asgar's presentation was similarly polished, and I couldn't help but wonder how these two managed to look so affluent, given their situation. I assumed they were among those who had come from comfortable circumstances and received funds from home while they awaited a time when Asgar could work.

We walked a few blocks to a tiny restaurant, which was spare and cheerless. There were aging metal tables sitting on yellowed linoleum tile. The owners, Samin's in-laws, led us to a downstairs room, where the smell of grease from the deep fat fryer had found a permanent home. Although it was neither cheerful nor inviting, the room was quiet, and there was plenty of space for the children to move around. Rana took Jamal out of the stroller and held him. Although Jamal was almost three, he was small for his age and unable to walk or sit up or talk because of his cerebral palsy. Shayan and Amir settled into a corner of the long table with pens and paper. Arian had warned me before we met about Amir. "He is a little busy. I hope you don't mind." I replied, truthfully, that my own son had been "a little busy" as a young child and that I liked being around spirited children. And truly, Amir needed all the space that was available. He began by dropping a glass of Coke onto the floor and, for the two hours we were together, demonstrated a commanding and almost enchanting presence. He engaged each of us at various times and found entertainment in every object and conversation. He moved from one table to another, experimenting with skipping and jumping and spinning. Periodically, Asgar picked him up and spoke softly to him in Farsi.

Arian was the only one in the two families who spoke English, so I awkwardly nodded at Rana on occasion with a smile. I wondered what she was thinking, and her expression didn't provide many clues. She was poised. Our hosts arrived with several small platters of seasoned rice piled high with meat. More awkwardness. I was a vegetarian, and I asked Arian whether he could ask for something without meat. He did and then talked about how much they missed cooking and eating traditional Afghan foods. He talked about their lives at the camp called Eleonas. He said he was lucky that only eight of them lived in the two-room caravan, because most of the caravans housed ten or twelve. He described how he tried to help at the camp by acting as a translator between residents and volunteers. A couple of days a week, he walked into the central part of the city to visit NGO offices, where he might find resources for the people at Eleonas. Once he was able to get Visa cards loaded with 300 euros for 20 families. Another time, an NGO gave him bags of shampoo and soap. Another served people with disabilities and provided Arian with 50 euros a month and diapers for Jamal. Arian paused on occasion to translate some of the content of our conversation. After finishing lunch, we took pictures of each other with our phones and walked back to the metro station together. I returned to my hotel, exhausted but full inside. Impressive, this young man who felt so comfortable in a world that had treated him so harshly.

The next day, I met Arian and his family at Eleonas Camp, a monotony of white metal caravans set on a vast expanse of asphalt in an industrial neighborhood west of central Athens. This was one of Greece's best camps because the caravans had private bathrooms and air conditioning, when the electricity was working. The security personnel at the camp did not permit me to leave the reception area at the gate, so we visited under a metal awning in the blistering Athens heat, another awkward but tender meeting. Amena had expressed an interest in photography, so I had brought her an extra point-and-shoot camera I had. She took pictures of us sitting on wooden spools that had once held copper telephone wire and served as furniture at the camp's front gate.

When I arrived back at my hotel that night, I spent some time on Arian's Facebook page. Clearly, he did not want to be defined by his difficult circumstances. He had posted page after page of photos that showed outings with his sons at an Athens beach, climbing the rocks around the Acropolis, mugging in sunglasses. Photos from his time in Afghanistan suggested a man full of energy for the good life. He wore dark business suits, posed with co-workers and brothers showing off a late-model car or enjoying a ride on an Arabian horse. I assumed these pictures had been taken during the month he had been working in Dubai.

By now, I felt great affection for Arian, and I sensed there was something special about him. In our communications, he was poetic but honest, charismatic but respectful. He seemed to have a second sense about people, and he was a survivor. In spite of the tragic turn of events in his life, he had dignity and seemed determined to succeed, whatever that might mean under the circumstances.

The day before I left Athens, Nanci and I agreed to meet Arian at an outdoor café in Monastiraki, the touristic neighborhood in the shadow of the Acropolis. Although I was always happy to return home, I hoped that the timing of my departure didn't mean an end to my friendship with Arian. When he arrived in Monastiraki, I could see him 20 yards distant, confident and smiling. As he walked toward me, I wanted to hug him. He was Muslim, and I didn't know the rules. When he approached me, I extended my arms in a way that would have permitted him to take my hands rather than accept a hug. But he understood, and he carefully put his arm around me. He seemed comfortable with everything he did. I felt relieved. We had broken a barrier that was normal between strangers and surely a more difficult one between a Muslim man and an American woman.

Arian sat down across from us at the table and declined our offer that he order lunch for himself. I was curious about this because he had been living on a lifeless diet of starches at the camp. I wondered whether his refusal was a way of signaling us that he wasn't meeting us for his personal comfort.

That day, he told us about his family's journey to Greece — the brutality of people at the borders, the duplicity of the smugglers, gun-toting militia, traversing mountains and deserts and water without adequate food or clothing. In his poetic way of speaking, he ended that part of the conversation by saying, "Our journey was to find safety. I didn't want to watch my children die. I didn't want them to watch me die. Everywhere, the sky is blue, and the earth is hard."

Arian talked about whether he could still have dreams because his life had become so confined by closed borders and the grind of his daily life in the camp. He wanted to talk about big things, like whether his sons would become educated men and how Greece would be unable to accommodate the thousands of people stranded within its borders.

The day before, I had researched Greek poets, hoping to find one whose message might seem relevant to Arian. I learned about Odysseus Elytis, a Greek Nobel Prize-winning poet who lived on Lesvos. That morning, I had found an English-language copy of his poems and gave it to Arian with a bookmarked passage:

You have a taste of tempest on your lips—But where did
*   you wander*
All day long in the hard reverie of stone and sea?
An eagle-bearing wind stripped the hills
Stripped your longing to the bone
And the pupils of your eyes received the message of
*   chimera*
Spotting memory with foam!

He thanked me for the book, and we sat together for another hour, poring over photos of our lives on each other's phones. He showed me a photo of myself that I had never seen before. It had been posted online after I'd spoken at a conference in California. He said he was proud of what he had learned online about my work as an administrative law judge. We took photos of ourselves and each other to remember this special day together.

Before I left Arian that day, I offered to help him live with his family outside the camp so he could find work. I didn't know what that would mean at the time, and I didn't think about the implications of taking a family out of a place where they received services, however meager, to a way of living that would cost more than just a monthly rent payment. They would need to buy food, acquire furniture, and pay utility bills. They would not have access to free clothing or diapers.

Without much evidence, I assumed Arian would navigate these kinds of problems. I trusted him without much more than a gut feeling. I believed Arian would be able to do a lot with a little help. I also believed he was a man who could make a difference in the lives of others. In the coming years, it would never be an easy path for him, but he did not let me down. Within a few weeks, I was calling him *joon*, a title of affection in Farsi.

Chapter 21
May 2016
Armen

AFTER LEAVING GREECE, I flew to Yerevan, Armenia, where I hoped to find a further connection with my grandfather. I didn't know what I was expecting to find when I arrived there. Modern Armenia is not the homeland of my family. Its current borders were defined following the fall of the Ottoman Empire in 1918. Much of the territory that had been historically inhabited by Armenians became part of the new state of Azerbaijan and what remained of Turkey. My ancestors' community of Chunkush had become part of Eastern Turkey, and the town of Chunkush was predominantly Kurdish. I didn't even know whether Armenia would feel Armenian to me — it had been occupied by the Soviet Union for 70 years, until 1991.

Having no expectation that I would find evidence of my Armenian family, I was nevertheless curious about whether and how I might feel a connection to the modern state called Armenia. I visited the ancient churches and spent time in Yerevan's public squares and parks. I walked across town to buy produce at the farmers' markets at the edges of the city. I visited museums and made up excuses to talk to shopkeepers and people in cafes. But the people in Yerevan were not like the Armenians I grew up with, who tended to be intellectual, sardonic, and a little noisy, generous with hugs, food, and laughter. The people in Yerevan felt stern and serious. They sat in cafes without laughing or gesticulating. Their public art was massive and heavy. Vendors shooed away old people trying to sell tiny bags of fruit. I sensed a creepy, elite class of men I wouldn't want to meet in a dark alley. I once tripped on the sidewalk in front of a dozen pedestrians, none of whom acknowledged my near miss with a gesture of any kind. Although I had never been to Russia, Armenia felt more Soviet than Armenian.

Armenia did, however, connect me with my refugee grandfather in a way I didn't expect, and with my refugee friends in Greece. Shortly before I arrived in Armenia, I had read an article about Armenians who had lived in Syria and escaped the war there by returning to the homeland of their grandparents and great-grandparents. An Armenian refugee from Syria had opened a restaurant in Yerevan called "Anteb," so I went there for lunch one day. I ate a Syrian salad called *fatoush*, made of fresh tomatoes, mint, and cucumbers, topped with crispy pita bread. When the waiter brought my check, I asked whether he knew of any Syrian Armenians who were refugees from the war in Syria. "I am one," he said. His name was Armen and he offered to talk to me.

Armen met me a few days later at a sidewalk café near Yerevan's main square. He was 27, with typical Armenian features — olive skinned with deep-set eyes and dark hair.

He was dressed modestly and presented himself as the kind of person who did not want to be noticed. As we talked that day, he did not often make eye contact and routinely covered his face with his hands.

Armen came from Aleppo, close to the Southwestern border of what was once Western Armenia, where the Ottoman Turks had systematically murdered more than a million Armenians and hundreds of thousands of Greeks. In 1915, Armen's grandparents left Western Armenia for Syria. Along the way, they lost each other in the desert. Six years later, they found each other in Aleppo.

Armen grew up in an Armenian neighborhood, attended good schools, and eventually began working for a software company, selling accounts on commission. His father was nearing retirement age after a career selling agricultural products. In 2011, normal citizens weary of the corruption of the Al-Assad regime staged what we now call "Arab Spring," which evolved into a many-sided war between the heavily armed governments, local rebels, Kurds, and religious extremists. By 2015, the Russian government was providing military support to the Assad regime, and, together, they bombed hundreds of civilian neighborhoods to shambles.

The citizens who wanted change became the victims. Hundreds of thousands of civilians died or were subjected to torture. Every day, Armen left his apartment for work and found evidence of new rounds of mortar shelling and missile fire in the neighborhoods of friends and family. His own neighborhood was occasionally a target as well. Armenians had originally supported the Assad regime, which reciprocated by setting up blockades in Armenian neighborhoods.

The blockades then became targets for Al-Assad's enemies, who pummeled the area with mortar shells.

By 2015, the war had caused 4 million Syrians to leave the country or to seek shelter in refugee camps. One of Armen's friends fled to Argentina and another to South Korea. Armen lost two college friends who had joined the military. A friend from work, Elisa, had escaped Aleppo through Turkey, where she and her family boarded a boat to the Greek Islands. The boat capsized, and Elisa swam in a life jacket for four hours back to the Turkish Coast. She lost her whole family. Armen's best friend, Krikor, died when his apartment was hit by mortar fire while he was sleeping. Krikor died 10 days before he was to join his brother in South Korea.

The war was causing Armen so much anxiety that he could barely get through the day. He heard bombs across town and wondered whether he would be next. He was haunted by the ghosts of his friends. He couldn't concentrate at work, and his sales commissions were no longer enough to live on. He had developed strange tics. He gulped air and then found himself holding his breath until he was almost sick. His eyes would dart across a room, and his arms moved on their own. He could no longer engage in any kind of normal conversation.

Armen told me he left because "I did not want to die," and no one had to tell him he was not tolerating the violence or the uncertainty. He could not imagine himself on a boat to Greece after Elisa's experience. The borders of many countries were closing. His parents had pled with him to go to Armenia. One day, Armen showed up at the Armenian Embassy in Aleppo with his passport, a report from his criminal-background check, and the certificate of his baptism in the Armenian Catholic Church. Armen did not need to seek asylum, and he was not a refugee. The Armenian government considered him a returning member of the diaspora. With great sorrow, Armen boarded a plane to Yerevan the following week. He left his family behind because they could not afford to leave. He missed them terribly and wondered whether he would ever see them again.

Armen told me he knew he was lucky compared to many other people who'd escaped the war in Syria. He lived in a safe place, he had his freedom, and he had a job. Armen had been welcomed by the country of his ancestors. But I knew the war was not behind him. When I asked him whether he thought he could make a good life for himself in Yerevan, he pulled on his cheeks and shut his eyes. "I do not think about my future anymore."

As I sat listening to Armen's story, I heard my grandfather, who never spoke of what happened to him or his family in Armenia, who never spoke of his feelings of loss and isolation or of the hardships he'd faced arriving in a new country with nothing but the clothes on his back. Armen helped me understand the pain my grandfather must have felt and how difficult it must have been for him to feel whole and have any peace of mind. I wanted to tell Armen that my grandfather had been a refugee and that he'd ultimately had a good life. In America, he had a successful small business and raised four children who went to college and had professional careers and good lives. I didn't tell him. For Armen, my grandfather's story would not have felt like encouragement. Instead, I told Armen that I believed in him and that he would find his happiness.

Chapter 22

Summer 2016

While I Was Away

I RETURNED TO THE BAY AREA in July, happy to spend time visiting friends and family after months of traveling alone. During this visit home, I realized that my experiences in Greece and my obvious commitment to Arian had created complications — or maybe highlighted those that already existed. I felt a special concern for how the changes in my life would affect my son, Gabe. He had graduated from college and was living with his girlfriend, Alex, in a cottage in the Oakland hills. He was working at a car-rental company, where he used his people skills to sell upgrades to rental cars. I believed this would be a good learning experience but one that would eventually bore him. I told him not to wear a tie with frayed edges. We argued about the disposition of my BMW, which he wanted, and we laughed about the otherwise small things that connected us. I felt such gratitude that my adorable all-American son seemed happy. Safe. Healthy. A stranger to war and persecution.

But I knew my ad hoc Greek family was already an emotional complication between Gabe and me, and I wanted to provide him with some assurance that he would always be the most important person in my life. This would require the kind of conversation that would be uncomfortable and that might even create more misunderstandings. Our occasional dinners together were cheerful and never seemed like the right time for serious discussion. I finally got up my courage during a family gathering that summer at a lake resort. There were 20 of us staying in several '70s-era condominiums. Our days there were full of food and laughter and games. With all the family activity, it was difficult to find a quiet moment, but one day Gabe and I ended up together alone on a bench along the lakeshore while we waited for his cousins to return the kayaks we had rented that afternoon.

Of course, by the time I was able talk to him, I didn't really know what to say. I told him I hoped he understood that he was the most important person in my life, and I explained a little bit about my relationship to Arian. He listened quietly, leaning over, looking at the sand. I paused and asked him how he felt about that. When he looked up at me, I could see he was feeling vulnerable and trying to find his own right words. After a few seconds, he politely replied, "Mom, it sounds like you have found a son who will talk to you a lot. And he was a television star. I am happy for you."

Gabe's response made me realize I had sent the wrong message somewhere along the way. My foolish hope had been that he would think of Arian as a brother, someone he might want to know and love. It appeared instead that I had profoundly shaken his confidence. I interpreted his response to mean he believed my relationship with Arian was a way to compensate for what I wasn't getting in my love for him. I felt small, insensitive. He was at a critical point on his path to adulthood, and having a "brother" who was, in his mind, things he was not, touched a raw nerve.

Gabe was so deeply a part of me that I had taken for granted his confidence in what we'd shared since he'd been a newborn. I promised myself that I would be more sensitive to his emotions and that I would make some special gestures in his direction. I didn't understand it at the time, but I made such a gesture a few weeks later, when I sold him my BMW for the price of a used Toyota. I knew that this a superficial way of connecting with him and that it wasn't going to make up for the emotional gaps. But I also knew it was meeting him on his own soil and acknowledging how his needs at this time of his life had nothing to do with Arian. After that, we returned to the usual ways we enjoyed each other's company — sharing the questions of our lives and annoying each other. Gabe didn't ask about Arian or talk about him again when I was home.

I learned a little about my relationships with other people in my life during this time as well. After Gabe, it was Vic whose understanding I needed most. He was family, a man who had been my partner before Gabe was born and who'd adopted Gabe when he was 14. And I never needed to doubt him. He was as solid as he had ever been and shared constant expressions of support and caring. He accepted that I did things my own way at times and didn't seem at all surprised at the changes I had made in my life.

Most of the other people in my life made it a point to provide expressions of encouragement and donated cash to spend on the people in Greece. A few became distant. For a while, I fretted over it, and then I let it go. I knew my life was unusual and, for my friends and family, probably hard to understand. For most of the previous two years, I had spent most of my days living in hotels or other people's apartments, in airports, in countries that were mysterious to most. Stranger than that, I had adopted a second family composed of people who, on the surface, had nothing in common with me.

But this life was beginning to feel normal to me. I half-jokingly referred to myself as "homeless" and corrected myself by saying the whole world was my home. I spent hours every week planning more adventures and the next visit to Greece. In spite of the wonderful familiarity of the people and places I loved in California, it all felt increasingly objective. That is, I saw it through the eyes of a visitor, with its casual affluence and natural beauty, as well as the waste and smug consumerism. Strangest of all, that summer, Donald Trump was conducting a presidential campaign of hate and fear, promising, among other things, to ban Muslims from immigrating to the United States and to create a register of Muslims who already lived there. It was hard to believe and harder to understand that this, too, was my country.

Traveling had always changed the lens through which I would see my own life at home, but I had brought home a lot more of Greece with me than I might have predicted. If I saw women in *hijabs* in a shop or heard a Farsi accent, I felt comforted. I was shocked at how much stuff Americans collected, so much more than they needed or even cared about. When I was shopping one day, I used the women's bathroom in a Macy's store and found myself calculating how many refugees could live comfortably in its two very large ante-rooms. The suite had heat, sanitary facilities, nice lighting, and comfortable furniture. It just needed a small kitchen. *At least eight*, I thought. Making the refugees' lives more comfortable seemed like just a logistics problem. If the people in my life would just give up the things they never used, there would be enough beds and dishes and blankets and couches and warm jackets for all of the refugees — and for all of the struggling Greeks as well.

Every day, my email inbox provided me with every one of the world's English-language news articles about the refugees in Greece, which I read to keep up with the evolution of the circumstances in Europe. A lot had changed from the days when Greece was a welcoming path to something better. After the Turkey-EU deal, Lesvos became a prison for the refugees who had arrived after March 20. The hope that Lesvos once offered to people traveling to Northern Europe was replaced by a feeling of hopelessness and uncertainty. There were many reports that Greece was sending refugees back to Turkey or Afghanistan without giving them an opportunity to apply for asylum, although this was a violation of international law. We continued to hear stories of police abuse, filthy living conditions, and inadequate food and medical care at Moria.

With the border closings, refugees on mainland Greece faced horrible circumstances as well. Thousands were living in an informal camp called "Idomeni," at the Macedonian border, each hoping unrealistically that Macedonia would eventually reopen the borders and permit them passage to northern Europe. Instead, border patrols took opportunities to brutalize, bully, and tear gas the people along the fence. It became widely known that the punishment for trying to cross was a severe beating by the Macedonian police. The conditions at the camp, which were widely reported in European news media, were nothing short of inhuman. Children begging shoeless and sick, tents sitting on top of mud, little sanitation or clean water. The only support at Idomeni was provided by independent volunteers and a handful of NGOs. The EU did nothing to help.

After the border closing, the Greek government convinced some to live in camps scattered around the country in isolated areas, many initially opened without electricity, sanitation, or security. Thousands of refugees were stuck in Athens as well without adequate support from the government or NGOs. Many lived on the streets, vulnerable to smugglers, the slave trade, and drug dealers. The UNHCR and the large NGOs made public pleas for more humane treatment of the refugees. The nations of the EU responded with indifference and, in some cases, victimization.

The conditions for so many people deepened my commitment to Arian and his family. While their circumstances remained difficult in some ways, they could have been so much worse, and a few hundred euros could make the difference between safety and homelessness.

During my time at home, I heard from Nanci, Anne-Lene, and Arian, sometimes several times a day. Arian created a group message for the six of us, who had become so close in so little time — Nanci, Anne-Lene, Arian, Hashem, Farshad, and me. I had told Arian about Auntie Dawn and how the small inheritance she'd left me allowed me to help him, so Arian called the group "Butterflies," a reference the others didn't quite understand, but it stuck. We used the group message to share photos, news, and endearments from three corners of the world. Farshad had joined a Greek soccer league. They had shared a big dinner at Arian's. Amir threw toys over the balcony fence. We took for granted that our sons would be adept at English, and they certainly learned fast although only Arian knew English at first — and because much of what he learned was by watching television, he was still learning how to write it. We used Google Translate when the messages were difficult, and we used a lot of emoticons — hearts, happy faces, cartoon dogs crying, with signs that said, "I miss you." One day Arian commented that he woke up to 83 messages.

Of course, I was most interested in how Arian was re-defining and restructuring his life. The term "refugee" was becoming associated with helplessness and problems, neither of which suited or described Arian. It took him only a few days to find a large two-bedroom apartment on the top floor of a typical Athens apartment building a few blocks north of Victoria Square in the center of Athens. It had new paint, hardwood floors, and a lot of light. He furnished it with donations from some of the volunteers he had met and bargains he found at the Sunday Bazaar.

Finding a landlord who would rent to him was a signifi-cant accomplishment, since he didn't have a job or evidence of income at the time. Arian always seemed to connect with the people he needed, and they always seemed to consider themselves lucky, as I did. His landlady, Anastasia, was an advocate for the family from the minute she met them.

Anastasia drove him to pick up furniture and get the utilities connected. She was a skilled physical therapist and taught Rana how to exercise Jamal's muscles so he would retain some of his physical functions. When Arian told me how much she was doing for him, I could only respond, "Of course. She is Greek."

Arian and Rana shared the apartment with Asgar and Samin for about a month. They needed the companionship, and Arian felt a commitment to the family. It wasn't long, however, before Arian understood that the arrangement was unworkable. Asgar had a short fuse that, in at least one instance, he could not manage. As a result, Arian ended up walking the streets in the middle of the night, looking for Samin and Amena after Asgar had beaten her for making a derogatory comment about one of his relatives. This incident would have been enough to change things, but Asgar did not seem motivated to contribute either resources or elbow grease to the maintenance of the household. Although Rana wanted Samin's company, Arian insisted the family move out, which I emphatically supported. He didn't need the additional responsibility and stress.

Arian had also become a visible part of the refugee community in Athens. He was compulsive about making connections and helping others find resources, and he was committed to finding a job, as unlikely as that might have been in the collapsed Greek economy. By April, Arian had gotten his "yellow card" from the Greek Asylum Services, which meant he was recognized as an asylum seeker and a legal resident until and unless he was officially denied asylum. Most refugees who arrived in Greece after the borders closed did not want asylum in Greece. They knew there were no jobs, very few social services, and no infrastructure for helping migrants integrate into local communities. Many waited to see whether the borders would open so they could move on to Northern Europe. Arian never believed the borders would reopen and had applied for asylum in Greece shortly after he arrived. This turned out to be foresighted. He avoided some of the bureaucratic chaos that accompanied the flood of applications that followed.

Arian's status as asylum-seeker entitled him to work, but he needed to endure an elaborate process of getting the Greek equivalent of a work permit. Anastasia was again invaluable. She helped Arian navigate the complex process of acquiring the legal documents he needed to work in bureaucratic Greece.

As soon as Arian had his work permit, he started volunteering his time at Piraeus Camp, where Nanci and Anne-Lene were volunteering. This young man who loved fast cars and had played a part in a television series texted me to say it had been his great privilege to be asked to wash dishes for an NGO. He let the NGO managers and volunteers know he was available to translate their conversations with people who spoke Farsi, Dari, Urdu, and Pashto. Within a few weeks, Arian was an official volunteer for Drop in the Ocean at Piraeus Camp. He sent me selfies that showed his work with other volunteers, proudly showing off his hi-vis vest and the friends he had met.

A few weeks later, he got a short-term assignment with *Medicins San Frontiers* (MSF) to act as translator during a vaccination campaign at one of the camps. More selfies in his MSF vest on the work site with doctors and children. MSF paid him 40 euros a day, which he sent home to his mother in Afghanistan. He told me he would never be able to work for a business again. He wanted only to serve people in need, and now he had a resume to show his commitment. I felt so happy and proud of him.

After the MSF job finished, Arian contacted the largest NGOs to find paid work at the camps and got an interview with Danish Refuge Council (DRC). DRC was under contract with the Greek Ministry to manage the operations at Elliniko Camp, which housed more than 3,000 refugees at the abandoned site of the 2002 Olympic Games, west of central Athens. I told Arian he seemed to have a special relationship with Danes because he loved Ecco shoes and Danish Anette had introduced us. DRC hired Arian as a "cultural mediator" at the Elliniko site. Most of Arian's work involved translating and problem solving. There were many problems where people had little hope of ever leading normal lives. He set up classes for the women and helped conduct a survey of the residents' skills. We all talked about the idea that the refugees could begin developing community and supporting themselves, although there was little in the way of leadership to bring people together.

DRC later moved Arian to work at Skaramangas Camp on what was called "protection." Protection work involved identifying people who were vulnerable, like pregnant women or unaccompanied minors, and making sure they were getting services. Part of the goal was to avoid exploitation of all kinds, which was becoming a problem in the camps and especially for the refugees living in squats and on the streets.

Arian had an insatiable appetite for working and helping people. One night on his way home, he found a young
couple on the street with a newborn who looked destitute.
He stopped and talked to them in Farsi and learned they
had just arrived after a nine-hour bus ride from the camp
at Idomeni. At the camp, they had been living in the mud
with the newborn and without medical care or food. The
sun was setting, so Arian took the family home to his apartment. They showered while Rana washed their clothes and
Arian made up an extra bed. They shared some of Jamal's
baby clothes and ate dinner together on the balcony of the
apartment. The next morning, Arian took them to Eleonas
in a taxi. At the camp, the Greek police refused to allow the
couple to stay, even with a newborn and knowing they might
otherwise be out on the street. The police at the gate knew
Arian from the time his family had lived at Eleonas, which
empowered Arian to argue with them until they agreed to
take the couple — "And that's it, Arian. Don't bring any more
people here." Some of Arian's friends at the camp promised
Arian they would take care of the new family.

During the months I was away, Arian became more like
a son to me. The relationship snuck up on me one small step
at a time over the course of, well, maybe two weeks. It all felt
very natural, although I knew Arian was pushing things along.
That last day in Athens, when Nanci and I met him for the
lunch at which he didn't eat, we had talked about Hashem
calling Nanci "mom." By then, I knew Arian and I were
developing a similar relationship, but I told Arian, "I am not
sure how I feel about you calling me 'Mom.' I don't want you

to feel we are in a hierarchical relationship." He nodded and said he understood. A week later, he was calling me "Mom." I think he needed the comfort of a maternal relationship during this most stressful and challenging time of his life. But even more, I think he knew that our strangely evolving relationship needed a fence around it. He was smarter than me about such things. This wasn't a business relationship, and there was no shame in the kind of hierarchy that comes with family.

I got used to being called "Mom" quickly. Within a month, I was startled and concerned when Arian sent me a note that addressed me as "Kim." Without any analysis or calculation, I felt the deep commitment to him that comes with motherhood. It was all very confusing. I worried about him. Like any mother, I occasionally expressed disapproval or provided advice, which was graciously accepted. He should not let his children eat too much sugar. Jamal should not be left on the floor all day. Amir needed to be around other children.

We spent hours on phone calls talking about his work, his future, his family. He confided that he had no one else to talk to about his problems. He didn't want to worry his family in Kabul. He could not talk to Rana, because it was his job to take care of her. And his male friends had their own very serious challenges — as the big brother, he could not bother them with his troubles. Arian also needed a confidante who trusted him and understood him. So he told me what was on his active mind, including some things I probably didn't want to know. (Once he recounted how a flirtatious volunteer approached him by saying, "The first time we met, I was so attracted to you, but I could tell you were a little bit shy.

Let's get to know each other." He giggled when he told me his mischievous reply, "I think that is not such a good idea because, you see, I am still a little bit shy.")

Arian had so many stresses in his life. Some were what you might expect from a man with three children and a low-paying job in a strange and difficult city. He and Rana had the kinds of marital strains that come with parenting young children and with their very different ways of looking at the world. Rana remained a devout Muslim, largely isolated at home with the children, while Arian was increasingly adapting to a European perspective and way of life. He was often on the verge of the flu or a cold because he pushed himself so hard. He occasionally called in a panic that he would never be able to succeed in Greece or provide opportunities for his sons. He was worried about his family at home, especially his mother, who had high blood pressure and other health problems. One time that summer, he could not reach them for two days and called me in a panic. I knew he assumed the worst and felt culpable, so we talked several times about why they might not be available. The next day, Arian learned that the internet system in the family's Kabul neighborhood had been down.

But the things he talked about the most were the troubles of others. He sent me a photo of a man at the camp who could not use one of his arms because it had been shattered by one of Assad's bombs. He asked me to provide art supplies to a gifted ten-year-old who was painting on filthy cardboard he had found in a dumpster. He described the injustices he saw everywhere around him — how the incompetence of the Greek government was affecting people's lives, a woman who had to relieve herself in a cup at night because she feared she would be raped if she left her tent. He was expressing my own feelings, but his tone was one of compassion and worry, while mine was usually one of anger and frustration. I tried to listen and agree and then distract him. I could feel the level of stress bearing down on him, and he didn't need my political perspectives. He needed to be reminded of his strength.

From the beginning, money created complicated problems that I didn't anticipate and didn't always handle well. Arian liked to spend money, like most of us, even though he lived a very austere existence. I found it difficult to tell him he needed to economize so he could live on his own salary, which was about 900 euros a month after taxes. I once felt ashamed to have suggested he should stop buying toys and houseplants the same week I booked a safari in Tanzania. But I was nervous thinking about whether I would have enough for his family's uncertain future, whether that meant paying for Shayan to go to college in London or making sure his family had food and shelter in Kabul. There was no way at the time to predict how things might turn out. And I admit, I selfishly didn't want to compromise my freedom to travel comfortably or deny Gabe a secure future, either. But there were other reasons that were less financial and more sociological. I knew that Arian needed to lead a modest lifestyle to maintain his connection with the community he worked with and needed. Arian's relative comfort could create envy and distrust. It could create a pressure for him to share his good fortune with others, which he was bound to do by his nature. But in the back of my mind, I knew all of this analysis was mostly a way of rationalizing the inequality in our respective lives, inequality that reflected the circumstances to which we had each born. That is, I felt guilty.

To defuse some of the tension of these financial issues and the differences in our material worlds, Arian found ways to poke fun at his expensive tastes *and* mine. One day, we were talking on a video call when I was sitting in my car in San Francisco. After a few minutes, he asked, "Mom, what kind of car are you in? It looks pretty nice." I didn't usually make a fuss about the trappings of my California life, because I assumed it would create more longing in him. I replied, "It's a BMW, but it's old!" Later, he playfully told me he preferred the 700 series BMWs to the 300 series. Another time, he asked me whether I was going to bring him a Rolex watch when I returned to Athens because "I like being able to tell time without opening my phone." He loved photography and once commented that a $12,000 Hasselblad camera had "nice features."

Because our conversations were often so emotional and his life was full of work commitments and children and an ever-more-complex social life, I was at times conflicted about how often to contact Arian. I wanted him to know I was thinking of him, and I was always enriched by our conversations, but I didn't want him to feel beholden to me, to feel that I expected him to call me out of deference or take care of my emotional needs. He had enough to think about. One day, he called me to say he was upset for two reasons: he had a cold, and I hadn't called in several days. After that, I stayed closer.

I occasionally felt a nagging sensation of how I could be played in this situation. Arian was in a situation with his family that would make any conscientious man desperate. On top of that, Arian was a personality who leveraged any advantage under any circumstance. I had heard the stories of people who had helped others in poverty and ended up spending small fortunes to sustain unrealistic lifestyles. I knew I would be tested on this from time to time and reminded myself to remain trusting but vigilant about the specifics. I wondered what my own mother would have told me if she were here, and every time I tried to imagine her responses to my questions, I could only hear her say, "These are complications you have invited. You will figure it out."

Rana remained a bit of a mystery to me during this time, mainly because we didn't share a common language and we had not spent much time together before I left Greece. On a couple of occasions, I wrote her emails that Arian translated for her, mainly to say she was important to me. She was by nature reserved and modest. I knew from Arian that she had grown up in a conservative Muslim family and was quite religious. She always wore her *hijab* when men were present and did not go out alone. She was a determined housekeeper and cook. She prayed five times a day on a prayer rug and observed the rules of Islam.

I learned a little more about Rana when Arian told me about the couple's first encounters. He prefaced his story by explaining earnestly that "all the women wanted me," a disclosure I didn't doubt but laughed at for its lacking modesty. The two of them had worked at a school. He was a trainer, and she did some of the accounting. Rana did not wear makeup or alluring clothes to work, consistent with her sense of modesty. One day, Arian asked her why she didn't dress up like the other women in the office, to which she responded, "And who do you think you are?" Apparently, that was the trigger for a long-term relationship. Arian came home one day from a business trip to learn that his father had arranged for him to marry Rana a few weeks later. I knew instinctively that their marriage was difficult at times. But I also believed that the high-risk dreamer Arian needed the stability and rock-solid loyalty that Rana brought to their relationship.

During that summer, I stayed in close touch with Nanci, who had developed a very close "mother-son" relationship with Hashem. Nanci had met Hashem when she worked with Drop in the Ocean at Piraeus and Hashem lived at the camp in Piraeus. A 16-year-old at the camp received a text from Syria that his mother had died in a bombing by the Assad regime. This would have been tragic enough, but this young man had to share the information with his 12-year-old brother, who was deaf. The two were traveling alone. Hashem and Nanci heard what was happening and wanted to show that they cared about these two teenagers in distress. The boys didn't speak English, so Hashem stayed with them for the rest of the day. Over the course of the week, he checked in with the boys a couple of times a day to see how they were doing and then reported to Nanci in a sort of broken English.

Hashem had a thick mop of hair and bushy black eyebrows. He was athletic and built like a football player (American football, not soccer). Hashem had escaped from Syria, where he had once had a career teaching sports and math at a public school. After the Syrian rebellion called "Muslim Spring," he had been imprisoned and tortured for almost two years by the Assad regime. During that time, the woman he loved assumed he was dead and married another man. Two of his cousins died in Assad's prisons, and his brother-in-law was killed in one of Assad's bombing raids.

Hashem did not speak English when Nanci met him, but the two of them stumbled through misunderstandings and miscues with good humor. From the beginning of their friendship, Hashem felt an affection for Nanci that permitted playfulness. At Piraeus, Nanci was free with her advice to the young men who were traveling without mothers. She scolded them for smoking and reminded them to call home. Because of this, Hashem started calling her "Mama Nanci." At first, the name was a reference to her role around others. But within a short time, it described the role she played in Hashem's life. Eventually, even the volunteers were calling her "Mama Nanci," and I found myself trying to think of her as just "Nanci."

After the Greek government shut down the camp at Piraeus, Hashem moved to Skaramangas camp, considered by "POCs" (people of concern — refugees) to be one of the best camps. Still, it was not much. Skaramangas sat on a stretch of asphalt along the sea northwest of central Athens. The camp accommodated about 3,000 refugees in metal "caravans," each with two rooms and a bathroom, air conditioning, and hot water but no kitchen facilities. The Greek Ministry provided meals, inadequate and tasteless but food at least. The camp had no trees and no meeting places, so, during the harsh, hot summers and cold, windy winters, the only place to hang out was in a crowded caravan. The Greek Ministry did not provide laundry facilities, so 3,000 people either washed blue jeans and t-shirts by hand or paid a euro to clean their clothes in a tiny washing machine set up next to one of the caravans. A few enterprising residents set up kiosks that sold cigarettes and sandwiches along the asphalt equivalent of a boardwalk. Ten feet from the row of kiosks, the asphalt dropped precipitously into the restless sea. In the summer evenings, families and young people walked along this makeshift promenade. Sometimes the men danced or played music, engaging the children and challenging themselves to forget the trauma of their lives.

Hashem shared the caravan with six others. Lorin was a cheerful and stylish 30-something Kurd from Iraq who seemed able to cope with her stressful environment without a care. Marzia, quiet and generous with affection, had traveled the dangerous journey from Iraq with four children between the ages of six and thirteen. Her husband had been granted asylum in Germany, and Marzia had applied for "reunification" with him, a process that, in Greece, took more than 20 months. These unlikely roommates had originally gotten to know each other at Piraeus and had chosen to live together when they moved to Skaramangas.

Nanci also lived in Hashem's caravan for several weeks that summer. Non-residents were not permitted to stay after evening curfew at official Greek camps (if they were allowed in at all), but Nanci managed to escape the attention of the police at the gate, who, in fact, probably knew exactly what she was up to. Nanci's new roommates assigned her the best bunk in the room with the women and Marzia's daughter, Sarah. Hashem and the boys lived in the other room. When she stayed there, Nanci proposed to buy what was needed for a modest kitchen — a hot plate, a small refrigerator, and plates. Hashem argued with her about this. He didn't accept handouts. She prevailed by saying she would not eat the Greek Army's food and threatening to spend her money at a hotel instead. Hashem relented and built a counter adjacent to one of the bunk beds. It had a small sink and a couple of shelves, and they called it a kitchen. Thereafter, with two pots and a tiny cutting board, Hashem and Marzia made elaborate Syrian meals of rice pilaf, stewed meats and vegetables, and lemon-dressed salads. They spread out on a blanket on the floor and ate from communal plates. They sent us selfies of these meals in which they were smiling as if they were attending great events.

This evolving family also included a teenager named Farshad. Handsome and fit as a movie star, Farshad had been a soccer professional in a sports league in Afghanistan. He was always smiling and placed a high value on maintaining his good looks. He invariably spent the small stipends he got from the Greek government or one of the moms to buy black t-shirts and soccer attire, while others bought better food or phone top-ups. Farshad's voice had a cadence that suggested education and kindness and modesty. His mother had been granted asylum in Germany, and his siblings remained in Afghanistan. He was an "unaccompanied minor" and therefore qualified to apply for reunification with his mother. Farshad would wait more than a year for the Greek government to process his claim and for Germany to approve it.

Nanci first got to know Farshad because he lived in the caravan across from Hashem's. She consulted with him when he wanted to be smuggled to Germany and helped him with his paperwork. He quickly became a full-fledged member of the dinners in Hashem's caravan and grew close to Arian because they shared a common language and similar sense of self-assurance about the world. Over the course of a couple of months, Arian, Hashem, and Farshad became brothers just as Anne-Lene, Nanci, and I became their moms.

The whole thing was mystifying, and these unexpected relationships unleashed unexpected emotions in the moms. Nanci, Anne-Lene, and I spent hours talking on the phone and texting each other in the middle of the night to make sense of how our lives had changed and the mystery of how our new family had become so important to us. Were there other moms like us in Greece? What was it about Middle Eastern (Muslim? Youth?) culture that encouraged such unorthodox relationships? Why did we leave our loving families and our privileged lives to be with people whose experiences were so vastly different from our own in that damaged place called Athens?

In contrast, our new children seemed perfectly comfortable with our strange and wonderful relationships. We knew they had emotional stresses we couldn't even imagine, but they were consistently generous in spirit and adept at supporting us and each other. Although we stumbled through language and cultural differences at times, our new children trusted their instincts and ours.

Chapter 23
August 2016
Exarchia

I GREW UP BELIEVING LOVE — whether platonic, familial, or romantic — sprung from and was nurtured in some pretty rarified settings. You made friends sitting on a beach during summer vacation or over homework in a well-stocked school library. Weddings occurred in beautiful churches and flowery gardens. Families were created when children were born in sterile hospitals and came home to teddy-beared nurseries in yellow-striped receiving blankets. The extended family was composed of in-laws who held forth at Thanksgiving dinners in warm, carpeted dining rooms. So much of my life had been some variation of what was portrayed in American television of the 1960s and 1970s.

In Greece, I learned that the whole gritty world can be a petri dish for creating family. When I returned there that August, I decided to stay in Athens to work with people in the squats and on the streets. I could have found ways to help in a thousand different places, but I wanted to be near Arian and Rana. I rented a small apartment in a neighborhood called

"Exarchia," in the central part of the city. From Exarchia, I could walk to almost anything of interest to me in Athens, including Arian and Rana's apartment.

In some ways, Exarchia was a mess. Like so much of Athens, it featured filthy streets, garbage bins overflowing with refuse, and ugly cement buildings covered in graffiti. The streets smelled of auto fumes, cigarette smoke, and cat piss. Many of the Greeks who lived in the neighborhood were serious and unfriendly. It was a time of deepening economic crisis in Greece, with high unemployment rates and cutbacks in social programs and services of all kinds, and there was plenty of evidence of this in Exarchia. I eventually made a habit of carrying bags of food when I left my apartment to relieve a dark-skinned man or a gray-haired woman from going through the smelly garbage bins in the streets.

But Exarchia had personality traits I liked and had never encountered in any city neighborhood. Exarchia was full of intellectuals, university students, and artists who patronized local cafes day and night. The neighborhood was home to a dozen or more "squats," empty buildings that had been appropriated by anarchists for refugee accommodation. In the evenings, the tree-lined square was full of young people and families speaking different languages, eating, drinking, dancing. Refugee families gathered in the evenings in the expanse in front of the National Archaeological Museum, where their children could run and play among statues of Greek antiquity. Exarchia was a place of demonstrations, bookstores, and panhandling. All of this suited me.

On my first day in town, my new Greek landlady, Vivian, took me on a walk to show me where to get the cheapest fresh orange juice and the best produce. Vivian was a "sand bird." Like many Athenians, she spent the oppressively hot Greek summers on a Greek island and rented out the family property in Athens to tourists and, these days, volunteers. She was probably 70 but had an enthusiasm for life and a kindness that felt more like Lesvos than Athens. Vivian left me with the keys and the phone number of a friend. I went out to buy groceries, unpacked, and then mentally paced all afternoon, waiting to see Arian at the end of his workday. He was to arrive at 6:30. At 6:25, I looked out the window of my second-floor apartment and saw him across the street, leaning on a post and waiting for me to look out the window. I had forgotten to tell him which button to push for the door buzzer. He waved and smiled, and I ran downstairs.

Arian followed me upstairs, and I opened a couple of beers. We sat down at opposite ends of the small couch in the living room and grinned at each other. At first, I was uncomfortable with the impropriety of this picture. As a mature, independent American woman — a person of privilege in a world of inequality — I felt safe assuming the risks that come with unusual relationships (although I think I know what my mother would have said). In conservative Afghan culture, however, men were not permitted to engage in informalities with unaccompanied women except those in their immediate families. I learned, however, that Arian was never anxious about what felt honest. And anyway, I was his mother.

Arian started the conversation by saying he wanted to discuss what it was about our relationship that was so special. At the time, I thought I understood this well enough to talk about it, and I was curious to know how Arian viewed it. Maybe, together, we could articulate the powerful connection we seemed to have. But then my mind went completely blank, and my mouth took over. I blurted out, "Yes, but first I need to clarify — it is not sexual!" Arian didn't need to pause to compose himself. He replied immediately with his usual authority and diplomacy. "Of course not, Mom."

Arian seamlessly changed the subject by saying he wanted to tell me about his life in Kabul, and I was eager to learn more about him and what made him so special. He talked about his childhood as the oldest of five children in an educated family that, by Afghan standards, was sometimes financially comfortable but usually struggling to survive.

I realized during this conversation that fear and exile had been an integral part of Arian's life, long before he'd left Afghanistan for Europe. The Soviet Union had come and gone by the time Arian was born in 1986, but the occupation and then withdrawal had left behind political chaos. His family was Shi'a Muslim, a minority in Afghanistan, and his father had worked for government. So when the Taliban gained control over most of the country, Arian's father fled to Pakistan. As the oldest son, Arian was expected to take care of the family — at age thirteen. He was sent to work at one of the rug-factory sweatshops. His job was to tie knots. After a few days, Arian decided the work was too grueling for the money he was being paid. He left and became a grape dealer. He met a man who sold Arian grapes in the field, which Arian sold to wine makers, a dangerous enterprise in Taliban-controlled Kabul. Arian sold the leftover fruit at a public market, which probably helped him develop the sense of ease he seemed to have in all kinds of transactions. As a grape dealer, Arian made enough money to support the family and even buy new furniture. When Arian's father returned from Pakistan, he assumed Arian's mother had accepted gifts from another man. The other man was his oldest son.

Shortly after Arian's father returned from Pakistan in 1999, the family fled to Iran, where Shi'a Muslims are a majority. In 2002, they returned to Kabul after the Americans and its allies invaded Afghanistan in 2001. Although Arian remembers the sound of bombs and the fear that accompanied them, he and his family felt relatively safe during the American war and under the regime of Hamid Karzai.

Arian's father was a complicated man, and Arian's relationship with him was conflicted. Arian told the story of his father sharing the family's firewood with a Hazera woman living in poverty with her children, even though it meant Arian's family might not have enough to last the winter. The Hazera were persecuted in Afghanistan, even by the Shia. Arian was proud of his father's philanthropy and sense of duty. But in spite of his philanthropy, Arian's father was a violent man by American standards. He routinely beat Arian and his brothers with an electric cord. When Arian explained this, he said, "Imagine beating your children so often that you had to replace the electric cord many times." I asked Arian how he felt about his father now. He replied that he admired and respected him as a man of principle and strength.

Arian's mother had been a hospital nurse for most of her adult life, until she developed her own health problems. When I first met Arian, he referred to her as "a doctor." I suspect this error was due to a misuse of language. But I also assumed

Arian was motivated to represent her in the best light possible, to him a woman of great knowledge and responsibility.
Arian described her as "not religious, and kind." I assumed
she had influenced Arian's views about the role of women,
which were more western than traditional Muslim.

Arian made it a point to tell me about some of the ways
women are oppressed in Taliban-controlled Afghanistan. He
explained that many men controlled and demeaned women
using their sexuality. One tradition that was especially offen-
sive to Arian involved requiring women to demonstrate their
virginity at the time of marriage. On the day of her wedding,
a bride was given a white silk scarf, which was to be returned
the morning after with blood on it. Women who did not
bleed on their wedding night were considered prostitutes and
thereafter subjected to cruelty and isolation. Many would
commit suicide. Polygamy remains common in some parts of
Afghanistan, and a woman may be put to death for going out
in public without a male relative or for leaving her husband.
Arian said he wished one of his children had been a girl so
he could raise her to be strong and independent.

That night, Arian talked again about a longing in him,
a dream to achieve something important. I understood
this — about him and myself. It was an important part of
the connection between us. We each saw something bigger
in ourselves, something that creates a drive and a romanti-
cism about the world. I knew from my own experience that
Arian's longing would never be satisfied, because with the
achievement of one goal, another would be just beyond that
horizon. This sense of self would be for him a gift and a

challenge. It was this personality trait that, in some, could lead to narcissism, addiction, or depression.

Arian's openness that evening was part of what made me feel so close to him. My assigned role as "second mother" seemed to open the door for such intimacy. The emotional component was confusing, and I was starting to understand there were practical considerations as well. I knew my responsibilities to my son, Gabe, but I wasn't sure what they were to Arian. Would I include him in my will and help his children through college? Would I get close to Rana the way I had grown close to Gabe's girlfriend, Alex? Did I expect Gabe to treat Arian as a brother and his children as nephews?

Some of the implications of my role were more immediate. I was uncertain about my role with Arian's family in Afghanistan. On occasion, I asked Arian, "How is your mother?" which was awkward enough because he was so protective of my adopted role in his life. Knowing this, I sometimes corrected myself by playfully adding, "your other mother." I wondered how his Other Mother — that is, the mother who bore him and assumed responsibility for him for his first 30 years — felt about me and the fact that her son referred to me as "mom" on his Facebook posts and sometimes posted poems about how much he loved me. When I asked him about this, he responded, "She is happy that you are a part of my life." I once spoke with her on a video call, which mostly involved a lot of smiling because of our language differences. Again, awkward. Did she hate me for being able to support her son in ways that she could not? Did my freedom and my connection to Arian threaten her confidence in her role? Was I a reminder of the sadness she felt about the dissolution of part of her family?

As time went on, the family issues became a little more complex. I knew Arian's family in Afghanistan was barely getting by and that Arian wanted to send them funds. In fact, he did send them funds on several occasions, and the funds were mine. I had to tell him I couldn't afford to support six more people, even occasionally and even though they lived in an economy where the cost of feeding six people was probably less than $200 a month. I worried that they expected me to help them as a member of the family who they probably assumed to be quite wealthy — and I was by their standards. Similar issues arose with our Athens family. If I was helping support Arian and his family, shouldn't I help Marzia and hers? Was I creating envy toward Arian, whose life in an Athens apartment was enviable to people living in camps? I felt guilty at times and internally defensive at others. I had to keep telling myself that I'd committed to only one thing — helping Arian get on his feet — and that I did the best I could for everyone else.

My role as Arian's other mother added some ironic perspective to my relationship with Gabe. From the time I'd adopted him in his infancy, I always knew I might have to be adaptable in how I defined my role as mother, especially if Gabe were to reunite with his birth mother. I accepted that, and yet I was never put to that test. Gabe and I bonded easily and immediately when I took him home, and he had never shown an interest in finding his birth family. With Gabe, the most complicated thing about being an adoptive mother was being a mother. Never an easy job.

Still, I had become a mother twice in two unconventional ways, and my two children were different from me in ways that were (unfortunately, still) significant for Americans. Gabe and I looked different. Arian and I grew up in wildly different worlds. I didn't know what this said about me except that I had a streak of eccentricity. I never felt compelled to add to the earth's population by giving birth. It didn't make sense to create a person who needed me when there were already so many in the world who needed me. I never felt I was missing anything by not having a biological connection to Gabe, and I never doubted that I was incapable of loving a child more than I loved Gabe.

I lay awake that evening listening to demonstrations by angry Greeks a couple of blocks from my apartment building. I could hear screams and explosions and authoritative voices over loudspeakers. I found an online site that showed bits and pieces of the proceedings as they unfolded. Hundreds of police congregated in riot gear as the demonstrators lobbed firebombs at them, and the police responded with tear gas. I learned later that this event was a regular feature in Athens in response to cutbacks in pensions, disability payments, and other types of government support.

In ironic contrast, our time with refugees of war in the following weeks were full of joy in an organic process of building an ad hoc family of unlikely members. Athens was sweltering, and, the Sunday after I arrived, Arian called to say the family members who were in Athens were going to Palaio Faliro, a long strip of beach about ten miles south of central Athens near Elliniko Camp. He wanted me to come. Arian and Rana packed a plastic cooler and large plastic bags with lunch, blankets, and juice for the kids, and we met the rest of the contingent before getting on a bus. As we headed southwest out of the city center, Amir flirted with one of the women and bounced up and down restlessly on his seat. Then he got was quiet. His eyes grew wide, and he leaned across the aisle toward his dad yelling, "Ow, ow!" I suspect this startled all of the Greek and English-speaking riders on the bus. I wanted to yell, "We are not hurting him, people!" Arian sensed this and laughed. "Mom, *ow* means "water." He loves the beach and remembers this is how we got there last month." For the rest of the hour-long bus ride, Amir reminded us frequently that we were going to the beach, and, when we arrived, he wiggled out of Hashem's hand and ran down the path toward the sea, pulling off his t-shirt. His passion for life was so profound that it was often hard to comprehend that he was less than 20 months old.

We followed Amir to a park adjacent to the beach and dropped our bags under a stand of trees on the lawn. Arian laid down several blankets and pulled out snacks for the children. The heat was oppressive — wet and windless. Most of us were removing any unnecessary clothing. I looked over at Rana, Marzia, and Lorin, who sat quietly in long-sleeved blouses, long skirts, and *hijabs*. Rana held Jamal across her lap, as she usually did, and smiled as if to say, "I am happy."

Hashem and Farshad were already on their way to the water with Shayan. Arian picked up Amir and gestured for me to follow. The young women did not get up. Arian shook his head when I paused to wait for them. From that gesture, and the way the women seemed rooted to the blanket, I guessed they intended to remain under the trees in the sweltering heat for the rest of the day. Joining Arian, I felt funny about this odd cultural circumstance. If I had been the mom in Afghanistan, I would have sat, covered head to toe, with the young women. But I had grown up with a kind of freedom and enjoyment these young women had never known. And it was too hot to sit! For the next several hours, I joined the men and the children, wading in the cool, salty water and digging holes in the sand with our fists. Farshad, Rafiq, Arian, and Hashem swam out about 100 yards, where they bobbed up and down, laughing and splashing like little boys.

That was the beginning of a summer full of togetherness and joy, mostly at dinners hosted by Arian and Rana in their apartment. Arian would invite the extended family to come to town from Skaramangas camp, and often a few volunteers or colleagues as well. He moved chairs and the long plastic dining-room table out to the apartment's long veranda so we could enjoy the evening breezes and the fiery Athens sunsets. Rana cooked wonderful Afghan dishes — rice pilaf, kebabs, and vegetables stewed in thick sauces made of fresh tomatoes or mushrooms. Dinner always included fresh salads seasoned with onion slices and lemon juice. Rana made a special effort to cook vegetarian dishes for me, and, sometimes, she would make my favorite Afghan dish, *mantoo*, a dumpling filled with meat or vegetables and topped with yogurt and spicy lentils. Arian had discovered the Louisiana hot sauce called "Tabasco" and dribbled it over everything.

I loved to cook, and, at first, I would ask Rana if I could help. She always replied with a sort of low-level alarm and without a comma, "Mom no!" At home my women friends cooked together as a way of enjoying each other's company and sharing our culinary ideas. But for Rana, serving me meals and exempting me from cleanup duties were her way of honoring me, and I eventually almost enjoyed it. I did enjoy the extra time I had those evenings to spend with Arian, who would share stories and ideas, each one leading to another, while Amir pulled on his ear and Shayan draped himself over his father's broad shoulders.

Occasionally, I made dinner at Nanci's with Hashem. Hashem loved to cook and had a lot of opinions about cooking, which he backed up with technical skills and a lot of compliments from eaters. The plan for the evening usually involved an agreement early in the day that "Kim and Hashem will cook because Mama Nanci does not like to cook." I shopped on my way to Nanci's apartment, and Hashem would have stocked the shelves at Nanci's. Hashem and I might agree who was cooking what or we might agree to share responsibilities for cooking a single dish. From there, I would proceed to cut a tomato. Hashem would quietly walk over to where I was working and say, "Have you tried cutting it like this?" I would say,"Sure — that seems like a good way," and he would say "Yes. You will see!" The same thing would happen when I seasoned the eggplant or boiled the pasta. When Hashem referred to "Kim's salad," I would say "That is not *my* salad!" We playfully referred to each other as "My Chef," but my title was honorary. Hashem was the better cook.

These evenings were full of laughter and good cheer. We never talked about the challenges of our lives, which seemed so far away when we were together (and mine were inconsequential compared to the ones the young people faced). No one scolded the children or complained about world politics or the Greek government's incompetence. When Marzia was there with the children, Sarah and Amir would get us dancing, and Arian would turn on the music, usually an eclectic mix of Afghan folk songs, American pop music, and traditional ballads from all over the globe. On Halloween, we painted the children's faces and dressed them in angel's wings and devil horns.

One night, as I sat watching the children dance, the joy and love in the room felt almost physical. I felt so proud to be a part of this tribe, so able to live in the moment and to open their hearts to each other, to me. Without knowing it or understanding it, Nanci, Anne-Lene, and I had created this unlikely family of three generations, five countries, and six languages.

Chapter 24

October 2016

Metaphors

My travels had always provided me with new ways of seeing things, and my experiences in Greece heightened the sense of connectedness between people and places and ideas, which would, at times, force me to consider my own small truths. On my way home from Athens that fall, I stopped in Berlin for a few days, where a small moment led to some larger realizations.

I had found a small hotel in a trendy area of East Berlin, the kind of place that identifies itself in marketing materials as "boutique." I would be among the oldest people in the hotel and even the neighborhood, as I often was. I chose such neighborhoods in large cities to get a sense of the people who would someday be running things. And if I couldn't be with friends on these trips, I could get vicarious pleasure from the neighborhood buzz.

Arriving in my hotel room, I found two fortune cookies on the bed pillows. The Chinese would call that "auspi-
cious." I loved the fortunes in fortune cookies and, over the
previous 30 years, I had saved hundreds of them, stashed in
covered clay pots and wooden boxes. For my birthday many
years before, Vic gave me one that said, "You will win the
Miss Universe title but not accept it," which had layers of
meaning for me. No, I would never win any beauty contests,
but, yes, I must always assume I could. When I would win,
I would have the humility and wisdom to reject that kind
of showy affirmation. I had taped this fortune to my office
computer when I worked for the state. One day I came to
work to find a new computer on my desk, which normally
would have been a pleasant surprise. Instead, I spent an hour
that day going through a roomful of dead computer parts
looking for it, but I never found the fortune that I'd taped to
my computer screen. Years later, I ordered 50 custom-made
fortune cookies with fortunes inside that said, "You will win
the Miss Universe title but not accept it."

I believed my Berlin fortune would connect me to something. I picked up one of the crispy cookies and I opened it.
The fortune read, "A metaphor could save your life." Bingo.
Before I opened the second fortune cookie, I turned on the
video function on my camera and filmed myself opening the
second one with a voice-over. "Hi, Arian. I love fortunes.
I have hundreds of them. I just opened one in my Berlin
hotel room, and I am opening a second one for you." The
fortune inside the cookie that was Arian's said, "A metaphor
could save your life." Before overthinking it, I sent the video
to Arian. He sent me back a message that said, "Wow."

Berlin was beautiful and clean and civilized. I spent a couple of days doing the things tourists do — walking, eating, museums. Of course, I visited what is left of the Berlin Wall, which was built in 1961 to stop the migration of East Berliners to West Berlin. East Berlin was part of the Soviet Union, and West Berlin was capitalist. On June 12, 1987, American President Ronald Reagan — no champion of the underdog — famously gave a speech in front of Berlin's Brandenburg Gate and said, "Mr. Gorbachev, tear down this wall!" Mr. Gorbachev ignored President Reagan, but two years later, after escalating protests and demonstrations, the Soviets opened the gates. People from East Berlin poured into West Berlin in an historic moment that celebrated the new freedom of East Berliners to join the vibrant economy of the west after years of deprivation and austerity on the other side of the wall.

The pieces of the original wall that hadn't been knocked over with bulldozers had become a memorial, covered in art and graffiti that celebrated freedom and hope for humanity, with paintings of all kinds of people and all kinds of inspiring quotes. "Many small people who in many small places do many small things can alter the face of the world." "One love Israel." "In the beginning was freedom." One of the sections presented sorrowful portraits of Syrians who had lost everything, including limbs.

It was so tragically ironic that Berlin's most popular tourist attraction celebrated the same kind of freedom that Germany and the rest of Europe were now trying to deny refugees of war. Countries all over the globe were building walls to keep out the less fortunate, among them, the United States,

Hungary, Macedonia, Israel, Spain, Austria, and the United Kingdom. There was not much to distinguish these wall builders from the Soviet Union in the 1960s. Germany itself had constructed a virtual wall when Angela Merkel signed and advocated for the EU-Turkey deal. In the moment, it was obvious to me but not much consolation that history would take as dim a view of these walls as it did the Berlin wall.

By now, Greece was often a filter that gave meaning to whatever was in front of me. The Berlin Wall obviously symbolized the politics of the refugees coming to Europe, but it also suggested what was so important to me about my relationship with Arian — but only after I realized what the fortune-cookie video suggested about my relationship with him. The fortune-cookie video felt clever and poignant in the moment but awkward when I reflected on it later. Had I ever sent that kind of video message to Gabe? Would I? The answers were "No" and "No." I understood too late that it assumed a type of intimacy that I didn't and couldn't share with the son I had raised. I would not have assigned the second fortune cookie to Gabe or sent him a video of me opening it up for him.

When I realized that I may have stepped over a line, I also realized there were other significant distinctions in the way I felt about Gabe and managed my relationship with him. Gabe would always be a reflection of me and on me. Because I raised him, Gabe's happiness and sorrows, his mistakes and his talents and his successes were partly mine. Mothers and sons never quite unravel, and this can be a source of great strain between them if they are not themselves empowered or at least philosophical. Gabe emphatically — and with gestures of deep anger — pulled away from me as an adolescent. To me, this was a sign that the normal process of separation that comes with growing up was difficult for him because of his deep love for me. The love between us endured as the anger and confusion subsided. And, of course, it did, one step at a time, not perfect but progressively better.

Arian, on the other hand, was not a reflection of me. He came to me after 30 years of learning and growing without me. By the time I met him, Arian was an independent, full-fledged adult with children of his own. The bond between us involved what each of us brought to our relationship as adults. This, of course, is what happens between friends and lovers. We were neither of those. But neither were we mother and son.

According to the conventions of our very different cultures and the very different lives we had led, we should have never become close. I grew up in affluent communities in an educated and mostly happy household. I had never felt hungry and had choices in every aspect of my life. I was able to take for granted a feeling of safety. In contrast, Arian grew up in a stressful family situation and worked from the time he was 13. His country had been at war his whole life, requiring his family to flee to Pakistan and then Iran. His marriage was arranged, and the women in his life had limited freedoms.

In spite of our different experiences in life, we developed a profoundly deep connection in a matter of months. Arian sought emotional support at that difficult time of his life, living without his parents or friends in a culture he would struggle to understand. But he didn't choose a soft and nurturing mother figure. I believed he needed someone to affirm something essential inside him. I understood what that was, even when I wasn't sure how to describe it or define it. When Arian commented on our relationship, he didn't refer to the affection I showed his family or the times I sat with Jamal in the hospital (although I know he appreciated such gestures). He said, "Mom, you have affirmed me. You have given me back my dignity and pride." He didn't say, "Mom, you made a nice dinner tonight." He said "Mom, I think it's amazing that you travel around the world alone and you crunch up wads of money in your pockets."

I eventually understood I was probably the only person in Arian's life who accepted his flaws as an integral part of what was so special about him. Vision, drive, and charisma are partners of vanity, risk-taking, and a tendency to overlook some of the details of life that are important to others. I accepted all of it and realized I understood Arian because of how we were alike (although I shared his personality traits in lesser measure). In that way, Arian affirmed the person I thought I needed to dial back — the independent person who heard a voice in the distance. In my family and in my career, I had many times gotten the message that this most essential person in me created trouble for the people I cared about. Not that it changed me much — but this was the person Arian seemed to value, just as I affirmed that person in him.

But there was something else that was more important about my relationship with Arian, something that was not just self-affirming. My love for Arian was outside of the conventions in my life. It did not begin with a set of expectations or rules, the kind we assume in our relationships with parents or friends, a husband or a colleague. I had never learned how I was "supposed" to manage a relationship with a man from a different culture who was more than 30 years younger than me. Arian and I created a way of knowing each other and caring for each other brick by brick. This freewheeling relationship cracked something open in me. I felt a deeper and more expansive love for others. I was able to more readily accept the things in my life that were painful and to free myself of some of the filters that confined my emotions. I cried more. I laughed more. I felt friendlier.

Arian and I were not friends or lovers, and yet our relationship was really not one of mother and son. So what were we to each other? I asked myself this many times and could never provide an answer that fit well in the conventions of my culture or experience. After a while, I just accepted that I didn't know how to define our relationship. It was a connection that didn't have a definition. The Berlin Wall was gone, and the pieces of it that remained represented freedom for people who had been confined by circumstances. Some kind of wall had collapsed inside me as well, giving me freedom to love in an expansive, new way.

Chapter 25
Fall 2016
Jamal

SOMETIMES THE light-heartedness of our family get-togethers allowed us to forget that each of the young people in our ad hoc family faced serious problems, whether emotional, physical, or logistical. All of them had suffered deep emotional trauma so far in their young lives and one, Jamal, had a severe physical disability that would require a lifetime of special attention. That fall, I realized how much I took for granted my well-being as well as the way the world would treat me if I needed professional care. People called "refugees" — and most Greeks — were not so lucky.

The night after I returned to Athens in early October, Arian and Rana organized one of their wonderful dinners. Nanci and Anne-Lene were in town, and the crowd from Skaramangas came to the city — Hashem, Marzia, and her children, Lorin and Farshad — as well as a couple of Arian's colleagues from work. We ate and drank and laughed as usual.

Rana had made all kinds of Afghan dishes and played the quiet hostess. But something was not quite right. I saw less of her than usual, and each time I looked for her, she was holding Jamal in the bedroom or on the couch.

Jamal had been sick with a cold for more than a week. His lungs were compromised from cerebral palsy, a condition that occurred as the result of untreated jaundice during the week after his birth. Because Jamal's lungs did not process fluids as they should have, he was especially vulnerable to infections and pneumonia. When I saw Jamal that night, I worried. Jamal was the sunniest of personalities. He was a child who normally responded to every smile, every gesture of affection, and every bit of sweet-talking. That night, he was listless and inattentive. His breathing was labored, and his complexion was sallow. I asked Arian about this, and he explained that a doctor at the local clinic had suggested Jamal might need to be hospitalized if symptoms hadn't improved by later in the week.

The next morning, Arian was at work, and Shayan was at school when I returned to the apartment. Farshad had stayed the night and was sleeping in the extra room. I accepted Rana's offer of tea and played with Amir for a few minutes, but I was there to see how Jamal was doing. He was lying on the mattress in the living room, and he was worse. He was gasping for air, and his complexion was gray. I asked Rana whether she had taken him to the doctor in the past week, and she said she had. I later learned the doctor had advised that Jamal should be admitted to the hospital if his condition didn't improve. By today. Rana understood me when I stood up and announced that we were going to the hospital. I could see that she was relieved, as she quickly and quietly tossed a few things into a bag and wrapped Jamal in a blanket. We woke Farshad, who agreed to stay with Amir.

When we arrived at the city's children's hospital, Rana knew the door to the emergency room because Jamal had been there for the same reason a few months before. When the admitting nurse saw Jamal, she didn't make us wait our turn with the dozens of people on the rickety couches outside the emergency room. She led us to an examination room, where three doctors spent five minutes before they said they Jamal needed to be admitted for treatment. They asked a lot of questions, and one of them recognized Jamal from the time he had been admitted in March. I didn't need to know Greek to figure out that the two others were arguing about whether Jamal should have been admitted when he was examined at the hospital a week before. We called Arian and asked him to come to the hospital as soon as he was able to leave work.

Jamal was in the hospital for twelve days. Until the tenth day, I didn't think he would make it. He didn't sleep or eat. He lost a lot of weight that he couldn't afford to lose, and his muscles stiffened day by day. He didn't smile, and he didn't have the strength to cry.

The hospital was a train wreck. The building and facilities were run down and depressing, with dirty, peeling paint and linoleum that curled up along seams. There was no soap or toilet paper in the rooms. Medical equipment was old, and some of it was literally scotch-taped together. Many members of the medical staff seemed exhausted and impatient. Parents were responsible for monitoring drug dosages, drug reactions, and changes in their children's conditions. Although the medical staff had a good reputation for their technical skills, I wondered every day how different things would be if Jamal were in a hospital in the United States. I remembered the care Gabe got when he had been in the hospital for surgery on his knees — the constant attention from medical staff, the immaculate facilities and the best technology. Cheerful nurses and doctors explained every step of the process and the significance of each. When Gabe had surgery, I never worried. For 12 days, I worried constantly about Jamal.

I developed a new love and respect for Rana during those 12 days in the hospital. Throughout, she was steadfast and never complained. She stayed every night, all night, and most days, listening to children crying and screaming up and down the halls. At the hospital, she had no access to a shower or healthy foods unless one of us was there to give her a break. Because she didn't speak English or Greek, she was not able to read, and she could not communicate with any of the other parents or medical professionals. She was completely isolated for most of those 12 days.

Coincidentally, Rana's long-awaited asylum interview had been scheduled for the second day of Jamal's hospital stay. If she had tried to change the date, she might have to wait another two or three months before she would have the opportunity to complete this very important last stage of the asylum claims process. The morning of her interview, she awoke at 5 a.m., took a taxi home to shower and change clothes, and then traveled to the edge of the city, where she stood in line for four hours before enduring a two-hour interview that she later described as "easy." In contrast, I was exhausted after sitting with Jamal and a book that day.

The logistics of managing Jamal's hospital stay were difficult for the family even after Rana's interview. Arian took a few days off work to be at home with the boys, who would not have done well with any of the rest of us. Neither had ever spent more than a couple of hours away from their mother. Amir pined for his mother for days. When Arian had to return to work on the fourth day, Marzia moved from Skaramangas to the apartment with her children. Sarah and Jaham delighted the boys and made them forget how much they missed their mom.

I went to the hospital most afternoons to take food and clothing, and visit. A few times, I stayed with Jamal for five or six hours so Rana could go home to be with the boys. During these times, Jamal was miserable. Too weak to cry, he made squeaking noises and shook in agitation. I sang John Lennon's "Beautiful Boy" to him over and over again. I held him. I rocked him. He frowned at me and waved his fist. I read to him and rubbed his back. He made more squeaking noises and refused to sleep for long hours, in spite of his exhaustion. Jamal made the point that I was no substitute for his mother. I waited months before he forgave me for trying, but it didn't matter. He survived.

Chapter 26

Fall 2016

Mohammed's Tambour

ONE OF THE GREAT PLEASURES of my travels was the chance to have a small but significant encounter with someone special. The prospect for these encounters was one of the selfish things that motivated me to continue with my volunteer work in Greece, which I formalized that fall in a way that was as easy as it was unplanned.

Over the years, I had worked with the Multicultural Institute (MI), a small NGO in Berkeley, California, that provided services to Central American immigrant families in the Bay Area. Most of those families were headed by men who were day laborers. They sat in front of lumberyards and hardware stores hoping for a little work. Most were undocumented. Father Rigo was the executive director and a Franciscan priest. He was the kind of person who could talk to a man with a fifth-grade education one minute and a roomful of PhDs the next. He was committed, philosophical, full of joy and kindness. I knew from sitting on MI's board that he was also a good manager and leader. He had a combination of talents that is unusual among nonprofit directors.

When I was back in California, I invited Father Rigo to lunch one day to ask him whether he would consider creating a program to support my work in Greece if I agreed to fund it. I needed some structure, and I needed to be able to say, "I can't do that because the money I have is from an NGO program that won't permit it." And since I was going to spend the money anyway, it might as well be tax deductible. Father Rigo lit up. "The work you are doing is consistent with our mission, and the program will make us truly multicultural!" A few weeks later, we made a presentation to MI's board and "Hope on the Ground" was official. Nanci and I volunteered and paid our own expenses, so we could use the modest donated funds to support refugees.

This program turned our Athens family into a little SWAT team. We heard about urgent short-term needs — sometimes from Facebook sites with names like "Information Point for Athens Volunteers" and "Refugees Relief Action Forum" — sometimes from NGOs or other independent volunteers we had gotten to know. We helped with small problems that required quick responses and weren't being addressed by an NGO or government. The problem was usually something that needed only a small amount of cash and a little time. I met a man with six-month-old twins who lived in an abandoned building with his wife and another couple. They had no money. When I met him at one of the squats, he was desperate for baby formula because MSF had run out, and his babies were hungry. He didn't say it at first, but he didn't have any grown-up food, either. So we spent an hour shopping at the produce markets and a supermarket that sold discounted baby formula.

Another time, Arian paid cab fare for a pregnant woman who was bleeding, because Greek ambulances did not show up at the camps for several hours. Hashem rounded up blankets for some young people living in the streets at Victoria Square. One day, Arian learned from his brother in Turkey that a couple of teenagers were in Athens with nothing but their cell phones and the clothes they were wearing. After work, Arian met the boys at Victoria Square and got them a room in a hostel until he convinced an NGO to provide longer-term support. We found a compassionate dentist who filled dozens of teeth and pulled dozens of others for almost nothing and scheduled patients on short notice to treat people with infections and constant pain.

At first, we also tried to provide information to refugees in Athens about the asylum claims process. We had heard that none of the big NGOs were focusing on this, and we had heard many stories to suggest that asylum seekers might be wrongly denied asylum if they didn't know how to prepare for their asylum interview or how the process worked. Good information was important, partly because the process was complicated. It involved several steps, each with long lead times, long lines, and long interviews. The Greek Asylum Service (GAS) assumed refugees would somehow find out when the rules changed and never seemed to anticipate how or whether its procedures would work. It once directed 50,000 recently arrived refugees to "pre-register" their asylum claims on a single Skype line. The line was not always operational, and none of the camps had Wi-Fi service. So refugees spent their scarce resources on cell data services while they waited for hours trying to get a Skype connection.

GAS also required refugees to show up for interviews in the office closest to where they entered the Greek mainland. This required people who had crossed the land border with Bulgaria, for example, and had been subsequently assigned (by the same Greek government) to a camp in Athens, for example, to travel 800 miles to and from Thessaloniki for a two-hour interview. The Greek government did not provide transportation or housing for this. Nanci and another volunteer once spent days trying to convince the GAS office in Athens that a woman who was nine months pregnant could not travel 400 miles to Thessaloniki the following week. They succeeded, but it was an odd victory to celebrate.

For the few months after the EU signed the deal with Turkey, the refugees remaining in Greece had little access to information except what a handful of volunteers could provide ad hoc. One of the information heroes during this time was an affable English woman named Sharon, who ran a small NGO called RefuComm. She was a 50-something blonde with good bone structure and a tangle of shoulder-length silver hair that fell over drapy cotton blouses. She was a den mother by nature and always had a small contingent of refugees and volunteers in her care when she was in Athens — and she worried about all of them like crazy when she was at home with her family in Germany. Before the borders closed, she had done a lot of work with refugees who entered Greece by way of the Balkan Route. At that time, Sharon focused on providing information about resources that would be useful on the journey north — for example, where to find clean water or a bus station. She made the point that people who have never traveled 1,000 miles without money or belongings cannot imagine the logistics problems. When the borders closed, she shifted gears. She created RefuComm to focus on how the process of asylum claims operated in Greece.

Nanci and I thought Sharon might be a good connection, not only because of the work she was officially doing with her NGO but also because she was interested in the shifting needs of the community and the individuals she met. Over the coming months, we frequently shared information and ideas with Sharon. Arian translated some of her documents, and we helped her produce a film on the asylum interview. The film was Arian's first professional "performance" since he had left Afghanistan, and he was impressive. The day before filming, Arian read the script I'd written. In the film, he spoke for 10 minutes according to the content of the script as if he were speaking off the cuff. A real actor.

We learned a lot from Sharon and the informational materials she had created for RefuComm. I drafted some ideas for workshop presentations and a script for individual consultations about how to prepare for the asylum interview. We scheduled a couple of workshops at a community center called "Orange House," which provided housing and other resources for women and children. The director was eager to host these workshops and sent an email out to several other organizations a couple of days in advance. We would lead the workshops in English but have an Arabic translator at one workshop and a Farsi translator at the other.

We had about 10 attendees show up to the Arabic session. Most were from NGOs, including a couple of lawyers. It went well, and I enjoyed the back-and-forth with people who either knew the law or knew what questions to ask — but we had hoped to reach refugees. At some point that day, we realized that most Arabic speakers were Syrians, and practically no Syrians were seeking asylum in Greece. They applied for "relocation," which provided the opportunity for them to apply for asylum in another EU country.

Our Farsi session that day was more successful but not in the way we expected. Arian was our "translator," which meant he presented all the material himself. I was really proud of him for taking the time to support our effort, especially since he had learned more about the asylum claims process than we had. The Farsi session was attended by only six teenagers. They were eager students, and it turned out that they needed us. They had just been kicked out of a squat and were on the streets. This sounded like a job for Sharon, who knew more than we did about navigating the system that was supposed to protect unaccompanied minors. The same day, she got them an Airbnb apartment in the central part of town, and we stocked the refrigerator. Then she initiated negotiations with UNHCR and a large Greek NGO called "Metadrasi," and she didn't let up until they provided the boys with housing and services.

The workshops at Orange House were our last because we learned that some of the large NGOs were beginning to provide informational workshops to refugees at the camps, and they would surely do a better job than we could. We decided we would re-focus our efforts on providing individual consultations. We didn't have the time or energy to market ourselves, but we did get some requests.

Working with refugees on preparing for asylum interviews was always a heart-wrenching experience. To help them with a presentation strategy would require them to relive events that were hard for me to comprehend — bombings, torture, loss of family and homeland. And yet they would do so quietly and without rage or blame.

I met a Kurdish man named Mohammed this way. One of the volunteers had contacted me to say Mohammed wanted some support preparing for his asylum interview. He lived with his wife, Manal, and two children at Skaramangas. I contacted Mohammed, and we scheduled a time to meet the following week at his caravan, which was close to Hashem's in the center of the camp. Mohammed didn't speak a lot of English, so I found a translator, who agreed to meet me at the camp. I arrived at Mohammed's caravan on a sunny, warm afternoon at the time we had arranged the previous week. I heard young children inside. One was crying in anger, and another was explaining something. I chuckled to myself that children are alike everywhere. I knocked on the door. When it opened, three youngsters in pigtails and dresses ran by me at three different speeds. Mohammed and Manal introduced themselves, and I handed Manal a bakery box of savory pastries. She smiled and then yelled at two of the girls to stop making noise. She raised her hand in warning. The third one was the daughter of a young woman seated on a mat in one of the two small rooms, and she ran to her mother.

Mohammed remained quiet through this and led me to the other side of the caravan, where his family of four lived. He placed a large pillow on the floor along the wall and invited me to sit. The cigarette smoke in the room was thick. My eyes burned. I thought about how it might be affecting the children's health. None of my business at this point.

I smiled at the children and asked Mohammed how old they were. "Khalil is three, and Jamil is almost five." These were unusual names to give to girls, but I said what I would have said had their names been "Samin" and "Mariam." "They are adorable girls." Looking up from under his eyebrows, Mohammed replied matter-of-factly, "They are not girls." Something about the way he said this suggested it was not his choice to dress his sons in girls' clothes but, as I learned later, he was a gentle and patient man.

I spent a couple of hours with Mohammed that day. We chatted briefly about the children and my visit to Greece. He could speak a little English, but a young woman named Goenev was there to translate. Manal could not speak English, but I had emphasized that it was important for her to join us. She would be interviewed separately by employees of the GAS, who would be looking for inconsistencies between her story and Mohammed's. I started into my presentation about what they could expect in the interviews and how they should focus their responses to questions on circumstances that corresponded to the criteria of international law. I explained that I wasn't a lawyer but read to him the main provisions of the United Nations Treaty that European countries adopted in 1951. Basically, to qualify for asylum in Europe, a refugee needed to make a convincing case that he or she was in danger in his or her home country and didn't receive the protection of government, and that returning home would present risks of death or further persecution. Mohammed and Manal might expect their interviews to include many pointed questions, and I emphasized that they should always tell the truth in every detail and feel comfortable saying, "I don't know" or "I don't remember." Manal was in and out of the room with the boys, who were by now quiet, each nibbling on a fistful of sweets.

So that we could connect the points of law with the family's story, I asked Mohammed to tell me what he could about what had happened to his family in Iraq. Mohammed explained that his family was Kurdish and had fled their home near Sinjar Mountain in 2014, when ISIS gained control over most of the region. They had lost their home and family members. The economy collapsed, so Mohammed could not earn enough money to support the family, and their lives were in danger. Mohammed took his family to Turkey, hoping to find work until they could save enough for passage to Europe. In Turkey, they were persecuted by the Turkish mafia, who threatened to take the children. Mohammed increasingly feared Erdogan's classification of Kurds as "terrorists." The Turkish police had told Mohammed they would not provide the family any protection from the men who were threatening them. It was obvious from Mohammed's story that the family would not be safe if they were to return to Iraq or Turkey.

After Mohammed shared his story, we talked more about how he might prepare for his interview. He agreed to write a narrative that I could help him edit, and he promised to talk to Manal about our conversation, so her own interview would focus on the most important circumstances of their lives in Iraq and Turkey.

Mohammed expressed his gratitude with his soft eyes and a hand over his heart. He said he wanted to play a video for me on his iPhone. Privately, I reacted with some nervousness thinking about what I might see on his video. Some of the refugees kept photos and videos of the horrors they had faced as evidence for their asylum claims. I wanted to be supportive, so I replied, of course, I wanted to see whatever he wanted to share. The video, however, was wonderful rather than horrible. It showed Mohammed playing a stringed instrument made from blonde- and cinnamon-colored woods. The body was built like an oblong bowl with a wooden cover. The music was soulful and mysterious, with complex and surprising progressions. It reminded me of the music I had heard in Turkey when I saw the Sufis dance. I didn't have to know much about the instrument or music to know that Mohammed was a talented musician.

As the music played, Mohammed had tears in his eyes. Mohammed said the instrument was a Persian tambour. He had not been able to carry his tambour from Turkey when they were smuggled to Greece, and he missed being able to play music because it was so much a part of his spirit. I thanked him for playing the video for me, and he thanked me for our time together. We promised to meet again, and I left for dinner at Hashem's caravan.

Shortly after I met with Mohammed, I was walking to my Exarchia apartment from one of the squats and noticed a shop with a dozen stringed instruments in the window. One of them looked like the tambour in Mohammed's video, so I went inside. The shopkeeper would not have been out of place in Haight-Ashbury in the '60s. He had a long ponytail and a beard and wore a leather vest over a worn-out t-shirt. I asked him about the instrument in the window, and he said it was a Persian tambour. I told him why I wanted it and, like any Greek, he reduced the price on the tag by 40 percent. He put the instrument in a new black canvas bag that fit perfectly. I was so happy at the thought of seeing Mohammed's reaction.

The following week, I returned to Skaramangas for one of the dinners in Hashem's caravan. After I arrived, I took the tambour in the black canvas bag to Mohammed's caravan. I handed him the instrument and said it was a gift from someone important in my life who loved music. And that was the truth. I had an account for such gifts from the estate of my Auntie Dawn's, the butterfly who taught music in Afghanistan.

Mohammed pulled the tambour out of its bag, and his face lit up. He closed his eyes and held the instrument high on his chest. He rubbed his hands along its strings and neck. He remained quiet for long seconds. My recent experiences with other Muslim men during my time in Greece led me to wonder whether I had created too much awkwardness for him by asking him to accept this gift. I didn't want him to feel he had to respond in the moment, so I told him Hashem's caravan was waiting for me and that I would come back another day. He put out his hand and said, "I want to tell you that you have brought great joy to me in two ways." He paused, looked down, and then slowly lifted his head. "First, I feel great joy that I will be able to play the tambour again. But more important, I feel joy that you have honored my soul and understand something important inside me." There was nothing for me to say except what I felt. "It is my privilege to know you and to have heard your music."

After that, Mohammed kept in touch with text messages and photos of the boys. He sent me many short videos sharing his musical gifts. Shortly afterward, he and his family were granted asylum and permitted to relocate in Germany. In the photographs he sent after that, his sons did not wear pigtails or dresses.

Chapter 27
Fall 2016
Squats

FOR THE REFUGEES IN ATHENS, as for the rest of us, life presented trade-offs between creature comforts and the less tangible — freedom, dignity, and a sense of belonging. The squats in Athens were an expression of these trade-offs. By mid-2016, a dozen or more of them provided shelter and community to thousands of refugees. They were usually appropriated by neighborhood anarchists, who then set up loose management structures and rules in the name of anarchy. Some refugees lived in squats because they could not get into a government camp, which were typically overcrowded from the day they opened. Some lived in the squats by choice, because the squats emphasized self-reliance and dignity ahead of cheap calories. There was no police presence, no NGOs controlling the agenda, no isolation from the Greek community. Of course, there were risks of all kinds for people living in the squats. The residents were vulnerable to drug dealers, small-time mafia, and the dangers of living in buildings with aging wiring, rodents, and crumbling sewage facilities. Each was overcrowded, often housing six or eight people in a room, often without furniture, mattresses, or hot water.

I had gotten to know about Oniro squat in the usual way — a solicitation on a Facebook page. The residents hadn't gotten enough food for the week from the central warehouse and had been eating little but rice and potatoes for two days. They needed produce, dairy products, and baby formula. I had access to the MI funds by this time, and I could help if I could be assured that the food would go to the residents instead of the Sunday Bazaar — a weekly outdoor market in Athens where volunteers consistently reported seeing goods for sale that they believed had been originally donated to refugee families. A young man named Abed answered my Facebook message, and we agreed on a time to meet that afternoon.

Oniro had been an abandoned hotel and was only a few blocks from my apartment on the north edge of Exarchia. It had 30 small rooms on five narrow floors and housed about 120 people, mostly Arabic-speaking. When I arrived, a couple of kids were sitting quietly on the single stair that separated the doorway from the filthy street curb. They smiled and let me through. The smell of sewage in the lobby was overpowering. I later learned that the pipes from the upstairs bathrooms were rotting and that the line to the street had problems that could be remedied only with funds that were out of range and city permits that would never be granted. The hotel walls were lined with faux wood paneling that had probably been installed in the 1970s, and the lobby floor was covered with a worn, wine-colored carpet. The oppressive heat seemed to have entered through the front door and accumulated in the lobby since sunrise.

I found Abed sitting at a makeshift desk in a small storeroom behind the stairway. He was thin and muscled, with soft eyes and a sympathetic smile. He stood up and thanked me for coming. My eyes began burning from a thick cloud of cigarette smoke, and I instinctively put my hand over my nose. Abed sensed my discomfort and shooed his smoking colleague out of the room. He poured me a plastic cup of tea and then spent several minutes explaining how the squat got provisions from the central warehouse at Elliniko. Usually, the squat received enough donated food to last four or five days of the week. The large NGOs managed a central warehouse, where they organized food donations. They were providing food to the squats but not enough, and they were not always able to provide all of the essentials like baby formula, cooking oil, and shampoo. Abed showed me the requests he'd sent to the warehouse and the responses he'd received. He was so eager to show me how account- able he was, I gave him some cash. The next day, he went to the "Syrian store" near Monastiraki and sent me photos of his purchases — tomatoes, toilet paper, eggs, and baby formula. The next time I saw him, he gave me the receipts. I dropped in on him unannounced to make sure what I saw in the photos ended up on the shelves of the storeroom, and I was happy to see that they had.

For the next month, Abed sent me lists of what he needed, and I provided him cash to buy produce and eggs, cooking oil, and baby formula. Sometimes his lists included sugar, which I told him I would not buy. Syrians loved sweet tea, but so many of the children had rotting teeth and were eating packaged junk food from the local corner markets.

One day over coffee, I talked to Abed about how so many of the men were spending the little cash they had on cigarettes instead of food for their children. Smoking was a big problem in the refugee community. Most of the refugee men I met smoked, and most of them smoked indoors around the children. I suggested that Abed ask the men who smoked to contribute 40 euros a month for supplemental food supplies. It took me about three seconds to realize that my suggestion was a mistake. Abed looked at me without responding, and I understood from his silence that he was in no position to impose such conditions on the residents at the squat. I knew there was no economic logic in the lives of the refugees living in Greece. People were in a constant state of stress, and smoking offered some relief. I realized, too late, that it was quite patronizing of me to imply that my donations of food would be conditioned on what I thought was appropriate resident behavior. Not really in the anarchist spirit, either.

Abed moved on by mentioning that the squat's 30-year-old washing machine finally died and the squat's 120 residents could not wash their clothes. I bounced back. I had funds for a washing machine. The next day, we hopped on a bus to a shop north of town. We purchased a new washing machine that the store owners installed at Oniro later that afternoon.

The kind of short-term partnership I had with Oniro and Abed was not uncommon. There were hundreds of independent volunteers supporting the development of community and daily welfare in the squats. And, as on Lesvos, the squats provided heartening examples of people helping people in ways that promoted dignity and defied economic self-interest. But as always, there were examples of the worst of humanity as well. The squats were becoming dangerous places for reasons other than rats and drug dealers. They were occasionally targets for domestic terrorism.

Notara 26 was a squat a few blocks from my apartment in Exarchia, a four-story structure at the intersection of two quiet residential streets. It was once an office building, with cheap metal siding and large glass windows. Each squat had a reputation of one kind or another, and my impression of Notara 26 was that it was a strong community of refugees with a lot of good support from independent volunteers. One day, I walked by it after what appeared to have been a fire. The side of the building had triangles of black soot over window frames, and the bottom two floors were gutted. A dozen young people were throwing charred debris out of second-story windows and hauling buckets of ashes to dumpsters. I asked one of the workers what had happened. The night before, the building had been deliberately set on fire with Molotov cocktails. Firebombed. More than 100 people were inside sleeping, among them, many children. And here it was, eight hours after the fire began. There were no firefighters at the site investigating the source of the arson, no police investigating this crime of attempted murder, no journalists with cameras or microphones. In a way, the lack of response by the community was more horrifying than the violence.

I asked one of the workers where the residents would be sleeping that night. A young man in a grimy t-shirt with a shovel said they would be able to sleep on the top floors. What? People escaping the terrors of war were going to sleep in a building set on fire the night before? When I was there, the damage was so extensive, I couldn't imagine how the residents and volunteers would restore this building to a livable space. I knew they would get no help from government or insurance companies. In the weeks that followed, I never saw a single article in any newspaper or heard of any outrage by the people in the neighborhood. The police had been informed of witnesses to the crime and never followed up or provided any protection to the people at the squat.

One day, I walked by the building after taking the long way home from Nanci's apartment. The bottom two floors had been fully reconstructed. Children played on a new floor, and residents sat on couches. I walked in and said I was surprised at how much they had accomplished in such a short time. I asked how they did it. She replied, "We just kept working until it was done."

Two months later, Jasmine squat was firebombed while 400 residents slept. No police investigation, no fire department investigation, no newspaper articles. One of the women living alone at Jasmine squat, Amena, sent me a note asking for help. She was terrified: "We escape from Syria, escape from death, escape from war, and come to die in Greece." The same morning, I asked Arian to inquire about whether Amena and her son could move to Skaramangas. A few days later, he reported that she would be able to move into a caravan there. But Amena declined the offer. She explained that she preferred her freedom and independence to the security of the camp. I understood.

Chapter 28

Fall 2016

Education

WHEN GABE WAS IN third grade, he came home from school one day and announced that he had written my biography. I should have been nervous. Gabe had always been honest about my shortcomings. But I was interested, and I asked Gabe whether I would be able to read it. He replied, "No, you don't need to read it. It's very short. I can tell you what it says." "OK, and what does it say?" He looked at me with a grin. "It says you are ready to learn." Fifteen years later, I was learning how much more there was to learn and also how much I learned from the people in my Greek life who were called "my students."

I had never considered myself to be a good teacher. In the classes I had taught over the years, I was prone to announcements and lectures rather than the collaborative teaching styles that I believed were more effective and creative. But I did know that teaching was a way to learn and, in Athens that fall, I wanted a project where I could do more than run around buying and delivering. I responded to a Facebook post from a young woman named Kanwal, who was looking for someone to teach English at Jasmine, one of the squats, which was later firebombed. There was always a need for English classes in Athens because the refugees realized the value of a language that had become almost universal. I had never taught language classes, but I knew there were resources online. I could figure out a month's worth of one-hour lessons, and I liked the idea of getting to know a group of people in the squat. Sign me up.

Jasmine squat was an abandoned school building a few blocks from my apartment on the edge of Exarchia. The building was classic 1920s Mediterranean architecture, three stories, built of stucco, with a red tile roof. Unlike the squats that housed people in office buildings or hotels, Jasmine featured a central asphalt courtyard that had been built as a playground. This provided some open space for light to get into the building and a community meeting place for the residents. Because the space was visible from the street and the rooms inside, the property had a feeling of openness and fostered familiarity between the residents. It also provided a play area for the children and young adults. There was usually a group dribbling a ball underneath the basketball hoop or kicking a soccer ball up and down the length of the courtyard.

Jasmine housed almost 400 refugees, including about 150 children. Like most squats, the leadership at the squat was unclear and fluid, but Kanwal had volunteered to manage the squat's programs and volunteers. She facilitated my transition to English professor by saying I could watch her for a few days and ease myself into it. Five minutes into my first day in the classroom, she left. And it worked out OK.

The class was a mixed bag. It had natural light and tall windows that provided fresh air. Someone had painted it a cheerful turquoise, and there were 20 small chairs and tables. The blackboard, which was there from the time the building had been used as a school, was serviceable, although someone had nailed four smaller pieces of "white board" on top of it. The biggest problem turned out to be the parties that were hosted in the room late at night. In the mornings when we arrived, we cleaned up cigarette butts and what remained of fast-food containers. The floor was always filthy. Still, it was a real classroom, and that fact alone might facilitate learning.

An enterprising young Syrian man named Ahmad helped me in the classroom by describing, in the students' native Arabic, some of the complexities of English grammar. "*Shabab!*" he would say — "Guys!" Ahmad was 19, tall and handsome. He had been an engineering student at the university in Damascus. He had lost his family home to one of Assad's bombs and fled to Greece with his 12-year-old brother — I never asked about his parents. Shrapnel had damaged Ahmad's spine, and he experienced extreme pain at times. Syrian and Greek doctors had told him he would be permanently paralyzed if he didn't get surgery within six months. He didn't want Greek doctors operating on his back. After my experience in the hospital where Jamal was treated, I understood his concerns. I also knew the Greek government was probably not going to get Ahmad to Northern Europe before the six months was up.

My students at Jasmine School squat were enthusiastic and funny. Like most of the people I met, they were young men. They called me "My Teacher" and treated me with great

deference. My students were motivated and so adept that I
routinely assumed they knew a lot more than they did. One
of them, a 40-year-old Palestinian, asked me to marry him.
The others laughed and told me to beware because he had a
very jealous wife back home in Gaza. As I often did, I wrote
a sentence on the board for the students to fill in the blank.
The sentence was "I am going to _____." My
suitor replied, "I am NOT going to Gaza!" which led to howls
from the rest of the class.

After about a week, the class started filling up for short
periods with children who stayed long enough for the distribution of snacks. One day at the beginning of class, I wrote on
the blackboard, "Twelve students came to class on Monday.
I brought 25 bananas to class on Monday. Each student got
one banana. I left class on Monday with no bananas." I asked
the students to explain my math. Three eight-year-old boys
sitting near the door thought this was hilarious.

The young men in my class seemed to care deeply for each
other. One of them was honored with a birthday celebration
after class one day. Someone brought a cake and candles,
and the men danced with each other to the beat of several
drums and hand clapping. At times, it was hard to believe
these people had left their homes, their countries, and their
families. They were so full of spirit and love.

Ahmad later asked whether I could help teach English
to the children at Jasmine School. It didn't seem to matter
that I only had six weeks remaining in Greece before I would
have to leave the Schengen area. He explained that the Greek
public schools did not want to admit those who didn't speak
any English or Greek. The few children who had enrolled in

local schools had been ignored by the teachers and taunted by some of the children. The goal of "your school, Kim" would be to prepare the kids to enroll in Greek public schools. Practically hours after I told Ahmad I would help, another volunteer in Athens told me about an English NGO that had funds to support the school. Within a couple of days, I sent the executive director at Leros Solidarity Network a proposal, and a few days later he got his board to approve funding for it — $1400 for school supplies and a modest stipend for an Arabic-speaking teacher. If things went well, we might be able to get more.

This teaching experience would be a little more difficult for me. I had never taught children's classes, and I wasn't one of those people who had a natural gift with kids. But I knew if I needed help, I would get it, and I did. Ahmad found a Jasmine squat resident who had taught English classes at an elementary school in Syria. Together, we were a great team. Rafah was methodical and skilled at teaching. I was enthusiastic and came up with minor innovations the kids liked — games and star stickers and props (although the globe disappeared the day after I bought it.) Within a few weeks, we had volunteers eagerly helping in the classroom, including Hashem, Nanci, and Anne-Lene. It was easy to create materials for the kids' classes. I downloaded some study guides I found online and modified them to account for cultural issues and the children's circumstances. These kids did not need to learn words like "shopping mall" or "Christmas tree," but they did need to learn words like "tent" and "bus."

The kids were wonderful. Once we got going, they arrived in class 20 minutes early and sat quietly in their chairs with the pencils and notebooks we had given them. When I arrived each morning, Rafah led them in a good-morning song Nanci had taught them. The older kids helped the younger kids, and they all negotiated for more star stickers. Three girls in the front seats always hand their hands in the air, and, like any teacher, I felt I knew these girls were college material.

One of the inducements for school was the simple breakfast we provided each day. It was the only meal most of the children got before 2 p.m. We usually handed each child a piece of fruit, a hardboiled egg, and a piece of flatbread. Occasionally, we bought spinach pies at a local bakery and boxed juices. I made lentils one day, which were not popular. Rafah explained that, in Syria, lentils were eaten only when mixed in with rice. Like many kids who live in poverty, Jasmine kids ate junk food when healthy calories were not available. They frequently arrived in class with packaged cookies or candy, and there was plenty of evidence that soda was a staple. Consequently, many of the children had black, rotting teeth and a lack of color in their cheeks. The Greek government did not provide dental care, and the services provided by NGOs were usually oversubscribed. Getting an appointment might mean waiting weeks or months. This seemed like one of those gaps in services that we could fill.

I understood how difficult it must have been for the kids who tried to attend Greek public schools because of my own efforts to enroll Arian's six-year-old son, Shayan, into a neighborhood public school. In Greece, as in all European countries, education is compulsory between the ages of six and 16 without regard for a child's legal status, skills, race, living situation, disabilities or nationality. However, many

Greek schools seemed unwilling to follow the law. I initially offered to help Arian and Rana with this since I was English speaking and, after 25 years in government, felt adept at dealing with bureaucracy. I wrongly assumed registering a single child for school would require an hour or two of my time. Getting Shayan registered in his local public school ultimately required weeks of work by three pushy, determined English- and Greek-speaking advocates.

My first challenge was trying to determine which school Shayan would attend. This required an entire day of phone calls and walking through the neighborhood where Arian and Rana had their apartment. Late in the afternoon, I met a helpful teacher at a middle school who made a series of phone calls for me and wouldn't take "no" for an answer. The district office confirmed that the only thing we needed to provide the school was identification and evidence that Shayan had been vaccinated. I was also informed that, because of Shayan's young age, it was not important that he speak Greek or English.

The next day, Rana and I went to the elementary school, about three blocks from the apartment with the requisite documents. After waiting for almost an hour without being acknowledged by any of the staff, I took the initiative to knock on an open door and introduce myself to a woman who appeared to be the school administrator. The woman did not introduce herself or invite me to sit down. While I explained my objective, she stared at Rana and the boys standing outside the door. She said Shayan was not welcome at the school because he didn't speak English. He would have to attend a school miles from his home. I informed her that the district office told me he did not need to speak English to register at his neighborhood school. She made a phone call. Although I didn't understand the Greek phone conversation, her disappointment was obvious and a small victory for me. As she hung up the phone, she said she had changed her mind about the school across town. "The child" might be able to attend her school, but she needed to provide evidence that he had attended school in Kabul, a doctor's certificate to say he was healthy, and a copy of the lease on the family's apartment. And then she asked me why I cared about whether Shayan was in school. I told her my view that children need to be educated and that Greek law required them to be in school. Thinking I could appeal to her humanity, I added that Shayan was like a family member to me. She furrowed her brow and replied, "This is not about love." I responded, "I understand that. For you, it is about compliance with Greek law." For the first time, I was grateful that Rana and her children did not understand English.

The next day, I left Athens for California, feeling confident that we had everything in order for Shayan to attend school the following week. I explained to Arian what Rana needed to take to the school, and he assured me that they had what was required. But when Rana returned to the school with the required documents, she was told to come back a week later because the school was too busy to register Shayan so that he could attend the first day of school. When Arian heard this, he did not wait a week. He took a morning off work and went to the school himself. This time, the school required a copy of his passport and more documentation about Arian's residency. Arian was prepared for more resistance and told the

administrator he would return the next day with his lawyer —
and he had one lined up. The administrator contacted Arian
later that day to say he did not need to bring in his lawyer.

Shayan attended school the following week. Even though
the school was in a neighborhood where hundreds of refugee
children lived, Shayan was the only refugee child attending
the school. And still, he thrived. The photos Arian sent to
me in the following weeks showed a different child from the
one I'd left in Athens. His face was relaxed and smiling. He
held himself with confidence. Within a few weeks, Shayan's
teachers were reporting to Arian that Shayan was a very successful student, and a few months later, Shayan was speaking
Greek. He knew, as I did, how good it felt to learn.

Chapter 29

Fall 2016

Daughters

MY RELATIONSHIPS WITH the women in my work and social life had always been more along the lines of sisterly than competitive. I wanted the women in my life to be empowered, to have the kinds of opportunities that I had. For that reason, I expected to get close to the refugee women in Greece. But I never got really close to any, and my observations of their circumstances led me to conclude that very few would be able to overcome the traditional roles they had learned in their home countries. It would be up to their daughters to have choices and be educated.

A practical problem was communication. Few of the women in the camps and squats came to Greece knowing English, and not many seemed motivated to learn it. Cultural differences created barriers as well. Most of the refugees in Greece had come from traditional Muslim backgrounds, especially those from Afghanistan. Many Muslim women in traditional communities grew up with the understanding that the men in their lives were responsible for taking care

of the worldly needs of the family. Muslim men grew up
learning the same thing and therefore did not assume that
women would take the initiative to do anything outside the
four corners of the family's domestic life — which in any
event could be a big responsibility for women with several
children living in such difficult circumstances. In our family
relationships, this meant that the moms' relationships with
the daughters were limited to helping with dinners or the
children. For me, this was wonderful for short periods, but
sitting quietly with a group of women and children just did
not suit me. I wanted to be out delivering food to the squats
or teaching English or having a beer at the café.

Although my personal experiences didn't support the
west's stereotype that Muslim men oppress women, it was all
relative. Many American women, myself among them, would
feel oppressed in the world of the Muslim women I knew —
not because it was inherently oppressive but because many
American women have grown up with different expectations.
In some cases, what might have appeared to be oppression
was just tradition. Arian encouraged Rana to go out without
her *hijab* and to dress in whatever way was comfortable for
her. But being in the presence of unrelated men without her
head covered was not comfortable for her — the same way
an American woman might be uncomfortable in public
without a shirt.

The men I knew in the refugee community were young,
and the ones I got to know were consistently respectful
of the women around them. I didn't assume they would
encourage empowered women, either, but, unlike most of
their fathers, most had learned a lot about gender equality

from television or their smart phones, and most were eager to adopt western values. Arian was fascinated by my self-reliance and occasionally expressed a wish that Rana could feel more equal in their partnership and have a more worldly outlook. Farshad's relationships with women were much more western than Afghan and in ways that would not have been acceptable in his home country. That is, he was a bit of a Romeo — although his sweethearts did not seem to include Muslim women. Generally, the young men I got to know didn't seem to have any interest in being confined to traditional Muslim culture, which they associated in many cases with the people who persecuted them — the Taliban, ISIS, Daesh. Arian expressed it well: "Yes, I am a Muslim, and I love my God, but I follow the rules of my religion according to what I believe is right."

I did hear of husbands abusing their wives, although I wondered how the incidence of abuse in the Greek refugee community compared to that in any stressed-out, destitute community, notwithstanding national origin or religious views. Still, domestic violence was apparently accepted in some Muslim communities (as it was in some non-Muslim communities). When Asgar beat Samin that night in Arian and Rana's apartment, he was indignant that Arian challenged his right to manage his marriage in whatever way suited him. Arian dealt with this kind of attitude in his work at the camps and once told me, "One of my jobs is to tell the men in the camp that they are in Europe now and if they beat their wives or their children, they could go to jail." He once cried as he told me the story of two teenage girls in the camp who had been raped by smugglers and then shunned by some of the residents, who referred to the girls as "prostitutes."

By American standards, the women I was around might not have been empowered by their short time in Europe, but some had gained a new perspective on their lives. Some women who were alone in Greece were waiting for permission to reunite with husbands who had made it to Germany, and I know that many were not eager to reunite with their husbands, a sign that they were reconsidering their traditional relationships.

Our daughters — Rana, Marzia, and Lorin — were strong women, and, over the course of the year, I watched them adjust and grow. All three were energetic and loving, and they assumed a lot of responsibility for domestic tasks. When they arrived in Greece, they might have been traditional in some ways but not so traditional in others. Rana had been an accountant in Kabul, and Marzia had served in the Kurdish military. Both Marzia and Lorin traveled to Greece without husbands or fathers, requiring them to assume responsibilities for themselves and their children that would normally have been assigned to the men in their lives.

Rana, of course, was married to a man who encouraged her independence, but she was so demure at times that I wondered whether she could overcome the cultural constraints she felt. The logistical ones might be even more of a challenge. Caring for three young children limited her freedom, emotionally, intellectually, and in practical ways. If Rana had been at home in Kabul, she would have had the company of her mother and sisters and female cousins. Living in an apartment in Athens, she didn't have an automatic community of female support.

Because of the language barriers and our different ways of moving in the world, I knew I needed to take the initiative to get to know Rana better, and it wasn't something that came easily to me. As an American, my first instinct was to invite her to go shopping. I had mixed feelings about this because I didn't want to create a consumer of a woman who had so little in the way of long-term resources. But at the time, her clothes — probably used when she got them — were getting shabby, and she needed to get out of the apartment. Every time I suggested a shopping adventure, she expressed interest, but she reminded me that we needed Arian to watch the boys for a few hours. This was not going to be an easy assignment. Although Shayan could take care of himself, Jamal needed the kind of attention infants needed, and Amir's activity level required nearly constant supervision. By summer, Farshad had become comfortable with sleepovers at Rana and Arian's apartment, so we picked a day when Farshad was there to support Arian.

Our shopping adventure was, for me, quite routine. We took a taxi to Athens' outdoor pedestrian mall on Ermou Street, where Rana would have a lot of choices and see a lot of city activity. In addition to a variety of international clothing stores, the mall was full of street vendors, musicians, and coffeehouses. At first, Rana didn't say anything, and she didn't ask for anything, although I sensed the experience was, from the beginning, powerful and entertaining. As we walked through the mall, I periodically asked her which store windows interested her, and she replied, "Mom, you" meaning, "Mom — you decide." I picked a large store that catered to young tastes and that I knew had the kind of clothes she liked — fitted but modest tops that fell below her hips and skinny pants that covered her ankles.

Once inside, she didn't need my encouragement. She seemed to enjoy flipping through the racks and trying on a variety of styles ("but no black, Mom"). She popped her head out of the dressing room to ask me what I thought and posed with pride. She settled on three tunic tops and two pairs of skinny pants, all of which could be dressed up for an interview with a lawyer or worn for a walk around the block. When we left the store and returned to the mall, she seemed to feel more comfortable and surprised me by pulling me into a store that sold makeup and fragrance. At the suggestion of the clerk, she sat on a high chrome stool while the clerk applied face powder, eye shadow, and mascara. She looked gorgeous.

For me, shopping is not an inherently fun or energizing way to spend an afternoon, so I was relieved when Rana indicated that she was ready to go home. As our taxi made its way back to the apartment, she put her hand on my shoulder and thanked me. I asked her whether she missed shopping in Kabul. In her limited English, she let me know that she hadn't been clothes shopping since she had become pregnant with Shayan, seven years before. And how did she buy clothes? "Arian bought, Mom."

Over the coming months, I could see Rana's confidence building. She occasionally had a dinner out with Arian or took the boys to a local community center for refugee women. She grew closer to Lorin and Marzia, who occasionally helped her manage the children. Lorin eventually spent part of every week at the apartment, providing Rana with companionship and more freedom to get out on her own.

One day when I was home in California, Arian called me and said, "Guess what, Mom? Rana is out shopping by herself today. It's the first time." I was delighted, of course, and I said so. Always honest without regard for his personal safety, he replied, "I hope you are glad that she is becoming independent."

After that, I knew I had originally underestimated Rana as she changed in the way she viewed herself and her role — and in ways that were unusual in the community of refugees I knew. She took classes in English and Greek, and she began volunteering at a community center for refugee women. She learned what Jamal needed to overcome some of his disabilities and committed herself to what must have been an exhausting regime of physical therapy, requiring her to travel for hours on a bus to get to the clinic. Her messages to me evolved from, "Hi, Mom, haw are you" to selfies where she mugged wearing funny hats or makeup. She even wore a swimsuit to the beach during the summer of 2017. Rana's emerging worldliness was possible only because her husband encouraged her and she had a family income, however modest.

One day in early 2017, Arian called me to say, "Mom, guess what Rana did! She helped a refugee family get an apartment! Do you believe that?" I did.

These signs of strength were encouraging, but I never believed the women who were already mothers would ever feel the kind of self-reliance and empowerment that most American and European women take for granted. These women needed to understand their rights and their opportunities. Neither the Greek government nor the NGOs were providing information or resources to empower women.

I inquired all over about whether and what NGOs were doing to encourage women's leadership and empowerment. The responses I got were, "We are conducting cooking classes," "We are conducting sewing classes," and "We are conducting photography classes."

Although the challenges were probably overwhelming for the women refugees, Marzia's ten-year-old daughter Sarah gave me hope that the girls would pick up where their mothers would leave off. I never got to know Sarah well, but I saw much in her in our brief encounters. She had learned three languages. She played keyboards and soccer. She was as social as a cruise-ship hostess. One summer evening, we had a family dinner at Skaramangas in the caravan where Hashem, Lorin, Marzia, and the children lived. Arian and Rana were there with the children. As was the custom, we let Rana and Lorin take charge of the cooking. I asked for an assignment, and Lorin handed me an armful of vegetables. I pulled out a cutting board and sat on the floor, where everything related to food began and ended, chopping peppers and onions while I listened to Sarah and her brothers chattering on the bunk beds next to me.

After dinner, as the sun started to set, several of us left the caravan to walk down to the causeway along the water, where there were other members of the camp community and fresh air. Sarah sidled up alongside me and took my hand. The heat pulsed off the cement, and the air felt orange. Farshad and Hashem waved at us as they left to swim in the seawater at the far end of the causeway. Watching them walk away, Sarah grabbed two chunks of her long, wavy hair with two hands. Then she dropped her hair and threaded her arm through one of mine and looked up at me without her usual smile. She picked up her pace and began talking with a cadence that I did not recognize as hers — quick and staccato. Sarah had good English-speaking skills, but I was straining to understand her words over the sound of the wind and the whitecaps lapping along the sea wall. But I understood every word once I understood the subject of her chatter. I also understood she was not talking to me but to someone deep inside her. "Swimming? Why, why are they swimming in this water? I know this water. I know it is not for swimming. Sometimes others swim in this water, but I would never swim here. This water is not for swimming. Swimming, swimming. Why do they swim here?" She continued to chatter this way for several minutes. I put my arm around her and took one of her hands in mine. I felt helpless, as if nothing I could say would relieve her of the anxiety she was feeling.

Then she stopped as abruptly as she had started. "Would you like to dance, Kim?" I was relieved that she sounded like Sarah again. "Yes," I said, "but I am not a dancer. You will have to teach me." And she did, one step at a time, until we were twirling and gliding in a half-graceful (Sarah), half-awkward (me) two-step. She was enchanted and enchanting. I asked her how she had learned to dance and why she was such a good teacher. "Because my dad taught me everything, and I will see him soon when we travel to Germany."

When we took a break from dancing, I asked her what she wanted to be when she grew up. "When I grow up, I want to come back here and swim in this sea."

Chapter 30

Fall 2016

Back to Lesvos

A S A YOUNG ADULT, I visited the small university town of Claremont, California, where I had lived for most of the first ten years of my life. During that visit, I drove by the old house, and, as anyone who has made a similar pilgrimage could have predicted, I was surprised by its small size and modest presentation. Didn't I live in a spacious new tract house with a giant porch and professional landscaping? The experience turned out to be very unromantic.

Maybe we can never go home again, but we can indulge in what was there that was special. And maybe we owe it to ourselves to understand what had to change, whether in fact or in our interpretations. When I decided to return to Lesvos in October, I was motivated to revisit the feelings that had been so powerful for me the previous winter. But ultimately, I learned more about what had changed there in a short time and why some of the magic there — the magic that was unrelated to the island's natural beauty and wonderful community — was gone forever.

Nanci wanted to join me, hoping to get away from the intensity of Athens and, like me, curious about what she would feel on the island. When I mentioned our plans to Arian, he asked whether he could join us. It seemed like a good idea. He needed a break more than I did, and we would be able to spend some time together, something that had become increasingly difficult with the demands of his work and family.

But there were reasons to tell Arian to stay at home. We did not invite Hashem and Farshad because we worried about the risk that they might be detained at the airport. Unlike Arian, Hashem and Farshad did not have their "yellow cards" because they had not sought asylum in Greece. Taking Arian on a rural retreat might create some jealousy and longing for the brothers left behind. Hashem, in particular, would be sensitive to Nanci vacationing with Arian. I was also aware that I was taking Arian away from Rana and the boys. Rana needed some relief as much as Arian did, but hauling three young children on a plane for two days to a cold island was not going to provide relief to anyone. I dismissed my concerns after talking to Arian about them — when he wanted something, he figured out ways to deal with complications.

But I did have one concern I needed to resolve for my own peace of mind. We were traveling with a refugee to an island that had become a virtual prison for refugees. Legally, Arian was permitted to travel anywhere within Greece, but our experience in Greece did not inspire great confidence that Greek authorities were consistently committed to the rule of law. I worried that Greek officials might find some pretense to detain him. When I mentioned this to Arian, he said he had already talked to an attorney at work, who'd assured him he should not have any problem, *inshallah*.

A few days later, we were on our way — but not without incident. At the airport, the three of us breezed through the first two security checks. But as Nanci and I ambled down the ramp to board the plane, we turned around when we realized that Arian was no longer behind us. Fearing Arian may have been detained, I rushed back to the desk at the gate. There Arian stood, calmly and diplomatically negotiating with the Aegean Air agent. When he saw me, he lowered his eyes. "Mom. I do not have my yellow card. I have Shayan's." Arian had noticed this for the first time at the gate — although none of the security people had. We were in the largest airport of a country that had been flooded with more than a million undocumented strangers, and yet three security officials had not compared Arian's ID with the name on his ticket. This was so Greek in a way — "We are not very good managers because we have more important things to consider." I liked it.

At the desk, Arian described the circumstance to the Aegean Air agent. He knew getting onto the plane at that point could have landed him in a Greek prison, and, although none of the security personnel had caught it, someone in Lesvos might and then prohibit him from returning to Athens. The line of passengers waiting to get through the gate watched quietly and patiently. I showed the agent a photo of Arian's yellow card stored on my phone. She said she could not accept a photo of an identification card. We sorrowfully began to say our goodbyes.

As Arian pushed his backpack higher on his shoulder, the Aegean Air agent looked up from her computer screen and said, "No — wait. I think I can fix this. Do you have any other ID with a photo?" Arian slowly riffled through his wallet. Dog-eared receipts, a few euro bills, an ATM card with my name on it. He held himself with such dignity and softness. Looking up, he handed the agent an expired Athens transit pass. "I am sorry. This is all I have." The agent took the card and began typing on her computer. She handed back the card to Arian and gave him a big smile. "You can get on the plane, and you will be able to return." He got to Lesvos, and he got back to Athens, too.

Arriving on Lesvos that day felt like arriving home. I felt a special kind of intimacy with every corner of it. Driving through Mytilene, I saw the man who cleaned windshields at the traffic signal. I saw the coffeehouse where I'd first met Panagiotis. When we passed City Hall, I remembered the giant kite with the peace sign painted on it that adorned the stairway to the mayor's office. Even as I was here breathing the air and feeling every bump in the road, I felt a longing for whatever it was that connected me to this place.

We arrived late in the day at our rental, a traditional stone house on Molyvos Hill with red shutters and a balcony that seemed to hang over the sea. Nanci and I assigned Arian the bedroom with the largest bed, a veranda, and a view of the sea. He protested that it was not appropriate for him to occupy the nicest room in the house. I thanked him for how he honored my role in the family and told him he didn't have a choice.

The next morning, we all slept late. For breakfast, Arian made *shakshuka*, a middle-eastern dish of eggs in a pool of caramelized onions and tomatoes. When I asked Arian whether it felt good to sleep late, he said, "Yes," — almost as good as waking up to Amir's little hands pulling on his ears.

The sky was clear and sunny as we walked down the hill to the car sitting in the parking lot along the waterfront. I could tell by the way Arian looked at the car that he wanted to drive. I pretended not to notice. He didn't have a driver's license, and any infraction of Greek laws could jeopardize his prospects for remaining in Europe. After I got in the car and put the key in the ignition, he said, "Mom, please get out of the car and look over there." He had never given me a reason to feel distrust, so I got out of the car and looked out toward the sea. In the corner of my vision, I watched him get into the car. I heard the engine start and saw the car move forward and backward in the parking space. The engine stopped, and Arian crawled out of the car with a silly smile on his face. "Thank you, Mom."

The day was full of joy and sorrow. We first stopped at the life-jacket graveyard up the dirt road behind the Donkey Farm sign. At the top of the hill, we parked the car and stood on a grassless, treeless rise overlooking half a million life jackets that formed two 30-foot hills. Hundreds of small boats of wood and deflated plastic sat silent on the perimeter. I felt my chest tighten and wondered where all these people were now, how many life jackets did not make it to land, how many would never get this far now that NATO patrols had replaced our beach patrols. The bright orange of the life jackets had faded to tan, many covered with a thin layer of mud.

Walking past a 12-foot-deep metal refuse bin, we heard the cry of a distressed cat coming from the bottom. As we leaned over the top of the bin, a scrawny calico jumped frantically at the side of the bin, trying to escape, and then retreated into a pile of rubble. Arian found a wooden beam and placed it strategically at an angle from the top of the rubble to the lip of the bin. We kitty-kittied with no response. She was afraid. We walked back to the car confident that she, at least, would find her path to freedom.

We drove through the coastal mountains to the tiny harbor town of Skala Sykamania, where fishermen had famously pulled terrified people out of the water and hauled raggedy boats into the tiny harbor. Approaching the town's tiny harbor was a middle-aged man dressed in an orange sheath and pumps the color of the life jackets. I remembered hearing that this was Dmitri, the community's cross-dresser.

We drank coffee at a café next to the dock, enjoying the sun and sea breeze. Just before we left, a Coast Guard boat arrived with dozens of young men who had come across on a rubber raft. They were wet and cold and scared. This was a contrast to my experiences with refugees coming in on the boats — kissing the ground, hugging the volunteers, and triumphantly texting home to say they were safe. These men were Iraqi Kurds, and they would be taken to Moria. The refugees always knew in advance what to expect on Lesvos. Their 15-foot raft was moored in a slip across from where we were sitting. Arian walked over to it and stood for a very long few seconds. Then he climbed into it and asked Nanci to take a picture.

We drove back toward Molyvos in silence and stopped at Limantziki Beach. The tents and equipment were gone. It was just a beach now. The flock of brown sheep that came down to the water for salt were not in sight. No cats. Arian stood for a very long time on the shore, looking toward Turkey.

We scrambled up the hill overlooking the beach, tip-toeing in hopes of avoiding snakes. The couch the Germans had made from a rubber dinghy had fallen from the cliff where we would sit looking for boats. The couch was hanging on its side just above the surf. Arian asked me if I wanted him to go down and get it. No! I begged him not to climb on the cliffs. "But I am from Afghanistan, and I grew up with mountains, so I know how to climb cliffs." "And I am from America, where you are an unacceptable insurance risk!" Just being at Limantziki felt risky enough with the emotions it brought back.

I saw Natasha briefly when she was on her way to work at Donkey Warehouse. She was still wearing her black beret. We hugged and promised to see each other later in the weekend, but I didn't see her again.

Our last stop was the Aphrodite Hotel. We walked down the packed-dirt lane through a double line of palm trees to the hotel beach where hundreds of boats had arrived. The beach was quiet and clean, and the water hitting the gravel made little flapping sounds. The hotel was closed for the season, but, as we headed back to the car, Panagiotis pulled up in his truck. He had been working on something. He was in overalls instead of his creased khakis. As he got out of the car, he gave me a smile of recognition and rubbed his hands on the bib of his overalls. I wanted to hug him as I had many times only months ago, but it didn't feel right. We shook hands and chatted for a few minutes. He looked serious and resigned, and he didn't have any good news. The hotel's business was down 70% this year. Tour agencies had diverted vacationers to islands where refugees did not land. Charter flights from Amsterdam and Oslo had been cancelled. The family had not been able to hire staff to run the hotel that summer. His father had been very sick. I wanted to spend more time with him, but I had the feeling I was a reminder of what had been so difficult for him and his family. I said goodbye and wondered whether I would ever see him again.

The next day, Nanci and I visited the Kempsons. Not much had changed at their little farm except that it was quiet — no buzz of volunteers or ongoing sense of urgency. The plastic storage room was still there with shelves of sorted clothing in labeled boxes. We sat outside near Eric's workshop with steaming cups of tea. Eric said the island had changed, and the people running the refugee-support operations no longer seemed motivated by a sense of humanity. They were paid to be there. He said the hotel owners in town had made sure Hotel Elpis did not get operating permits. He had been fined $10,000 for operating the hotel without permits and said the only time refugees had been there was after the island police asked him to shelter them. The boats were coming in again, he said, "hundreds of people are arriving every week, but no one is talking about it." He expected more boats with the collapse of the EU-Turkey deal. He described a Turkish Coast Guard boat entering Greek waters illegally to intercept a boat of refugees. He felt sidelined. He felt the refugees had been sidelined.

It was the first time I had been able to have more than a casual conversation with the Kempsons, although nothing they shared surprised me. I could feel their sense of loss. The loss of an opportunity to feel solidarity, to feel valued, to really make a difference in people's lives. They had been at the center of something important, something that had been destroyed for the wrong reasons.

As we drove through the familiar olive groves and sheep pastures, I felt sorrow and love. I remembered the feelings of common purpose and humanity. I had felt a sense of purpose and community I had never known before, and I had learned a little about the heroism of a handful of Greeks and half a million people in blue jeans and *hijabs*. Although so much about what was important to me about Lesvos had changed, one of those half million people in blue jeans was with me. I knew he would keep me connected to some of what was so special for me about the time of my life I spent on Lesvos.

V

ELEUTHEROMANIA

An Intense Desire for Freedom

Chapter 31

November 2016

Complications

ONE OF THE WONDERS of our ad hoc family was the simple joy of being together. Those who were refugees desperately needed relief from the stresses in their lives and the uncertainties about how their lives might unfold. I needed them as antidote to the noise in my brain that often kept me from just enjoying life without any particular plan or agenda. Living in the moment, as we did when we were together, discouraged thoughts about how things could change. And they did change.

It started with a pitch-perfect trip in November to the historic site of Delphi, the ancient sanctuary of the Greek gods Apollo and Athena. Delphi was only 120 miles north of Athens, located in some of Greece's most beautiful countryside. I had asked Nanci and Anne-Lene about a visit to Delphi a couple of times, and we had always managed to avoid making a commitment. But we needed another break from the grind and grit of Athens, so one day I told them we were going, and I gave them a date. They were happy to get out of town. We invited Arian, Hashem, and Farshad. All three responded to our invitation with the enthusiasm of children on their way to Disneyland. Except for Arian's weekend on Lesvos, none of them had been any place with natural beauty during their 10 months in Greece. In fact, it had probably been many months or years since any of them had been in a place of safety and beauty.

On a bright sunny day, we picked up our rental cars south of downtown, two brand-new small SUVs. While Nanci and I did the paperwork inside, our sons took the opportunity to take selfies next to the cars as if they had just purchased them. It seemed they never missed an opportunity to imagine themselves in the kind of lives they wanted to live.

Arian and Farshad rode with me. Anne-Lene and Hashem rode with Nanci. The road to Delphi was mostly fast and modern, bisecting a valley in the central part of Greece that goes to the Macedonian border. The topography was familiar — hilly, rugged, and open, like parts of central Lesvos. It also reminded me of my California. As we hit the highway, Arian turned on a radio station that played New Orleans jazz and Chicago blues. "I went down to the crossroad, fell down on my knees…" The open road and the familiarity of my American music was exhilarating for me, and I began singing and tapping my hands on the steering wheel. Arian smiled, "Mom, I think I have found your favorite playlist."

Farshad was in the backseat, navigating and texting Hashem. Forty minutes into the drive, Farshad announced, "They are way behind us, near the turnoff." There was a playfully competitive tone in his voice. Seconds later, Nanci's car breezed past us. GPS in Greece.

We approached the small tourist town of Delphi sitting in the shadow of the ruins, which are perched on a high plateau in a mountain range over a spectacular gorge. It was easy to see why the Greeks considered Delphi the center of the earth and one of its holiest places. The whole area exuded a sort of mysticism. We quickly checked into our hotel and then hiked down the road to watch the sun set into the mountains before enjoying a dinner overlooking the gorge. I laughed to myself at the picture we presented — three aging white women with three swarthy young men sporting "high and tight" haircuts and fitted t-shirts. And yet we did not have a moment of awkwardness of any kind, with each other or with those in the community.

That night we stayed up late playing poker and gin rummy, sitting at a large, round table in the lobby. Each of us was either genuinely competitive or playing along at being competitive. We laughed until we hurt.

The next day, we walked to the Delphi ruins, where kings and priests consulted with the Oracle. On our walk back to the hotel, we took a detour down a dirt road that rambled into the gorge. Arian and Nanci climbed an almond tree. Farshad scratched "Butterflies" and our names into the side of a soft rock.

Everything seemed so incredibly uncomplicated at that time, just before everything wasn't.

Shortly after the Delphi adventure, I returned home to California. My time at home again highlighted the inequities of my two worlds. I enjoyed the beauty and wealth of my California community and the simple pleasures of spending time with my family and friends. At the same time, my second family in Greece was struggling. I imagined how difficult it must have been for Hashem and Farshad to return to the camp after spending almost two months in the comfort of Nanci's apartment. At Skaramangas, they had no privacy or quiet moments. Skaramangas had no trees, no place to go where people weren't in various stages of stress or trauma. They had none of the emotional support Mama Nanci and the family gatherings provided. Worse — especially for Hashem — at Skaramangas, they were people who needed help.

Hashem and Arian's relationship had become strained, perhaps in part because Arian's work assignment at Skaramangas was a reminder that Hashem did not have a job. Hashem accused Arian of insensitivity, and, when I talked to Arian about it, he admitted making a comment that he believed a brother should understand as playful. Farshad called me, obviously near tears, to say that he didn't know what to do about his brothers — he was in the middle of a problem he didn't understand, each one of his brothers stubbornly refusing to reconcile with the other.

Things got more complicated after someone stole Farshad's wallet from his caravan. The circumstances were suspicious because Farshad had just been paid for a month's work with the soccer club, and the wallet had been hidden in an unlikely place. What was worse for Farshad than losing the money was losing his Greek identification. To get a new one, he had to stand in long lines and await a replacement during a time he was hoping the German government would grant him reunification with his mother. Hashem believed the police suspected his involvement, and some suspected Farshad's cousin was involved. His cousin's wallet went missing a few days later. This was not the happy, optimistic group we had lived with for two months.

Arian called one afternoon, as he did a few times a week. He spoke with a great deal of stress in his voice, and I could hear what sounded like a lot of street noise. He began a plaintive description of his fears that he would be stuck in Greece forever, unable to provide his children a good education and a secure life. He couldn't bear the thought that he would never have opportunities to have a good job. His friend, Ahmad, had been successfully smuggled to Sweden, and Rana's brother had just been granted asylum in Germany. A group of men at one of the squats was about to leave for Norway with fake identification. He had heard stories of so many others making it to Northern Europe with smugglers. "Mom, the EU is going to apply Dublin III beginning in March. Until then, Sweden and Germany are not sending back refugees to Greece."

Dublin III was the EU agreement that permitted EU countries to return refugees to the country where they'd first set foot on EU shores. That was almost always Greece and Italy because of the proximity of their borders to Africa and the Middle East. For the previous two years, the Northern European countries had declined their privilege to send back refugees according to Dublin III because of Greece's well-deserved reputation for incompetence in its asylum claims procedures. Before the borders closed, this circumstance encouraged refugees to make their way north on foot or by public transportation. Although it was a long and difficult journey by any measure, it was safe and cheap compared to the options that had become available after the borders closed in February 2016. Smugglers were, again, the beneficiaries of EU policies to deter refugee arrivals. Refugees paid as much as $5,000 for a fake passport and a $40 airplane ticket. For $2,000, refugees could risk death — tied to the bottom of a freight truck.

I stifled my urge to say, "Arian, you should thank your lucky stars if you are granted asylum in Greece." I didn't stifle my urge to say, "I understand you are restless and struggling, but you cannot leave your wife and children for a risky journey that could leave them alone in Greece for a year."

As I paced between the kitchen and the living room, up the stairs, and back to the kitchen, the conversation continued like this for more than an hour. Arian said he would never have a chance to succeed in Greece, and I understood why he felt this way. I had never appreciated the claim that "anyone can succeed in the United States" until I wasn't in the United States. Of course, not everyone succeeds in the United States, but Arian was exactly the kind of person who could. And the United States might be one of the only places in the world where he would have that chance — if he could ever get in.

Greece, on the other hand, did not appear to provide opportunities to anyone but its elite, and it certainly showed no signs of acknowledging the skills and talents of the 60,000 refugees it could have deployed to almost every imaginable task and profession. I didn't say any of this, of course, and, given Arian's almost-unerring instincts about almost everything in his life, I didn't need to. Instead, I said with honest conviction that he would succeed anywhere he would find himself and that he would have opportunities to live in other places if he could be patient. Arian replied by saying, "But I don't have anyone in my life supporting me." He allowed me to sit through several seconds of silence. "Arian, no one?" And then he didn't pause. "Mom, you are me. I am you." And in the moment, I understood how betrayed he felt by the world — and how I felt so safe in it.

I glanced out the Southern California living room window and saw a street-cleaning truck passing by. The sign on the door said, "Athens Services." At the end of the conversation, Arian agreed to think about his options for a few days and to keep calling. I agreed to investigate Canada's sponsorship program, which had been wildly successful at creating community while saving lives. (I later learned from the Canadian government's website that Afghans could not participate in its sponsorship program or apply for asylum except in some very unusual circumstances. Asylum in Canada was, for practical purposes, offered only to Syrians and Iraqis and people referred by the UNHCR. The UNHCR referred only Syrians and Iraqis.)

Arian had always told me he did not accept that he was unlucky to have been born in a country at war or to have been exiled from his country or to have the responsibility of raising a child who was permanently disabled due to medical incompetence. He did not consider himself lucky to have been born strong and smart or to have met an American woman who wanted to help him get himself going in Greece. Arian said, "A man makes his own luck. I will succeed or fail on my own." It was this outlook on life that made it so difficult for him to wait for the Greek bureaucracy to declare his fate or for the EU to reconsider its inhumanity. And here I was, one of the most impatient people in my life, suggesting that Arian slow it down.

The day after our long phone call, Arian texted me that he had received a call from GAS to report to its offices the next day. It would give him a written copy of the decision on his asylum claim. For all of the work I had done investigating Greece's asylum claims procedures, I had no idea what this meant. Was it a good sign or a bad sign? Twenty-four hours is a long time to think about such things. On the one hand, he had a strong case under international law. On the other hand, the asylum claims process had become increasingly politicized, and we had not been able to provide documentation of some of Arian's claims.

I contacted Nanci and Anne-Lene for moral support and let Hashem and Farshad know that his brother needed them to be close, whatever the outcome. I had tried to engage an attorney in Greece in case he needed to appeal. But none of this felt reassuring. I was almost 7,000 miles away when Arian needed me to be with him.

Chapter 32
Winter 2016–17
Betrayals

I BEGAN MY CAREER IN government in 1982, motivated by my belief in the good government can do. It ended 33 years later in surrender. That's not to say I didn't see a lot of good during my career — and I certainly came across many good people wanting to do good things. But I also learned how government consolidates power and money in ways that overwhelm good people wanting to do good things. The good-people-doing-good-work is what motivated me to travel to Lesvos in late 2015, and I found what I was looking for. Soon after I arrived, however, the power and the money prevailed, and, by 2017, the situation was ever more desperate for refugees.

That winter, hundreds died trying to cross from Northern Africa, while the European Commission focused its efforts on ways to keep people out of the EU. Border patrols in eastern Europe beat refugees mercilessly. The French police stole blankets from refugees living in the streets of Paris. The island of Lesvos continued as a shameful metaphor for

Europe's change of heart toward people running from war. That winter, many of the residents — prisoners — of Moria slept on the ground in the kind of flimsy tents we bought at the Chinese store for $15. The snow fell night after night. Several young men died. The media attention and the local outcry did nothing to change the conditions there that winter in spite of the promises of the Greek Ministry.

At the same time, Afghanistan seemed to be descending into civil war. Suicide bombings were common, and the American Embassy pulled out of Kabul. The Taliban had taken control of several Afghan provinces, blocking roads, shutting down supplies of water and electricity, and engaging in hand-to-hand fighting. The Taliban had made public statements about how the election of Donald Trump in the US created recruitment opportunities for Taliban fighters. At the same time, the Afghan government in Kabul was increasingly allying itself with the Taliban. Out of the blue, the Trump administration marketed an attack on Afghanistan by touting its weapon of choice as "the mother of all bombs."

As the drama unfolded in Afghanistan, the Turkey-EU deal was falling apart because of Erdogan's very public acts of oppression and human-rights violations. Fearing Erdogan might make good on his public statements that he would turn loose boatloads of refugees to cross into Greece, the EU announced another of its deals, which, like the EU-Turkey deal, was designed to keep refugees off of its soil regardless of the consequences for human lives. In an agreement between the EU and the Afghan government, the EU would send back tens of thousands of Afghan refugees to Afghanistan.

For its cooperation, Afghanistan would receive $16 billion over four years.

On December 13, 2016, Arian reported to the Katahaki office of GAS, where he waited in line with hundreds of others for six hours. Arian texted me at 4:30 a.m. California time to tell me the Greek government had denied his asylum claim. He added that he felt "hopeless." He said, "It is my bad luck," something I never thought I would hear him say.

This terrifying announcement was not a shock to me intellectually. For months, I had prepared myself for this outcome. I knew Arian's deportation to Afghanistan could be a death sentence and, even if he survived, I might not see him again. I didn't know whether I had the kind of courage needed to travel to Afghanistan, given the escalating violence there. An American woman would be an easy target for kidnappers, and my presence might create additional risks for Arian.

But these equations did not prepare me for the physical response I felt when Arian told me. I felt nauseous — the same kind of pressure and pain in my chest that I had felt when my brother died on the same day in 1989. Like Arian, he was 30. Holding back tears, I knew I had to let go of my pain and these metaphysical explanations to be strong and present for Arian. I replied, "Of course, Arian, you will appeal. You must not worry."

In the middle of this bureaucratic, heartless ordeal, Rana contacted Arian to say that she and Shayan were at the hospital. The doctors had suggested Shayan might need emergency surgery. He had a high fever and severe pain in his joints and stomach. Arian could not leave the GAS office for the hospital without creating a risk that he would give up his right to an attorney. I wondered how much more he could take.

For the next several hours, Arian and I texted back and forth while he waited in line at the GAS office to be assigned an appeals attorney. At the end of two hours, he was called by his case number to one of several attorneys. She handed Arian a piece of paper and said, "I will call you within 30 days." Despite Arian's repeated requests, she refused to give Arian her name or her contact information. Arian had only 30 days to file an appeal, which was a complex legal document that required a deep understanding of the individual's case. I told Arian we would engage another lawyer, but, privately, I did not know whether we would find one. I had already spent hours soliciting legal help, even promising to pay. The one attorney who agreed to represent him backed out at the last minute. Legal help for refugees in Greece was scarce.

Arian left for the hospital. Shayan did not need surgery. The hospital sent him home with a bottle of antibiotics. I felt little confidence in a group of doctors who moved so quickly from a plan to operate to a prescription for antibiotics, but I didn't say anything. Having been relieved of the prospects for Shayan's hospitalization, Arian's mind was free to indulge in the fears that accompanied the Greek government's rejection of his asylum claim. During our phone call, Arian recounted the threats on his life he had received from the Taliban, which was gaining strength all over Afghanistan. He was recognizable everywhere because of his work in television. Of course, I agreed with him that he had a strong case for asylum, perhaps now more than ever. I also told them the process was as much a political one as a legal one at this point. He needed a backup plan. He could never return to Afghanistan. "I will kill myself before I let them kill me."

Turkey was not an option, either. Refugees who were arriving to Greece from the Turkish coast told stories of abuse and exploitation. Many of the three million refugees there were living desperate lives. We had heard that the only work refugees were finding was back-breaking work in the farm fields, which did not pay enough to live on. Refugees were not being provided adequate services, and the Turkish economy was floundering under Erdogan's increasingly despotic rule. Arian said he could never take his children to a country where he could not provide them with education and the hope of a safe and comfortable life.

I knew Arian had a strong case under international law, but, without an attorney, his prospects were slim. The decision and the transcript from his eight-hour interview were in Greek. I had tried for the prior six months to engage a Greek attorney. The only one I found who said she might be able to help told me — after Arian's decision had been issued — that she was too busy to talk with him. She suggested he rely on the attorney who had not given him her name and would not contact him until Day 28 of a 30-day appeal window. I didn't sleep for two nights, knowing Arian and Rana would be in worse emotional shape.

Then something happened that was better than anything we could have hoped for. Arian called me to say he had met with his boss at work, a Greek attorney named Erica who had worked for the GAS for 25 years. She sat with Arian and read the GAS decision denying Arian's asylum claim. Within a few minutes, she found two glaring legal errors in the analysis supporting the denial. She believed appellate judges would find "reversible error" in the decision. Then she went on her computer and, within minutes, found evidence of Arian's time as a television actor that neither of us had been able to find. The clips of his role as "Bashir" on a NATO-funded production would support Arian's claim that he would be at risk of facing renewed persecution if he were deported back to Afghanistan. Erica said he did not have to worry. Erica's boss told Arian that Erica would need to use only "the amount of her knowledge that is in the tiniest corner of the finger of her left hand." He told Arian they would support his appeal to the highest court.

When Arian told me this, I could hear the gratitude in his voice. "Mom, I respect these people more than anyone, and they want to help me." They had affirmed all the work he had done and the goodwill he had tried to share. "If my appeal is denied and I am deported, I could face it now. And Mom, this is all because of you. You gave me back my power. It's all you." I reminded him that the only thing I could take credit for was recognizing his depth and spirit. The rest was what he had done for himself. We cried together and then laughed with relief and joy.

Later that day, Anne-Lene texted Nanci and me to say she would make a surprise visit to Athens that week. She would take a deck of cards, and we were hopeful that she could get our sons together in one room laughing again.

Chapter 33

Winter-Summer 2017

What I Would Keep

I hope for nothing. I fear nothing. I am free.
— Nikos Kazantakis, **author of** *Zorba the Greek*

WHEN I LEFT GREECE in November, I knew instinctively that I had experienced something that, like the light of a church candle or the exuberance of new love, could not last. Our family had come together at a time when, strangely, our respective needs and circumstances harmonized. When we were together, we were barely conscious or inquiring because we did not need to be. It all seemed so easy. With or without the strains that would eventually arise in our complicated relationships, the family was destined for dissolution — for good reasons and sad ones.

In January, Farshad heard from the German authorities. He was granted his request for reunification with his mother in Germany and would be given his travel papers in summer. He described how she cried when he told her. We all cried.

For happiness. For sadness. This was the best possible outcome for Farshad. He would be with his mother in a country where he would have opportunities to finish his education and continue his soccer career. He had the motivation and the social skills to begin a new life in Germany.

Farshad wasn't able to leave for Germany for more than eight months after he was granted reunification with his mother, creating a lot of anxiety for him. And as Europe began making slow progress toward settling refugees in permanent communities, I knew the inevitable changes in everyone's lives would contribute to the strains in the family that were already building. When I returned to Greece in February, Hashem and Farshad were growing apart just as Hashem and Arian had become distant. Farshad was spending a lot of time with his soccer team and coaching a group of children at Skaramangas. Hashem was working part time with an NGO that taught music to the kids at the camp. He was also managing what had become a small business enterprise, operating the washing machine we had purchased. Since Skaramangas had three washing machines for more than 3,000 residents, Hashem had more business than he could handle.

Arian still kept in touch with his refugee brothers, mostly when he saw them at the camp during his work hours. The dinners and sleepovers at his apartment, however, were rare. Lorin moved back to the camp. I did not learn why, but this change in Rana's life might have been one of the triggers for what happened shortly after I returned to Greece.

I had spent my first week in Athens to visit and help in the squats and then retreated to the historic seaside town of Nafplio, about two hours' drive west of Athens on the peninsula called the Peloponnese. Nafplio's cobblestone streets were lined with cafes and *tavernas* and two-story Venetian-style houses. I rented a tiny apartment overlooking the Argolic Gulf and, on weekdays, lived like a retired American, but restless. I bought produce at the outdoor market on Wednesdays, wrote essays that would never be published, and shared dinners at outdoor cafes with a local shopkeeper who became a friend.

One night, as I was getting ready for bed, Arian called. I could hear street noise in the background, and Arian's voice was strained. "Mom, I am calling you for help. I have lost everything. I have lost my life." And then he began sobbing. I had a few seconds to foolishly hope that he had lost another phone. When he could speak, he explained that he had arrived home from work that night to an empty apartment. A short time later, he received a message from Rana saying she and the boys would not return. He found Rana's wedding ring on a pillow in the middle of the living room.

Rana's decision to leave with the children was a shock, even though I knew theirs was not a comfortable marriage. In spite of their very different temperaments and perspectives, I assumed they had found an accommodation in order to make the best of things for their sons and in recognition that they needed each other. But Arian's late nights with friends and his friendships with young women, however innocent, would have made any wife suspicious. I had believed him when he told me he was faithful and doing what he believed he needed to do for his career. I guessed that Rana did not.

Arian spoke almost incoherently on the phone about his efforts to find Rana during the previous two hours. I told

him I understood he was feeling deep sorrow but to go home
so he would be safe. I was always fearful when he was on
the streets of Athens in the middle of the night, more with
regard to the Athens police than anything else, and he was
at greater risk in a state of panic. I told him he must not try
to find Rana. If he contacted her, he must not say anything
that could sound like a threat.

Over the next few days, Arian blamed himself for everything and promised to change. He said he could not live
without his sons, literally. He pleaded with me to help. I told
him he must take care of himself and hope that Rana would
realize that she could not live comfortably without an income
and that her sons needed their father.

The morning after she left the house, I began sending
messages to Rana to tell her I loved her and worried about
the boys. At first, she would reply only that everyone was
"fine." A couple of days later, she sent me a message saying
she was "tired of his high life." I was not surprised. I knew
her Muslim faith guided her views on how the family should
conduct itself. Arian was more European than Muslim in so
many ways. The traits that had served him so well in his work
were also the source of the strain in his marriage. Although
his behavior was not justification for taking a man's children
from him, I assumed Rana did not have the confidence or
the skills to negotiate with hm. She had a moment of courage, and she took it.

There was some irony here, of course. She had told Arian,
"You gave me my freedom, and so I used it to leave you."
I wondered whether she understood that the price of freedom
is responsibility. I also felt a sense of guilt. The cash I was

sending was probably facilitating Arian's evenings out, in spite of my stipulation that the money was for emergencies.

Besides the guilt, I felt anger. I didn't know Rana well enough to get a sense of whether she was making a statement or was naïve enough to believe her children would be better off living in poverty, without a father. On the other hand, poverty might be better than abuse. I didn't believe Arian could have abused them, but I also knew that Rana might consider Arian's partying and neglect unacceptably hurtful. They had all been through so much. I worried about how this would contribute to the stresses in their lives, especially the lives of the boys.

I tried to focus on more practical and analytical issues. Although Rana described her life with Arian as "torture," she did not claim physical abuse toward her or the children. Rana may have been justified in her bitter feelings toward him, but the law would not sanction what she had done with that as a defense. I was also disturbed when Arian told me that an NGO was advising Rana that she would qualify for relocation to another country. Of course, she didn't share everything, but the NGO should have also told her that her rights would depend on the result of a legal process that would have to include Arian. But a legal approach could be only a last resort. In the meantime, I believed even a discussion of law would create more strains between Arian and Rana, and add to Rana's feelings of betrayal and isolation.

My place in this family was tested that week. I knew I could not assume the benign supporting role I had been playing, and I felt a responsibility to be maternal in a "tough love" kind of way. On Sunday, I met Arian in the busy Monastiraki neighborhood for coffee. I could see immediately that he was exhausted. His eyes were puffy, and his complexion was sallow. To my surprise, he also had a new "high and tight" haircut (a style I hated because I could not help be reminded of Adolf Hitler and Kim Jong Un). The haircut seemed like an invitation for me to address the effects of his vanity, which was a source of so much stress in his marriage. After we hugged and settled at a street-side table, I started by saying, "You are not going to like what I am going to say, but I will say it because I love you." I started by being specific. "Why are you spending time and money on a haircut during this crisis? How do you think Rana will feel about that?" I was already exhausted.

As always, Arian reacted with patience and apparent acceptance. "Mom, I did this because I am hoping Rana will come home. I got a haircut for her." To me, this was a metaphor for their misunderstandings. She wanted a man who was reverent and loyal. He seemed to think she wanted the sensual, edgy man who was so attractive to the women in his work place. Or maybe he was fooling himself — he wanted her to want that kind of husband and got a haircut to make himself feel better.

The haircut led to my bigger message. Rather than trying to convince Rana that he could not live without her and focus on his feelings of guilt, he needed to see the world through her eyes. She needed to know that he understood her pain and why she couldn't tolerate a continuation of the isolation she felt. I knew all of this was ironic coming from me, someone who had failed in two marriages and a live-in relationship.

Later that day, I met Rana in Exarchia Square. She was wearing blue jeans and her *hijab*, without makeup or jewelry.

I saw her across the square with Amir and an NGO worker. As they approached me, Amir flew into my arms and squeezed me around the neck. Although I had seen him the week before, I felt as though I hadn't held him in months. Rana's expression was one of peace brought on by exhaustion. The NGO worker introduced herself and then left us.

We crossed the street to a bakery, where we bought slices of pizza and sat at a tiny table on the sidewalk. The conversation was awkward because of our language differences. "Mom, I am so tired. And Arian sees many women." I replied, "Of course, you are tired. Raising three young children is so hard." I told her I understood her anger at Arian's behavior and said I thought he understood it as well. I said the traits that made him difficult were the ones that also made him so special. They would both need to compromise. I mentioned that Shayan needed to be back in school because of how it helped him overcome his trauma and feel a sense of belonging in Greece. Rana suggested in broken English that she would meet with an attorney the next day. She had been staying in a hotel but would have to move to a communal living arrangement if she did not move home. She would have no privacy and little access to many of the comforts of life that she and the boys had in their lives at home.

As we spoke, Amir leapt from his chair every 30 or 40 seconds and ran toward the street. I realized Rana would have left him at the shelter if she had wanted a long conversation that was free of distractions. I suggested we walk and gave Amir the handle to my wheeled suitcase, which I had filled with fresh food for Rana and the boys. The full suitcase probably weighed more than he did, but Amir was delighted.

We walked for half a mile while he navigated the crowded sidewalks and cobblestones with great determination. I had to remind myself again that he was only two.

After we arrived at the hotel where Rana and the boys were staying, I hugged Rana and thanked her for meeting with me. Then I walked down the hill to meet Arian in Exarchia Square before I headed for the bus back to Nafplio. Over a pot of tea, I told him about my conversation with Rana and my sense that she had not made up her mind about anything. I didn't tell him that I felt that I had failed in trying to provide her with the kind of support she needed from me. Arian's intuitive, extroverted personality made it easy for me to navigate our unusual relationship in a way that was not possible with Rana, as much as I loved her. I handed him a 50-euro bill for the tea and told him it was the only bill I had. I knew he was out of cash. I had told him the week before that he was spending too much of my money on things he didn't need and that I was able to provide money for emergencies and special situations only. My timing turned out to be terrible, of course. I hailed a cab for the ride to the bus terminal so I could get back to Nafplio.

The next day was *Nowruz*, an Afghan holiday that takes place on the vernal equinox. *Nowruz* means "New Year," a reference to a time of renewal rather than a date on the calendar. It is a time of "deep cleaning," literally and metaphorically: the observant clean their houses and usher out the emotional problems of the previous year. It is also a time of reunification and sharing. I knew it would be a difficult day for Arian in particular, who loved the social component of every holiday and would be desperately missing his family.

That morning, Arian and I exchanged brief greetings in electronic messages as we usually did, and then I didn't hear from him for the rest of the day, as I expected to. As I poured myself a glass of wine that evening, I checked my messages. Arian had sent a beautiful photo of himself and Rana. He didn't send a written message with the photo. I could tell by his haircut that he had taken the photo that day. They were both beaming. They would try again. I was so grateful.

When I later talked to Arian about this, he was philosophical. He explained, in words that I myself might have used to explain, that Rana needed to assert her rights in her marriage and that it was a sign of her growing empowerment, which he supported. He understood that her time away had been a bridge toward better understanding and toward compromise between the two cultures of their lives — one they were born into and one that Arian loved but remained somewhat strange and irreverent to Rana.

On weekends, I took the bus back to Athens to be with friends and family there. The feeling was changing. Arian, Hashem, and Farshad anticipated the separation that was inevitable by focusing on other people and things in their lives. I felt a door closing on the time of joy and laughter we spent together. Unlike the evolution of our families at home, we did not have 18 or 20 years to prepare ourselves. We had given birth to this family less than a year before, and we had grown together quickly and deeply. We had developed intimate family relationships that included secrets and admonishments, insults and worry, laughter and dreams. We knew things would change, but, in those treasured moments, it never seemed possible. I wanted our sons to remain close to each other and to us. But like our children at home, these young people had to travel their own paths and to find those things in their lives that would empower them.

That summer, Marzia and her children were granted reunification with Marzia's husband in Germany, and Lorin was also granted relocation to Germany. They would live in a country that worked to integrate newcomers into German communities and where they might be able to live independently. The children might have a chance to be educated and to become German citizens.

A month later, Hashem was granted his request for relocation. He was assigned to France, which initially caused additional stress for him. Although France was a wealthy country where he might expect to eventually find community and peace, he would be going there alone, not knowing anyone and not speaking the language. He had built community in Greece. He had been the head of a household at Skaramangas Camp. In France, he would have to start over again for a second time in the span of a couple of years. But when I called him the week after he arrived, he sounded relieved. "I live in a very small village. Everything is clean and beautiful here. There are other refugees in my apartment building, and the French people are very nice to me. And French is easy to learn. You will visit."

Arian filed his appeal in June 2017. A grant of asylum would allow him and his family to remain in Greece. Although this was not the best outcome, considering the country's collapsed economy, it was infinitely better than deportation to Afghanistan. Arian and Rana might eventually have opportunities to apply for residency in other places, especially if Arian could get a work assignment in another EU country. Arian also applied for the US lottery, which annually provided 50,000 international candidates with an opportunity for resident status. Still, any such opportunities would probably take years, and the prospects for Afghans were not great because most countries did not officially acknowledge the war that was escalating there.

I left Greece that summer wondering what future visits would hold. The extended family we had created would be geographically dispersed. My frequent visits over the previous 20 months were motivated partly by a sense of urgency that if people like me didn't help, people would go hungry or lose hope. By mid-2017, circumstances weren't much better for refugees in Greece, but they had improved. The Greek government and the EU announced the NGOs would no longer be funded to provide refugee services. The Greek government would take over those functions. Given our experience with the Greek bureaucracy, this was not a good direction — and it would probably mean fewer opportunities for independent volunteers like me to help. The implementation of rules and management procedures would crowd out informal and more personal partnerships.

I knew I would return to Greece to visit Arian and his family, but I also knew they did not need my visits the way they had the previous year. Through spring and summer of 2017, my relationship with Arian evolved in a way that was probably predictable. We sent each other messages a couple of times a week and talked on the phone occasionally, but the frequent and emotional communications were behind us. I knew I had to let go, and the feeling was bittersweet.

But Arian's ability to get through his week without a need for my consolations and explicit encouragement was a sign of success: Arian was feeling strong, and, for the most part, he was living independently. He understandably continued to show signs of stress — he drank too much at times, purchased small luxuries with money he needed for necessities, and stayed out late on evenings he should have been with his family. But he was doing well in his job and was developing stronger bonds with Rana and the children. He continued to integrate himself into the community of refugees and NGO professionals, and to be a part of Greece. Others recognized his depth of character, and he was finding a balance between his affinity for western values and his commitment to Islam. These were his advantages in life, just as being born into a world of privilege had been mine.

The authenticity of our relationship had survived many tests over the previous year. At least, that is how I had interpreted things. I had been more concerned about my commitment to Arian and his family than I was about Arian's loyalty to me because it was easy for me to move on. Ultimately, however, Arian's struggle for survival and his drive for material success compromised his sense of loyalty to me. Arian continued to ask me for large sums of money while posting photos on Instagram, as he often did, of partying with his friends from work. Laughing, drinking, smoking *shisha* in new clothes, and fresh haircuts while Rana was home with the boys. He told me he had sent money to family in Afghanistan, Turkey, and Canada. Money that was not his to share. I was bitter about it at times but reminded myself that I had always known the whole person who was

Arian — smart, charismatic, generous, driven, and, at times, a self-centered hedonist.

Had I been foolish? Yes, but it didn't matter. Arian was born and raised in a world of war and oppression. He had always survived by his wits. I didn't doubt that he cared for me deeply, but I would have been fooling myself if I didn't consider myself a resource. The money I had given Arian tipped the balance just a bit — sharing some of what I had wouldn't change my life, but it had changed the lives of five people. And intentionally or not, they had changed mine. I knew that I would always love them and that I would always feel a special connection to Arian.

During my time at home in fall 2017, I felt conflicted about whether to remain nomadic or to settle back into my life in the Bay Area. I missed my friends and family, and the intellectual and cultural richness of my life at home. I thought about how I would live my life if I moved back home. Most of my friends and family worked long hours. I had no grandchildren there to care for. I dreaded the thought of slipping into a lifestyle of relative comfort and routine when I knew the bigger world had so much to teach me and give me. On Lesvos, I felt connected to something that transcended time and place, and the pain and terror of the people around me, something that put everything else in perspective, at least in the moment. In Athens, every circumstance and gesture seemed to align in harmony to create a family that was happy to be together, safe, and hopeful, as if our time together had no beginning or end.

The circumstances that opened the doors to these feelings changed, but, in quiet moments, I could feel them build inside me, and usually I cried. Greece had connected me to a big mystery, something I can only describe as a feeling of being a part of humanity. My experiences with the refugees there had freed me to be more accepting, more adventurous, more loving. My journey had also resolved one of the small mysteries in my life by connecting my refugee grandfather, whose story I could only ever imagine, with a young man whose story I was beginning to understand, anchoring my past to my future. With all of that, I felt more confident that I would know in the moment whether to pursue freedom or stability, intellect or heart, home or the road.

In Fall, refugee boats were arriving in ever-larger numbers on the Greek Island of Lesvos.

VI

EPILOGUE

2017

WE LIVE IN A WORLD OF conventions about who we can love and what love is. When I adopted my son in 1992, I thought I had reached the boundaries of the conventions of my American culture. And maybe it was this unconventional family-building 24 years before that set the stage for an even more unusual family relationship. That year in Greece, I had unintentionally found a kind of love that couldn't be explained in the context of what my life had previously taught me. It transcended class and culture, age and gender.

The story of my time in Greece and the people who became so much a part of my life is one of millions of stories about people who have been displaced by war and persecution. At the time of this writing, the UNHCR estimates that more than 65 million people have been forced from their communities, mostly in Africa, Asia, and the Middle East.

Millions more are at risk with the likely effects of climate change and the prospects for more war around the globe. (*"Global Trends: Forced Displacement 2015,"* Report of the United Nations High Command for Refugees)

The response of Europe's wealthy nations to this ongoing tragedy was initially one to model but, in a short time, evolved to one that seems to promise more global disaster. The circumstances at the camps on the Aegean Islands of Greece provide some insight. As refugees live in squalor month upon month with no prospect for a normal life, they grow desperate. Reports of suicides, police brutality, and desperation became common in 2017. People can live productively and with dignity in poverty if they have family and community and a reasonable hope of caring for their children. People cannot be expected to live peaceably in a constant state of fear, loss, and hopelessness. Many experts have predicted that the wealthy nations of the world are sowing the seeds of extremism: people without hope might be willing take their chances with someone who promises to feed their families and provides a sense of purpose — no matter what their political objective.

In spite of the disastrous conditions new arrivals face when they come to Europe, thousands continued to migrate there through 2017 without an end in sight. Their other choices — to remain in places like Somalia, Iraq, and Syria — were worse than a life of destitution and disdain in Europe. They continued to come as smugglers extracted their life savings and governments spent billions trying to keep them out. At some point, we would need to ask ourselves whether the resources wouldn't be better spent helping people settle in real communities with schools and jobs and opportunities to lead productive, meaningful lives.

Scientists are finding that humans have genetic memory, that the environmental influences of our ancestors may have been passed along to us. Whether our genetic memory extends to memories of violence and flight is not known. But most of us are the progeny of refugees and immigrants and, in some very deep place inside me, I understood the words I had heard so many times on the island of Lesvos: "I honor my refugee grandfather when I welcome my neighbors who are running from trouble." And that was enriching beyond expectation.

I Dream Awake

Day and night
I always dream with open eyes
And on top of the foaming waves
Of the wide turbulent sea,
And on the rolling
Desert sands,
And merrily riding on the gentle neck
Of a mighty lion,
Monarch of my heart,
I always see a floating child
Who is calling me!

— Jose Marti

References

A LTHOUGH I RELIED ON dozens of publications of all kinds for information, the following were especially helpful:

The Guardian, which covered Europe's refugee crisis with honesty, accuracy, and integrity.

The New York Times and The Washington Post

Fortress Europe, Matthew Carr, New Press, (September 4, 2012)

The New Odyssey: The Story of Europe's Refugee Crisis, Patrick Kingsley, Liveright Publishing Corporation (January 10, 2017)

The Great Fire: One American's Mission to Rescue Victims of the 20th Century's First Genocide, Lou Ureneck, Ecco (May 12, 2015)

Dust of My Feet, Richard Malcolm, several volumes, self-published between 1976 and 1986

Acknowledgements

Janet Econome for her encouragement and expert editorial guidance at every step of the way:

Karen Sokal-Gutierrez, Judy Logan and Eli Weissman for their valuable insights on my draft manuscript

Vic Weisser for supporting me always

Nanci Clifton and Anne-Lene Bjorkland, my forever Greekish sisters

The loving and courageous members of my Greekish refugee family and all of the world's refugees, who deserve solidarity and compassion and a safe place to live

Valerie Haynes-Perry for her motivational coaching

Marilyn Ruman — for talking me down off the ledge

Ann Jones — for talking me back onto the ledge

The generous people of Greece

And mostly to Gabe Malcolm — for teaching me life's most important lessons

I am also grateful to the people of Lesvos and the refugees who spent time sharing their memories and feelings with me, because the heroes of my story are people for whom memories are the subjects of nightmares and people who do not want to be identified as heroes.

CPSIA information can be obtained
at www.ICGtesting.com
Printed in the USA
FSHW04n0750120418
46815FS